THE BOOK OF ANGELS AND ARCHANGELS

Complete Guide to Practical Angelology
For Invocation, Manifestation, Assistance, and
Protection Through Heavenly Angels and Archangels

By
Natalia Martínez

All rights reserved. No part of this book may be reproduced or transmitted in any form or by any electronic or mechanical means, including photocopying, recording, or by any information storage or retrieval system, without written permission from the author.

Important disclaimer: This book is for educational and entertainment purposes only. The author has made every effort to provide complete, accurate, current, and reliable information, but this cannot be guaranteed. The author is not an expert in legal, financial, medical, or professional advice. The information in this book has been compiled from various sources, so it is important to consult a professional before trying any techniques described. By reading this book, you agree that the author is not responsible for any direct or indirect loss that may arise from the use of the information provided, such as errors or inaccuracies.

COPYRIGHT©JAXBIRD LLC

20241129

Contents

Preface 1

1. Introduction to Angelology: Fundamentals and Basic Concepts 4

Definition of Angelology 4

Etymological origin of the word "angel" 6

Divine messengers, beings of light, intermediaries 7

A brief historical overview of the belief in angels 9

Differences between angels, archangels, and other spiritual beings 11

The role of angels in the universe 12

How angels interact with humans 13

Angelic perception: signs and manifestations 15

Introductory Exercises to Angelic Perception 17

2. History of angels across cultures and religions 22

Angels in Judaism: from the Old Testament to Kabbalah 22

Angels in Christianity: evolution of angelic doctrine 25

Angels in Islam: the jinn and the malaikah 26

Celestial beings in Zoroastrianism and their influence 27

Devas and celestial beings in Hinduism and Buddhism 28

Angels in Norse and Greek mythology: parallels and differences 29

Evolution of the perception of angels in the Age of Aquarius 30

Angels in modern popular culture: influence on art and literature 32

3. Angelic Hierarchies: Understanding the Celestial Order 34

The celestial hierarchy according to Pseudo-Dionysius the Areopagite .. 34

The nine angelic orders 35

Specific functions of each angelic order 39

Angelic hierarchies in different religious traditions................ 41

How to interact with different levels of the hierarchy 43

Symbolism and attributes of each angelic order 44

The relationship between angelic hierarchies and human spiritual evolution... 45

Meditation to Connect with the Different Angelic Orders 48

4. The Seven Major Archangels: Profiles and Functions 52

Michael: Protection and Courage.. 52

Gabriel: Communication and Annunciation........................... 53

Raphael: Healing and Science 54

Uriel: Wisdom and Creativity 56

Jofiel: Beauty and Enlightenment... 57

Chamuel: Love and Relationships 58

Zadkiel: Freedom and Transmutation 59

Colors, days, and crystals associated with each archangel..... 60

Specific invocations for each archangel 62

How to work with the archangels in daily life........................ 64

Specific Invocation Prayers for the Seven Main Archangels 66

5. Guardian Angels: How to Identify and Connect with Yours . 71

Concept of guardian angels 71

Do we all have a guardian angel?.. 73

How to identify the signs of your guardian angel................... 74

Techniques for communicating with your guardian angel 75

Difference between guardian angel and spirit guide 76

How to strengthen the connection with your guardian angel.. 78

The name of your guardian angel: importance and
how to discover it 79

6. The language of angels: Symbols, numbers, and synchronicities 83

Common angelic symbols and their meanings 84

Angelic numerology: number sequences and their messages 85

Synchronicities as a form of angelic communication 87

Feathers, rainbows, and other angelic messages 88

Dreams and visions: decoding angelic messages 90

Developing intuition to interpret angelic messages 91

7. Spiritual Preparation for Angelic Work: Cleansing and Protection 95

Personal energy cleansing techniques 96

Creating a sacred space for angelic communication 97

Use of incense, candles, and essential oils in preparation 99

Meditations for protection and grounding 100

The importance of intention in angelic work 101

Mantras and affirmations to raise your vibration 102

Mantras and affirmations to raise your vibration 103

50 Powerful Mantras and Affirmations 104

Preparation Ritual for Angelic Work 108

8. Meditation techniques for tuning into angelic frequencies .. 113

Fundamentals of Angelic Meditation 113

Conscious Breathing to Raise Vibrational Frequency 114

Visualization of Light and Color in Angelic Meditation 115

Light Ladder Technique: Ascending to Angelic Realms 116

Exercise: Ascending to Angelic Realms
(Guided Astral Journey) 117

Meditation with angelic music and sounds 121

Using crystals in meditation to amplify the connection 122

Mindfulness practice for perceiving angelic presences 124

9. The Art of Angelic Invocation: Effective Rituals and Prayers 126

Structure of an effective invocation 127

Use of the sacred name in invocations 128

Specific invocations according to purpose 129

The power of repetition in angelic prayers 130

Creating your own personalized invocation ritual 132

Use of gestures and movements in invocation 133

Precautions and ethical considerations in angelic invocation 135

Example of an Angelic Invocation Ritual 136

10. Angelic decrees: Formulation and power of words 140

What are decrees and how do they work? 140

The science behind the power of words 141

Structure of an effective angelic decree 142

Decrees for different aspects of life: Health, Abundance, and Love 144

Health: Healing from the energetic plane 144

Abundance: Activating the Flow of Prosperity 145

Love: Attracting authentic connections 146

The role of emotion and visualization in decrees 147

Techniques to empower your decrees 148

Creating personalized decrees 149

Decrees assisted by the power of the Angels 150

11. Manifestation with Angelic Assistance: Principles and Practices 157

Universal Laws of Manifestation 157

The role of angels as catalysts for desires 159

Aligning personal will with angelic guidance 160

Creative visualization techniques with angels 162

Creating angelic vision boards 164

Angelic Manifestation Exercise: Anticipatory Gratitude 165

Successful manifestations with angelic help 170

12. Angels and Chakras: Energetic Alignment for Celestial Communication 172

Activation of the Third Eye with Cherubim 175

Harmonizing the Throat Chakra with the Thrones 176

Opening the Heart Chakra with the Dominations 177

Purification of the Chakras with Diamond Light 178

Angelic Cleansing of the Chakras 179

Activation of the Crown Chakra with the Lotus of Light 180

Opening the Heart Chakra with Gratitude 182

Solar Plexus Balance for Manifesting Angelic Guidance 183

Chakra Harmonization Meditation with Angelic Vibration 184

13. Angelology and astrology: Cosmic connections and planetary influences 186

Ruling angels of the zodiac signs 186

Taurus – Angel Anael 186

Gemini – Archangel Raphael 187

Cancer – Archangel Gabriel 187

Leo – Archangel Michael 188

Virgo – Angel Metatron 188

Libra – Angel Jofiel 188

Scorpio – Angel Azrael 189

Sagittarius – Angel Zadkiel 189

Capricorn – Angel Cassiel 189

Aquarius – Angel Uriel 190

Pisces – Angel Sandalphon 190

Planetary influences and their associated angels 190

Angelic work during planetary retrogrades 192

Angels of the astrological houses... 193

Angelic rituals to enhance favorable astrological transits 194

Karmic healing with angels according to the natal chart 195

Angels and lunar nodes: life purpose and karmic lessons 196

14. Angels in dreams: Interpretation and angelic dream work.. 199

Types of angelic dreams: messages, visits, teachings 199

Techniques for inducing angelic dreams 200

Interpretation of angelic symbols in dreams.. 201

Astral travel and angelic encounters during sleep 202

Angelic dream journal: methods of recording and analysis 204

Angel-guided dream healing.. 205

Problem solving through angelic consultations in dreams 206

The influence of lunar cycles and angelic symbols on problem solving 208

Lucid Dreaming Practices for Conscious Angelic Interactions 209

Exercise: Inducing Lucid Dreams for Angelic Encounters 210

15. Angelic Healing: Techniques and Protocols for Different Ailments 214

Fundamentals of angelic energy healing 214

Exercise: Harmonizing the Chakras with the
Seven Archangels... 216

Healing with Archangel Raphael 220

Exercise: Emerald Light Bath with Raphael 221

Techniques of Laying on of Hands with Angelic Assistance 223

Healing of the Seven Chakras with Angelic Laying
on of Hands.. 224

Distance Healing through Angelic Invocation.. 227

Exercise: Sending Angelic Healing Energy from a Distance 228

Exercise: Activating the Angelic Master Symbols 230

Release of Emotional Trauma with Angelic Help 232

Exercise: Releasing Emotional Trauma with the Help of Angels 233

Healing Relationships with the Help of Angels 236

Integrating angelic healing with other therapeutic modalities 240

16. Angels and Abundance: Manifestation of Prosperity and Abundance 243

Abundance from the Angelic Perspective 243

Angels Linked to Prosperity and Abundance 244

Releasing Limiting Beliefs about Money with Angelic Help 246

Angelic rituals to attract financial opportunities 248

Use of affirmations and decrees for abundance 249

Gratitude and generosity as keys to angelic abundance 250

Healing your relationship with money through angelic intervention 251

Creating an angel-guided abundance plan 252

Candle Ritual to Attract Financial Opportunities 253

Money Relationship Healing Ritual 255

20 affirmations and decrees for abundance 258

17. Angelic protection 261

The Protection of Archangel Michael and His Vibrational Power 262

Creation and Maintenance of Angelic Energy Shields 263

Cleansing and Consecration of Spaces with the Angelic Presence 264

Angelic Symbols and Seals as Methods of Protection 265

Energy Protection During Travel and Dangerous Situations 266

Protection Exercise with Sacred Symbols 267

18. Angels in Nature 275
Difference between angels, devas, and nature spirits 275
Communication with the angels of the four elements 276
Working with devas for the healing of the planet 278
Rituals for connecting with angels in natural environments 278
Angelic gardening: co-creation with plant devas 279
Healing ecosystems through angelic invocations 280
Communication with animals through angelic mediation 281
Eco-spirituality practices guided by angelic presences 282
Exercise: "Dialogue with the Elements" 283

19. Angelology in everyday life 286
Incorporating the angelic presence into your daily routine 286
Creating an altar or sacred space in the home 287
Morning and evening invocations for protection
and guidance 288
Using angelic intuition in decision-making 289
Angels at work: improving the work environment 289
No boundary between the sacred and the mundane 290
Conscious driving with angelic protection 291
Angelic cooking: preparing food with celestial energy 292
Conscious parenting: involving children in angelic awareness 293
The Angelic Map of the Home: Transforming
Everyday Spaces 295

20. Akashic Records and Angels: Accessing
Universal Wisdom 300
The Akashic Records and Their Relationship to Angels 300
Guardian Angels of the Akashic Records 301
Techniques for Accessing the Records with Angelic
Guidance 302

Reading and interpreting Akashic information 303
Healing past lives through records and angelic guidance 305
Discovering your life purpose through the records 306
Ethics and responsibility in accessing the Akashic records 307
Integrating Akashic wisdom into everyday life 309
Exercise: "Surrendering Emotional Traumas to the Angels" 310

21. Angels and Karma: Release of Patterns and Ancestral Healing 313

Karma from the angelic perspective 313
Identifying karmic patterns with the help of the angels 314
Healing ancestral lines with family guardian angels 316
Resolution of karmic contracts through angelic decrees 318
Transforming negative karma into lessons for growth 319
Creating positive karma with angelically inspired actions 320
Karmic release technique through angelic intervention: "Violet Flame of Liberation" 322
Ancestral Line Healing: "The Luminous Family Tree" 323
Resolution of karmic contracts: "Decree of Freedom" 323
Transformation of negative karma: "Angelic Alchemy" 324
Creating positive karma: "Angelic Seeding" 325
Meditation to dissolve attachments: "Cutting Ties" 326

23. Near-death experiences and angelic encounters: Evidence and testimonies 327

Overview of research on near-death experiences (NDEs) 327
Common patterns in angelic encounters during NDEs 328
Post-NDE life transformations and their relationship to angelology 330

Appendix 1 – Angelic Listing from Multiple Traditions 332

Appendix 2 – Angel Numerology 348

Appendix 3 – Creating Angelic Sigils 388

Appendix 4 – Seals of the 7 Archangels 395

Preface

Since time immemorial, humanity has sought guidance, protection, and comfort in the presence of celestial beings. The Book of Angels and Archangels: A Complete y Guide to Practical Angelology for Invocation, Manifestation, Assistance, and Protection through Celestial Angels and Archangels was born out of that search and offers a structured and accessible compendium for those who wish to understand and work with angelic energies from a practical and profound perspective.

This book is not only the result of years of research and experience in the field of spirituality, but also a reflection of a living connection with angels and archangels. Here are presented teachings that have been studied, experienced, and refined for the purpose of offering a clear and effective tool for those who wish to integrate angelology into their daily lives.

Throughout these pages, you will find a detailed journey covering everything from theoretical foundations to advanced practices of invocation and manifestation. It is not an abstract treatise or a collection of unrelated stories, but an orderly guide that provides structured knowledge and applicable techniques. Beyond theory, each chapter includes specific exercises, visualizations, and connection protocols so you can experience for yourself the influence and support of celestial beings.

One of the pillars of this work is its eminently practical approach. Angelology is not just knowledge to be studied, but a way of interacting directly with spiritual intelligences that can assist us in our personal growth and inner evolution. Therefore, this book is designed as a working guide that will allow you not only to understand the angelic world, but also to interact with it consciously and effectively.

To facilitate the integration of this knowledge, illustrations and diagrams have been included to complement the content, offering a visual representation of key concepts and angelic structures. These resources will help you visualize the celestial hierarchy, the methods of connection, and the energetic dynamics involved in communicating with angels and archangels.

You will also find appendices with complementary information that will enrich your experience and allow you to delve deeper into specific aspects of angelology. Whether you are looking for cross-references with other esoteric traditions or wish to explore advanced techniques, these sections will provide you with valuable elements to broaden your perspective.

In essence, this book is an invitation to discover and experience the presence of angels in an authentic and transformative way. It is a work that seeks to guide you in building a personal and profound bond with these luminous entities, providing you with clear tools so that this connection does not remain in the realm of theory, but becomes a tangible reality in your life.

May this journey through the angelic world be an enriching experience for you, full of light and expansion. Thank you for allowing me to share with you the fruits of my research and experience.

Sincerely,

Natalia Martínez

1. Introduction to Angelology: Fundamentals and Basic Concepts

Definition of Angelology

Angelology is the metaphysical study of beings of light who act as links between human consciousness and higher dimensions. These are not only spiritual entities, but also energetic forms that operate in harmony with universal principles. Unlike traditional theological approaches, which describe them from a dogmatic perspective, Angelology conceives them as intelligent energy patterns, vibrational structures that interact with matter and consciousness.

Its framework combines Hermetic teachings—a tradition that attributes knowledge of alchemy, philosophy, and mysticism to Hermes Trismegistus[1] —with principles of quantum physics, which explores the unpredictable behavior of particles at subatomic levels, and transpersonal

---

[1] Hermes Trismegistus is a mythical figure associated with esoteric wisdom. He is credited with texts such as the Corpus Hermeticum, the basis of Hermeticism.

psychology[2], which investigates experiences that connect the individual with a higher consciousness. From this perspective, angelology is not only a matter of faith, but an exploration of the mechanisms that govern the interaction between the spiritual and the material, allowing each person to experience these connections consciously and actively.

In the esoteric view, angels regulate the akashic flow, understood as a vast field of information that sustains reality as we perceive it. This idea resembles a cosmic archive where all the memory of the past, present, and future possibilities is stored. Their intervention in the quantum field occurs through vibrational resonance, which, in simple terms, means that they influence reality in a similar way to how the sound of a vibrating string can modify the surrounding environment. This principle finds parallels in scientific phenomena such as quantum entanglement—where separate particles can instantly affect each other—and in the theory of morphogenetic fields[3], which posits the existence of invisible patterns that guide the evolution and behavior of living beings. Thus, angels can be understood as programmers of reality, capable of operating in multiple dimensions at once, organizing events and probabilities in a manner analogous

---

[2] Transpersonal psychology, developed by authors such as Stanislav Grof, explores altered states of consciousness and spiritual experiences.
[3] Rupert Sheldrake proposed morphogenetic fields as energetic structures that influence biological and behavioral development.

to how a film director adjusts each scene to construct a coherent story.

Practical angelology is distinguished by its focus on conscious co-creation. Rather than limiting itself to passive devotion, it offers methods for aligning personal will with universal intelligence, allowing each individual to actively collaborate in the construction of their destiny. This participation turns the relationship with angels into a tool for transformation, where the microcosm of the human being tunes in to the macrocosm of the universe in a dynamic exchange of energy and purpose.

Etymological origin of the word "angel"

The origin of the word "angel" reflects its nature as an intermediary. It comes from the Greek *ángelos* (ἄγγελος), which originally referred to official messengers charged with transmitting royal decrees. Over time, this meaning shifted to the spiritual realm, describing divine emissaries who communicate the will of the sacred.

In the oldest records of humanity, such as the Sumerian tablets from the third millennium BC, the term *anunaki* appears, meaning "those who descended from heaven to Earth." Although in its original context it referred ly to beings linked to the transmission of knowledge, their function as intermediaries is similar to that which would later be attributed to angels in the Abrahamic traditions.

In Hebrew culture, the word *mal'akh* was used to refer to envoys or emissaries, but over time it acquired a spiritual connotation, becoming a key part of angelic theology. During the third century BC, in the Greek translation of the Hebrew sacred texts known as the Septuagint[4], the word *angelos* was adopted to refer to these beings, cementing their concept in early Christian tradition, where they became a fundamental part of the link between the divine and humanity.

Islam adds another dimension to this term with *mala'ika*, derived from the Arabic root l-'-k, related to light and speed, characteristics that reinforce the idea of angels as agile and luminous messengers. Recent studies have found parallels between these Semitic and Indo-European roots and the Sanskrit *anjali*, which means "offering" and is associated with gestures of reverence. This suggests a shared linguistic background, reflecting how different cultures have coincided in describing these beings as transmitters of divine messages and elevated energies.

Divine messengers, beings of light, intermediaries

Angels, in their role as divine messengers, act under the hermetic principle of correspondence: "As above, so

---

[4] Greek translation of the Hebrew Tanakh (3rd century BC), the basis of early Christian angelology.

below." This maxim means that what happens on the higher planes is reflected in the earthly world and vice versa. Their communication does not occur in conventional language, but through symbols, images, and energies that resonate in the consciousness of those who perceive them. Not only do they transmit words or visions, but they can also activate energy patterns in DNA, influence cellular memory, and harmonize the cycles of life with universal rhythms, as if they were tuners adjusting the symphony of existence.

The term "beings of light" is not just a metaphor, but a description of their energetic nature. In the field of biophotonics, light emissions have been identified in living organisms—tiny particles of light called photons—which some researchers consider to be the material basis for the interaction between consciousness and biology. From a more mystical perspective, it has been theorized that angels manipulate these subtle particles in the quantum vacuum to influence the manifestation of events aligned with the greater good.

As intermediaries, angels operate on three levels simultaneously: they connect individual consciousness with collective consciousness, serve as a bridge between the material plane and the spiritual , and filter cosmic energies to make them accessible to humanity. Their intervention is subtle and always respects free will. Rather than imposing guidelines, their influence manifests as gentle guidance, allowing each person to choose their own path. Their presence does not seek to replace human will, but to expand it, offering new possibilities and guiding those who seek to understand their true purpose.

A brief historical overview of the belief in angels

The earliest references to spiritual beings with functions similar to angels are found in ancient Mesopotamian civilizations such as Sumeria, Akkad, and Babylon. There, they spoke of the *apkallu*[5], antediluvian sages who served as guardians and transmitters of divine knowledge. These beings were considered intermediaries between humanity and the gods, charged with preserving wisdom about writing, architecture, and agriculture. In the *Epic of Gilgamesh*, one of the oldest texts in human history (dating from approximately 2100 BC), there are already references to the intervention of celestial entities in human affairs, establishing an archetype that would later be replicated in multiple traditions : the divine messenger who influences the destiny of humanity.

In Ancient Egypt, the concept of entities that existed between gods and humans was reflected in figures such as the *ba*, representations of the soul that transcended death, and the *netjeru*, deities that acted as guardians and guides. Similarly, Zoroastrianism, the ancient Persian religion

---

[5] Mesopotamian mythological beings considered mediators between gods and humans in cuneiform texts.

founded in the 6th century BCE by the prophet Zoroaster, introduced a dualistic system that distinguished between angels and demons. This classification profoundly influenced Judaism during the Second Temple period, giving rise to a hierarchical structure of celestial beings with specific names and functions, laying the foundations for the organized angelology that Christianity would later adopt.

During the Renaissance, a period of great cultural and spiritual expansion in Europe, philosophers such as Marsilio Ficino, Giovanni Pico della Mirandola, and[6] revisited and synthesized esoteric knowledge from different traditions. They integrated angelology with Hermetic thought, Neoplatonism—a current based on Plato's teachings with a mystical view of the cosmos—and Jewish Kabbalah, creating a more structured and complex angelic model. In the 20th century, this vision evolved further by merging with concepts from quantum physics—which explores the interconnection of particles at subatomic levels— r Jungian psychology, which introduced the idea of archetypes[7] as universal patterns in the collective unconscious. Based on these transdisciplinary approaches, some spiritual researchers began to reinterpret angels as expressions of the universal

---

[6] Ficino and Pico were key figures of the Renaissance who integrated Neoplatonic, Kabbalistic, and Hermetic ideas into their philosophy.

[7] Archetypes are universal patterns described by Carl Jung as primordial images present in the collective unconscious.

holographic mind, that is, manifestations of a cosmic intelligence that interacts with human consciousness.

Differences between angels, archangels, and other spiritual beings

Angels can be considered cosmic specialists, each with a specific function in reality: healing, protection, inspiration, among others. Their capacity for action is determined by their vibrational frequency—the energy level at which they operate—and by their "field of specialization," that is, the type of spiritual intervention they can perform. Unlike *devas*, entities from Eastern traditions linked to natural elements such as air, earth, and water, angels work with energy structures and universal patterns that transcend the purely physical.

Archangels, on the other hand, act as great coordinators. While angels work individually or on small missions, archangels oversee larger projects, ranging from guiding nations to protecting planetary evolutionary cycles. Their energy is more expansive and operates in multiple dimensions simultaneously, which means they can act on human collectives and historical processes, influencing spiritual development on a large scale.

Other spiritual beings with different functions include spiritual guides, who are evolved souls who have completed their cycle of incarnations and accompany people in their personal development. Devas, for their part, guard ecosystems and the forces of nature, ensuring planetary balance. In another category are the ascended masters, who, having lived human experiences in different incarnations, have attained a high degree of consciousness and continue to assist humanity from higher planes. Understanding these differences is key to choosing the appropriate methods of invocation or connection with each type of entity.

The role of angels in the universe

From a cosmic perspective, angels can be considered architects of the space-time structure. Their function is to maintain harmony between the divine plan and its manifestation in matter, ensuring that the cycles of creation and evolution follow a coherent order. Some theories inspired by theoretical physics, such as string theory, suggest that their work consists of stabilizing hidden dimensions within the fabric of the universe, acting as regulators of the fundamental laws of reality. This is equivalent to imagining that angels play a role similar to that of a mechanic who adjusts each gear of a large machine so that everything works in perfect synchrony.

On a human level, angels operate as karmic engineers, modifying the initial conditions of situations to promote learning without interfering with free will. In other words, they create opportunities for spiritual growth without imposing decisions. The theory of synchronicity, developed by psychologist Carl Jung, can help us understand this process: angels seem to intervene through "meaningful coincidences," events that align external experiences with internal processes of transformation, generating paths conducive to personal evolution.

On a planetary level, angels regulate the circulation of energies between dimensions. This manifests through the opening of star portals—access points to higher realities—and the activation of energy vortexes in sacred places or places of high electromagnetic activity. The so-called "crystalline Earth grid," an energy network that envelops and penetrates the planet, is kept in balance thanks to these angelic interactions. Their work translates into the regulation of telluric forces (energies coming from within the Earth) and cosmic forces (energies of celestial origin), ensuring that the connection between heaven and Earth remains active and accessible to humanity.

How angels interact with humans

The connection between angels and human beings is based on principles of energetic resonance and free will. In simple terms, this means that the angelic presence is perceived more intensely when a person's vibration aligns with that of these beings, but without them directly interfering with individual will. Their influence is subtle and respectful, functioning more as a guide than an imposition.

One of the main channels of angelic communication is the emotional field. Angels induce elevated states of unconditional love, serenity, and inner clarity, which facilitates personal transformation. Some theories in quantum biophysics suggest that this interaction occurs through the toroidal fields of the heart, energetic structures that generate harmonic patterns in consciousness, much like a tuned orchestra creates a perfect symphony.

On the mental plane, angels use universal symbols and archetypes that have been present in humanity throughout time. Images such as the dove, the lightning bolt, or the spiral act as codes that convey messages without the need for words. It is also believed that sacred geometric language—figures such as the flower of life or Platonic solids[8] —serves as a means of communication to activate deep memories in DNA and awaken innate knowledge. Neuroscience has identified correlations between mystical experiences and the simultaneous activation of certain brain regions[9] , such as the temporal lobes (associated with perception and memory) and the prefrontal cortex (related to decision-making and introspection). This suggests that angelic experiences have a real impact on how we interpret and process reality.

---

[8] The flower of life is a geometric symbol associated with universal patterns; Platonic solids represent fundamental forms in sacred geometry.
[9] Studies such as those by Newberg (2001) show activity in the temporal lobes during mystical experiences.

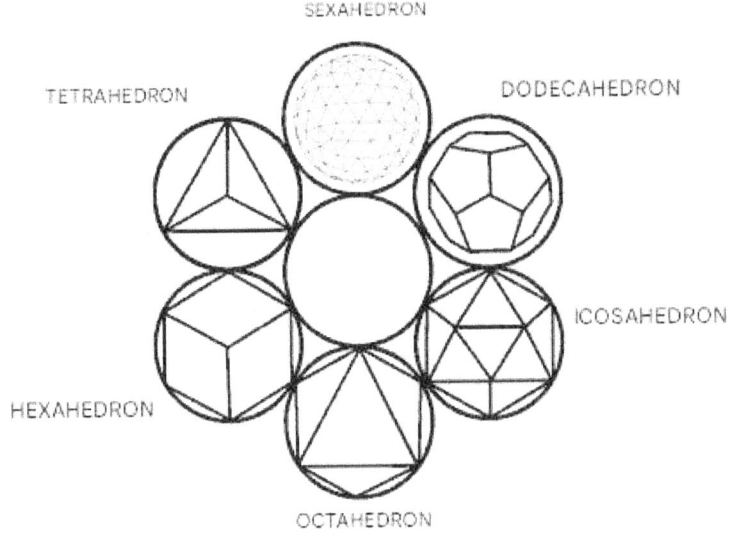

Flower of Life and Platonic Solids

On a physical level, the presence of angels can manifest itself through subtle light phenomena, such as flashes in peripheral vision or small spheres of light, known as *orbs*, which some people have captured in photographs. Changes in local electromagnetic fields have also been recorded using EMF (ElectroMagnetic Field) detectors, with fluctuations observed at times when a strong spiritual presence has been reported. Although these phenomena defy conventional scientific explanations, they invite us to consider that reality is interconnected at levels we do not yet fully understand.

Angelic perception: signs and manifestations

Perceiving the presence of angels requires developing *subtle vision*, an ability that allows one to capture energies beyond the visible spectrum. This inner sense is activated when the brain enters states of high receptivity, characterized by the synchronization of theta and gamma brain waves. Theta waves are related to meditation and intuition, while gamma waves are associated with moments of lucidity and inspiration. Since ancient times, some shamanic traditions have used methods such as ritual dance and music to induce these expanded states of consciousness, thus facilitating the perception of the invisible.

Angels communicate through symbolic signs that can appear in everyday life. Finding feathers in unexpected places, seeing repetitive patterns on clocks (such as 11:11 or 22:22), or receiving messages that seem to directly answer an internal question are some of the most common signs. These manifestations can be interpreted as reminders of spiritual alignment or as answers to concerns of the soul.

From an energetic perspective, these signs are believed to act as mnemonic cues within non-coding DNA, that is, in those parts of our genetic material that are not directly related to protein production but could store ancestral and spiritual information . Some hypotheses in epigenetics suggest that certain stimuli can activate latent memories in our genetic code, which would explain why some people feel immediate recognition when receiving an angelic sign.

In the contemporary world, technology has opened up new ways of perceiving the angelic presence. Interference in electronic devices has been documented, such as lights flashing for no apparent reason or unexpected sounds in audio recordings, which seem to respond to the presence of subtle energies. From an esoteric perspective, some researchers have proposed that these phenomena may be due to interactions with quantum information fields, suggesting that angels could even use digital media to transmit messages adapted to modern consciousness.

In this way, angelic perception is not a phenomenon exclusive to ancient times, but a reality that manifests itself in new and varied ways in everyday life. The key to recognizing it lies in inner openness and sensitivity to interpret the signs that constantly surround us.

Introductory Exercises to Angelic Perception

Meditation to Tune into Angelic Energy

This exercise will help you connect with the subtle vibrations of angels and expand your perception of their presence in your life.

Instructions:
1. **Prepare the space:**

Find a quiet place where you can be calm and undisturbed. Sit or lie down comfortably, keeping your back straight but relaxed. Place your hands gently on your lap or at your sides.

2. **Breathe consciously:**

Close your eyes and begin to breathe slowly and deeply. Inhale through your nose, allowing the air to fill your abdomen first and then your chest. Hold for a few moments and exhale slowly through your mouth. Feel your body relax more with each exhalation.

3. **Visualize the heavenly light:**

Imagine a white and golden light gently descending from above, penetrating your crown and filling your entire being. Feel how this divine light flows through every cell of your body, releasing blockages, dissipating tensions, and enveloping you in a deep sense of peace.

4. **Expand your energy:**

As you immerse yourself in this light, imagine your energy expanding beyond your body, connecting with an infinite field of love and wisdom: the angelic realm.

5. **Open your intention:**

From within, express mentally or aloud:

"Angels of light, I open my heart and mind to your love and guidance. Allow me to feel your presence in the way I can best understand it."

6. **Perceive without expectations:**

   Remain in a state of receptivity. Observe any sensations, images, emotions, or thoughts that arise. Do not analyze or judge, simply experience.

7. **Close with gratitude:**

   When you feel it is time to end, thank the angels for their presence and bring your awareness back to your physical body. Feel the contact with the ground, the air around you, the beating of your heart. Before opening your eyes, affirm internally:

   "I remain connected to angelic energy throughout the day."

Perform this meditation frequently to strengthen your connection with the angelic realm and refine your subtle perception.

2. Exercise for Connecting with Your Guardian Angel

Your guardian angel has been with you since the moment you were born, accompanying you every step of your life. This exercise will allow you to strengthen your bond with their loving presence.

Instructions:
1. **Find your sacred space:**

   Choose a place where you can be calm and free from distractions. It can be in your room, in a special corner of nature, or simply a quiet moment during the day.

2. **Breath awareness:**

   Close your eyes and focus your attention on your breathing. Don't try to change it, just observe it. Feel the air entering and leaving your body naturally, allowing you to anchor yourself in the present.

3. **Heart activation:**

   Bring your attention to the center of your chest, where your heart resides. Imagine that with each inhalation, a soft golden light expands from this point, radiating love and serenity throughout your being. Remain in this sensation for a few moments, allowing the light to dissolve any concerns.

4. **Invite your guardian angel:**

   From this state of openness, extend an invitation with love and trust:

5. *"Guardian angel, loving presence that has accompanied me since birth, I invite you to make yourself*

present in my consciousness. Let me feel you and know that you are here with me."

6. **Listen and perceive:**

   Remain silent and receptive. You may feel a change in temperature, a subtle tingling sensation on your skin, or a deep sense of calm. Perhaps a word, image, or emotion will spontaneously arise in your mind. Don't worry if you don't perceive something im r immediately; the bond with your angel grows stronger with practice.

7. **Close with gratitude:**

   To conclude, express a message of thanks:

   "Thank you, beloved angel, for always being by my side. Help me to remain aware of your presence throughout my life."

   Take a few deep breaths and, when you feel ready, open your eyes.

2. History of angels across cultures and religions

Angels in Judaism: from the Old Testament to Kabbalah

In Jewish tradition, angels are known as mal'akh, a Hebrew term meaning "messenger." Their main role is to serve as intermediaries between God and humanity, carrying divine messages or intervening at key moments in history. In the Old Testament, these beings are not limited to being abstract presences; on many occasions, they take human form and actively participate in earthly events[10].

An example of this can be found in chapters 18 and 19 of Genesis, which recounts the visit of three angels to Abraham. One of them announces the birth of Isaac, while the other two go to Sodom to warn Lot about the imminent destruction of the city. This interaction symbolizes the direct manifestation of divine will in the human world. Another significant passage is Jacob's vision in Genesis 28:12, where he contemplates a ladder connecting heaven and earth, up and down which angels ascend and descend.

---

[10] In texts such as Genesis 18-19, angels interact physically with humans, demonstrating their role as divine intermediaries in key events.

This dream reinforces the idea that angels not only convey messages, but also facilitate the connection between the spiritual and material planes.

Throughout rabbinic literature, angels take on more defined roles and are given specific names and functions. Among the most prominent are Michael, protector of Israel[11] and symbol of divine strength; Raphael, the heavenly healer, whose role in the Book of Tobit is fundamental in guiding and assisting Tobias in his mission; and Gabriel, the bearer of prophetic visions and revelations, especially in the Book of Daniel.

Kabbalah, the mystical tradition of Judaism, delves even deeper into the nature of angels, considering them energetic forces that operate through the Sefirot, the channels of divinity in the Tree of Life. In the Zohar, one of the most important Kabbalistic texts, angels are described as entities of light that maintain cosmic order and record human actions, functioning as bridges between spiritual experience and ethical behavior.

---

[11] The archangel Michael is mentioned in texts such as Daniel 10:13 and Revelation 12:7 as the leader of the heavenly hosts.

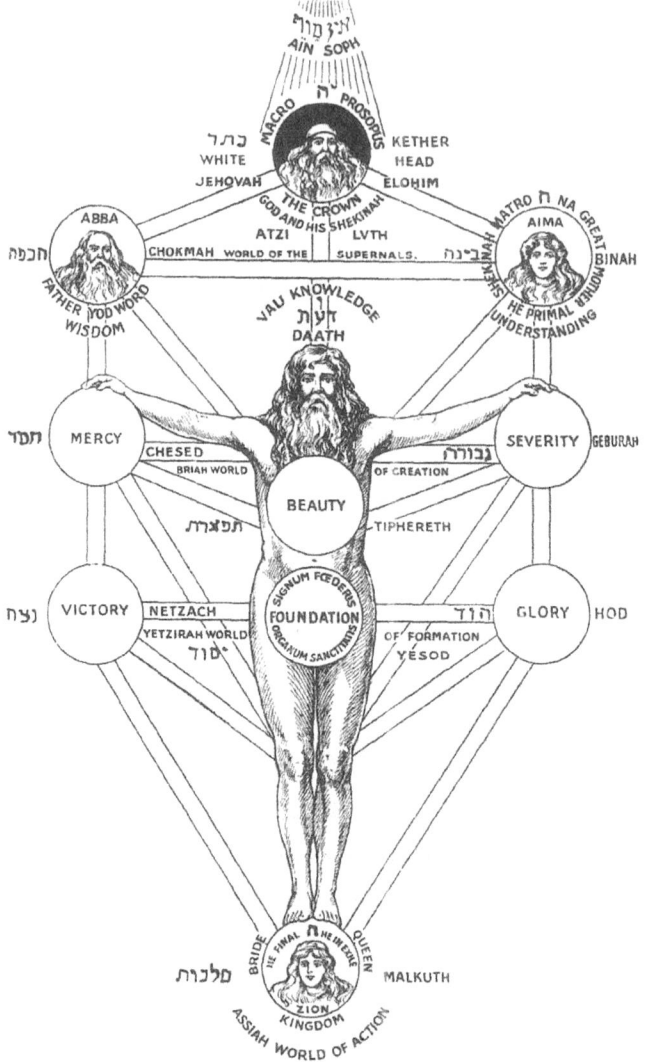

Tree of Life and the Sephirot

Angels in Christianity: evolution of angelic doctrine

Christianity adopted and reinterpreted Jewish angelology, giving these beings a more defined role within the plan of salvation. From the early centuries, angels were considered not only as messengers, but also as active participants in the redemption of humanity.

One of the milestones in the evolution of this doctrine was the work of Pseudo-Dionysius the Areopagite[12], a medieval Christian mystic who classified angels into celestial hierarchies. According to his system, seraphim represent God's burning love, cherubim guard sacred wisdom, and thrones embody divine authority. Later, Thomas Aquinas elaborated on these concepts, describing angels as "pure intellects," that is, beings without physical bodies whose existence is dedicated to the contemplation and worship of God.

The archangels Michael, Gabriel, and Raphael took on a central role in Christian tradition. Michael established himself as the heavenly warrior who fights against the forces of evil; Gabriel became the angel of the Annunciation, communicating to Mary her role in the birth

---

[12] Pseudo-Dionysius the Areopagite was a 5th-6th century Christian theologian and mystic, author of influential Neoplatonic texts on negative theology and celestial hierarchy, falsely attributed to a disciple of Paul.

of Jesus; and Raphael maintained his role as healer and spiritual guide.

The Council of Nicaea in 325 AD marked a crucial point in angelic doctrine, rejecting the idea that Christ could be considered an angel and affirming his absolute divinity. This reinforced the conception of angels as beings subordinate to God, whose main function is to serve and assist humanity.

Renaissance art reflected this view, depicting angels with an ethereal beauty that combined the human with the divine. Painters such as Fra Angelico and Sandro Botticelli portrayed them with androgynous and harmonious forms, conveying their heavenly nature through color, light, and the serene expression of their figures.

Angels in Islam: the jinn and the malaikah

In Islamic tradition, angels (malaikah) are described in the Quran as beings of light, created by God to carry out his commands without question. Unlike humans and jinn—the latter created from fire and endowed with free will—angels have no free will and operate exclusively as executors of the divine will.

[13] Jibril (Gabriel) is the most prominent angel in Islam, as he was responsible for revealing the Quran to the Prophet Muhammad in the cave of Hira, thus becoming the link between the divine and humanity. Mikail (Michael) governs natural phenomena and is associated with rain and the fertility of the earth. Israfil is the angel who will blow the trumpet on Judgment Day, marking the end of time.

In addition to angels, Islam recognizes the existence of jinn, invisible beings that can lean toward either good or evil. Their free will makes them similar to humans, and in some interpretations they are linked to demonic entities in other traditions.

Medieval Islamic theology established a precise hierarchy among angels, dividing them into different ranks, such as the hamalat al-'arsh (bearers of God's throne) and the muqarrabun (those closest to God). This structure reflects a vision in which the divine manifests itself both in the harmony of the cosmos and in the individual protection of each believer.

Celestial beings in Zoroastrianism and their influence

---

[13] According to Islamic tradition, Jibril transmitted the Quran to the prophet Muhammad over a period of 23 years, beginning in the cave of Hira.

Zoroastrianism, one of the oldest religions in the world, developed an angelological system that profoundly influenced Judaism and, consequently, Christian and Islamic traditions. Its supreme god, Ahura Mazda, delegated certain functions to the Amesha Spentas, divine entities representing essential cosmic principles.

Each Amesha Spenta embodies a sacred virtue: Vohu Manah symbolizes good thinking, Asha Vahishta symbolizes truth and justice, and Kshathra Vairya symbolizes sovereignty and protection. In addition, the Yazatas—venerable beings who act as intermediaries between heaven and earth—include figures such as Mithra, god of light and covenants, and Anahita, goddess of water and fertility.

During the Babylonian exile, contact with Zoroastrianism influenced the configuration of Jewish angelology, consolidating the figure of Michael as defender of the people of Israel and reinforcing the notion of a cosmic conflict between good and evil. The idea of fravashis, individual guardian spirits, also found parallels in the conception of protective angels.

Devas and celestial beings in Hinduism and Buddhism

In Hinduism, devas are deities representing forces of nature and cosmic principles. Agni is the god of fire, Vayu rules the winds, and Surya embodies solar energy. Unlike monotheistic angels, devas are not subordinate to a single god, but are part of an interconnected pantheon.

Buddhism, on the other hand, conceives of devas as inhabitants of higher planes within samsara, the cycle of reincarnation. Although they enjoy great power, they are still subject to karma and must eventually be reborn into other states of existence.

Other celestial beings include the apsaras, dancing nymphs who accompany the gods, and the gandharvas, divine musicians. In contrast, bodhisattvas embody infinite compassion and, in their desire to help others, postpone their entry into nirvana to guide beings toward enlightenment, fulfilling a role similar to that of guardian angels in other traditions.

Angels in Norse and Greek mythology: parallels and differences

Although there is no figure in Norse mythology equivalent to angels in the traditional sense, we do find entities that fulfill similar roles as mediators and guardians of destiny. The Valkyries, for example, are heavenly warriors who select the bravest fallen in battle to lead them to Valhalla, a majestic hall where warriors await Ragnarok, the final battle of the world. Their function symbolizes the direct connection between the human and the divine, ensuring that the worthy have a place in eternity.

Another related concept is that of the fylgjur, guardian spirits that accompany people throughout their lives, usually taking the form of a protective animal. These guardians are considered manifestations of destiny and, in many cases, reflect the character or luck of those who possess them.

On the other hand, Greek mythology introduces the notion of daimones, beings who act as intermediaries between gods and humans. Unlike angels in the Abrahamic tradition, daimones are not inherently benevolent or malevolent, but forces that can influence people's fortunes and destinies. Some, like guardian genies, protect and inspire mortals, while others can cause misfortune or confusion.

Within this pantheon, figures such as Hermes, the messenger of the gods, and Nike, the personification of victory, display characteristics that would later influence the Christian iconography of angels. However, in the Greek worldview, these beings were not mere executors of the divine will, but were part of a polytheistic system where multiple deities and forces coexisted in a complex structure of interactions.

Evolution of the perception of angels in the Age of Aquarius

The image of angels has constantly evolved over time, and in the so-called Age of Aquarius—interpreted by many as a new cycle of spiritual transformation—it has acquired meanings different from those of conventional religious traditions. In this context, angels are conceived as quantum archetypes, a term that seeks to merge concepts of modern physics with spiritual notions. The idea is that these beings are not external entities with a defined form, but rather patterns of consciousness present in the energy field of the universe and in the human psyche.

The New Age movement has played a key role in this reinterpretation, integrating ideas from Kabbalah—where angels are seen as emanations of the divine—theosophy—which establishes complex spiritual hierarchies—and Jungian psychology, which considers them manifestations of the collective unconscious. In this syncretic approach, angels are not figures to be worshipped, but spiritual guides with whom each individual can establish a direct relationship through intuition and meditation.

Within this current, authors such as Doreen Virtue[14] have promoted tools such as oracle cards and angelic communication techniques, presenting angels as "spiritual coaches" who help people in their inner growth. This vision emphasizes individual empowerment, moving away from dogmatic hierarchies and promoting an accessible and personalized spirituality.

---

[14] Doreen Virtue is a contemporary author known for popularizing modern methods of communicating with angels in the New Age movement.

Today, this perspective continues to gain followers, reflecting a collective search for connection with the transcendent without the need to adhere to traditional religious structures. Angels, far from being static figures, continue to transform themselves according to the spiritual needs of each era.

Angels in modern popular culture: influence on art and literature

The image of angels has been reworked in contemporary art and literature, in many cases moving away from its theological roots to adapt to new cultural contexts. Artists such as Louise Bourgeois have explored the iconography of winged beings from an introspective perspective, capturing the emotional and psychological dimensions of human beings in their works.

[15]In pop culture, angels have been reinterpreted in surprising ways. In the animated series Neon Genesis Evangelion, for example, these beings appear as enigmatic entities of extraterrestrial origin, merging the sacred with the technological and the apocalyptic. Series such as Supernatural and Good Omens have delved into the moral ambiguity of these beings, portraying them as complex

---

[15] Neon Genesis Evangelion is a Japanese series that reinterprets religious and philosophical concepts through a futuristic apocalyptic narrative.

entities with internal conflicts, far from the traditional image of immaculate divine messengers.

In literature, novels such as Dan Brown's Angels and Demons have intertwined angelology with plots of mystery and historical intrigue, while Donna Tartt's The Invention of Angels explores a more symbolic and philosophical view of these beings. In cinema, films such as Constantine and City of Angels[16] have humanized the figure of the angel, exploring existential dilemmas and the longing for transcendence in a world where the divine and the human intertwine.

This resurgence of the angelic figure in contemporary culture reflects a trend toward the exploration of the spiritual from a personal and artistic perspective. Far from being static representations, angels have evolved to become symbols of protection, transformation, and redemption, projecting human desires and aspirations onto the eternal mystery of the celestial.

---

[16] City of Angels (1998) explores themes of love and mortality from the perspective of an angel who wishes to experience human emotions.

3. Angelic Hierarchies: Understanding the Celestial Order

The celestial hierarchy according to Pseudo-Dionysius the Areopagite

The hierarchical system outlined by Pseudo-Dionysius in *De Coelesti Hierarchia* (5th-6th centuries AD) offers a structured view of the heavenly intelligences, organizing them into three spheres of three orders each. This model, which fuses Neoplatonic thought with Christian theology, describes how divine light and knowledge descend from the highest levels until they reach the human sphere.

Each triad fulfills a specific purpose in this process of spiritual transmission. The first is immersed in pure contemplation of the divine, the second is responsible for interpreting and shaping that knowledge, and the third acts directly in the material world, influencing human experience. This structure is not rigid or mechanical, but rather a living network of interconnected consciousness where each level empowers and collaborates with the next.

The higher hierarchies do not communicate directly with the lower ones, but rather employ symbols and archetypes that are adapted to the understanding of each order, thus ensuring a progressive transmission of divine knowledge. Imagine this process as a river flowing from the heights, filtering through different channels until it reaches humanity. In this flow, angels use sacred patterns, such as universal geometry, to facilitate the manifestation of knowledge on the earthly plane.

The nine angelic orders

1. Seraphim

Seraphim embody divine love in its purest and most incandescent form. Their name, derived from the Hebrew *saraph* ("to burn"), alludes to the flame of their absolute devotion. In Isaiah's prophetic vision (6:1-3), they surround God's throne chanting the *Trisagion*[17] —"Holy, Holy, Holy"—which generates extremely high-frequency vibrations capable of purifying and transforming everything they touch. Their energy is similar to a celestial melody that dissolves any shadow, reminding us of our connection to the unity of the universe.

2. Cherubim

---

[17] The Trisagion is a liturgical hymn that exalts divine holiness and is used in Eastern and Western Christian traditions.

The Cherubim[18] are the guardians of sacred knowledge and the repositories of cosmic wisdom. They are depicted with multiple eyes and wings, symbolizing their total vision and their ability to encompass all levels of existence. In Kabbalistic tradition, they are associated with *Binah*, the emanation of deep understanding. Not only do they guard knowledge, but they also decode it so that it can be transmitted in an understandable way to lower orders, acting as interpreters of divine thought.

3. Thrones

Thrones represent divine justice and the stability of the cosmos. They are also known as *Ophanim*[19] ("wheels"), as in apocalyptic texts they appear as rotating structures that support the heavenly throne. Imagine a perfect cosmic machinery, whose function is to stabilize realities and channel divine energy in harmony with the patterns of the universe. Their presence balances the forces of chaos and order, ensuring coherence in the manifestation of divine will.

4. Dominions

The Dominions are the architects of universal laws. They are credited with designing the principles that govern the

---

[18] Cherubim appear in Genesis 3:24 as guardians of Eden and in Ezekiel 10 as bearers of the divine throne.

[19] The Ophanim are described in Ezekiel 1:15-21 as wheels filled with eyes that accompany living beings in prophetic visions.

cosmos, establishing harmony between physical and spiritual laws. Their role is similar to that of divine engineers, ensuring that energy flows correctly between the different planes of existence. They are responsible for the structure of the natural order, from gravity to the interaction of souls in their evolutionary processes.

5. Virtues

Virtues are the facilitators of miracles and the guardians of divine grace. Their energy transforms the vibration of the material world to align it with higher states of consciousness. They are responsible for manifesting transcendental changes, such as spontaneous healings or meaningful synchronicities, turning faith and intention into tangible realities. Throughout history, they have been linked to the administration of the elements and the ability to elevate matter to more subtle levels.

6. Powers

Potencies are the guardians of karmic balance and the regulators of the dynamics between light and darkness. Their function is to protect the integrity of evolutionary processes, ensuring that no force alters the natural development of the soul. They are said to work by dismantling negative energy structures and dissipating egregores[20] —collective thought forms that can influence human consciousness— thus allowing humanity to advance without distorting interference.

7. Principalities

The Principalities[21] are the guardians of nations and cultures. Their influence extends to the growth of societies, the flourishing of artistic movements, and the advancement of ideas that transform history. They act as inspirers of spiritual revolutions and guardians of collective identity, influencing leaders and visionaries to align their actions with the common good. They are responsible for maintaining the connection between humanity and the higher forces that guide planetary evolution.

8. Archangels

Archangels coordinate large-scale missions on a planetary level. While angels assist individually, archangels operate in collective dimensions, intervening at critical moments in humanity's history. For example, Michael is known for his protection in times of conflict, and Raphael for his work in global healing. Their vibration encompasses multiple levels of existence, allowing them to

---

[20] Egregores are forms of collective thought that, according to esotericism, can positively or negatively influence group consciousness.

[21] According to Daniel 10:13, Principalities oversee regions or peoples; the "Prince of Persia" is mentioned as an example of this function.

simultaneously assist in different processes of transformation on Earth.

9. Angels

Angels are the messengers and guardians closest to humanity. Their role is to act directly in people's lives, offering guidance, protection, and support on a daily basis. They are said to work with each individual's energy field, adjusting their emotional and mental frequencies to align them with a higher purpose. They are the most tangible manifestation of heavenly assistance, reminding us that we are never alone on our journey.

Specific functions of each angelic order

Each angelic order fulfills a unique purpose within the vast fabric of the universe, functioning as specialized channels for the manifestation and regulation of divine energy. They are not just symbolic figures, but active agents that influence the structure of reality.

Seraphim, beyond their devotion to the divine, emit vibrations that not only praise but also shape the structure of the cosmos. Their song, more than an expression of worship, is a powerful frequency that influences the arrangement of galaxies and the harmony of the subtle planes of ex . It is as if their melody envelops the universe, maintaining order at the highest levels of existence.

Cherubim, guardians of wisdom, do not accumulate knowledge as a static archive, but sow it as ideas in the minds of those who are ready to receive them. These inspirations can manifest as scientific advances, spiritual revelations, or creative impulses that transform the course of humanity.

Thrones are agents of balance. Their function is to order energy, transform chaos into harmony, and establish cosmic structure through patterns that are reflected in everything from an individual's emotional balance to the stability of planetary systems. Their intervention can be perceived in times of crisis, when energies seem overwhelmed and need to be realigned.

The **Dominions** operate as the great organizers of the universal flow. They are the designers of the principles that govern existence, laying the foundation for the interaction between spiritual and natural laws. Their work ensures that the evolution of the cosmos follows a divine purpose without disorderly interference.

The **Virtues** are the force behind miracles and transcendental changes. They act as channels of divine grace and , materializing the highest prayers and desires in the physical world. Their influence is perceived in phenomena such as unexpected healings, meaningful synchronicities, and events that defy conventional logic.

Powers, on the other hand, are the guardians of energetic balance. They safeguard the stability of the collective consciousness, dismantling egregores or negative thought patterns that can affect humanity. Their work is comparable to that of those who clean a dark and dusty room, allowing light to penetrate and transform the space.

The **Principalities** intervene in the cultural and spiritual evolution of humanity. Not only do they protect nations and civilizations, but they also drive the great awakenings of history, such as the Renaissance or movements of ethical and social change. They are the spark that ignites the spirit of each era, ensuring that societies develop in tune with the divine plan.

The **Archangels** coordinate large-scale missions. While angels work with individuals, archangels manage collective processes, directing transformations on a planetary level. Their presence becomes evident at crucial moments in humanity, when a massive shift in consciousness or an adjustment in the Earth's energy is necessary.

Finally, **Angels**, who are closest to human beings, interact directly with everyday life. They act as guides, protectors, and inspirers, adjusting each individual's personal energy to help them find their way and strengthen their connection with the divine.

Angelic hierarchies in different religious traditions

Throughout history, various cultures have structured their own celestial hierarchies, reflecting the universality of the angelic presence in human thought.

In Judaism, we find figures such as the Chayot Ha Kodesh ("living beings") and the Ofanim ("wheels"), which emerge from the mystical tradition of the Merkabah, an esoteric vision of the celestial chariot where angels are part of a divine structure in constant motion.

Islam, although it does not establish a hierarchy as detailed as Christianity, recognizes the existence of the Malaikah (angels) and the Jinn, spiritual beings with their own nature. Figures such as Yibril (Gabriel) play an essential role in the revelation of divine messages, such as in the delivery of the Quran to the prophet Muhammad.

In Zoroastrianism, one of the oldest spiritual traditions, the Amesha Spentas[22] ("beneficial immortals") perform functions similar to those of archangels. Vohu Manah, symbol of good thought, stands out, whose task is to guide humanity towards virtue and harmony.

In Hinduism, the Devas[23] represent natural and cosmic forces that govern the universe, while in Buddhism the Bodhisattvas, although not angels in the Western sense,

---

[22] The Amesha Spentas are seen in Zoroastrianism as extensions of Ahura Mazda, each embodying fundamental virtues of the cosmos.

[23] The Devas are minor gods in the Hindu pantheon associated with natural elements; Agni (fire) and Surya (sun) are notable examples.

assume the role of spiritual guides who help souls in their evolution toward enlightenment.

Esoteric thought, especially in Hermetic angelology, has integrated these views. Kabbalah associates each of the sefirot with specific angelic choirs, while theosophy links them to higher planes of existence. Beyond doctrinal differences, all these perspectives reflect the same human concern: to understand the invisible forces that govern existence and their relationship with the divine.

How to interact with different levels of the hierarchy

Connecting with the different angelic levels requires expanding one's perception and tuning into higher frequencies. To interact with the higher spheres, such as the Seraphim and Cherubim, it is recommended to practice deep meditation, conscious fasting, and inner silence, methods that allow one to refine one's consciousness to perceive their subtle presence.

The intermediate orders, such as the Dominations and Virtues, can be contacted through symbolic tools, such as mandalas or sacred musical frequencies. Sound vibration and geometry act as keys that facilitate access to their energy.

The Archangels and Angels, on the other hand, respond to more direct invocations. Their names, when pronounced in

Hebrew—such as Mikael (Michael) or Gavriel (Gabriel)—generate a vibrational resonance that facilitates connection. They can also be called upon through specific colors, such as blue for Michael or gold for Uriel.

On the other hand, Thrones and Powers are linked to social action and community service. Their presence manifests itself in times of collective change, when order and justice need to be restored in the world.

Symbolism and attributes of each angelic order

Each angelic order has attributes and symbols that facilitate their recognition and connection:

- **Seraphim**: Spheres of fire, hexagrams, red-gold colors.

- **Cherubim**: Tetramorphs (lion, bull, eagle, human), emerald tones.

- **Thrones**: Concentric wheels, topaz, deep vibrations.

- **Dominations**: Scepters, lapis lazuli, the golden ratio.

- **Virtues**: Chalices, aquamarine, harmonic musical scales.

- **Powers**: Swords of light, amethyst, protective mantras.

- **Principalities**: Crowns, rose quartz, sacred geometry.
- **Archangels**: Trumpets, sapphire, names ending in "-el."
- **Angels**: Subtle wings, pearls, personal melodies.

These symbols are not merely decorative, but condense the vibrational essence of each order, serving as portals of connection with their energies.

The relationship between angelic hierarchies and human spiritual evolution

Each angelic order reflects an aspect of human spiritual development, acting as guides in the process of awakening consciousness. Just as sunlight illuminates the earth in different intensities depending on the season, the angelic hierarchies influence the evolution of the soul as it progresses on its path of understanding and transformation.

Seraphim represent the purest state of enlightenment. Their vibration resonates with absolute union with the divine, that moment when the veil of separation dissolves and the human being experiences the totality of the universe within themselves. It is the pinnacle of spiritual awakening, where unconditional love becomes the primordial force that guides everything.

Cherubim, on the other hand, symbolize transcendental wisdom, the profound knowledge that reveals the mysteries of existence. It is not intellectual knowledge, but a direct understanding of the nature of the cosmos. Those who attune themselves to this energy access an expansion of consciousness in which answers seem to come effortlessly, as if they had always been there, waiting to be remembered.

Thrones embody purpose, the ability to materialize in the physical world what has been understood on the higher planes. They are the connection between enlightenment and action, the bridge between vision and reality. Their energy drives those who have received the light of knowledge to turn it into service, into a tangible contribution to the balance of the universe.

This process of spiritual ascension does not occur in a linear or uniform manner. Rather, it is a dynamic movement in which different angelic hierarchies intervene according to the experiences and needs of each individual. For example, in times of crisis or profound transformation, the **Powers** act by dissolving karmic patterns and readjusting energy, like a current that cleanses and renews everything in its path.

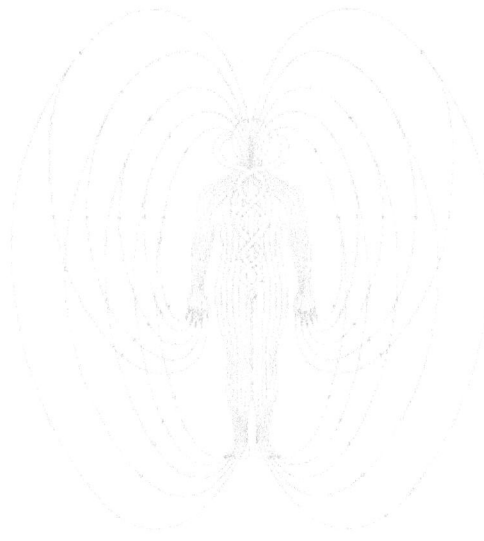

Aura

Each step in spiritual evolution strengthens the auric field[24], that energetic envelope that surrounds and defines each person. Attuning to the **Seraphim** raises the vibration of the soul, while connecting with the **Cherubim** activates higher understanding. The influence of the **Principalities**, on the other hand, can be felt in times of collective change, when the individual is driven to contribute to the awakening of their environment.

---

[24] Esoteric concept of a multicolored energy body that reflects physical, emotional, and spiritual states.

This mystical view of angelology reminds us that the universe is a living web, in which each being plays an essential role. From the highest dimensions to the most mundane, everything is interconnected by a greater purpose that unfolds in perfect harmony. The angelic hierarchies are not only guardians of the celestial order, but also companions on the path, guiding us through each stage of our spiritual growth.

Meditation to Connect with the Different Angelic Orders

This meditation will allow you to experience the vibration of each angelic choir, feeling their energy and allowing their teachings to integrate into your being. It is an inner journey in which you will experience the essence of each order, connecting with its light and its purpose in the divine plan.

Instructions:
1. Find a quiet place where you can sit comfortably without interruptions. If you wish, light a candle or place crystals that resonate with the intention of the meditation.

2. Close your eyes and breathe deeply. Inhale through your nose and exhale slowly through your mouth, allowing each breath to bring you into a state of peace and receptivity.

3. Visualize a bright white light above your head. It is the pure energy of the Divine Source. Feel it gently descend through the crown of your head, filling your entire body with its healing radiance.

4. In front of you, a golden path appears. It is the path that will take you through the different angelic levels. With confidence, take the first step and allow the energy of this journey to envelop you.

5. A red glow surrounds you. You have arrived in the realm of the **Seraphim**, the angels of pure love. Feel their embracing warmth, which dissolves any barriers in your heart. Their vibration awakens in you the ability to love unconditionally, reminding you that you are part of the divine unity.

6. Continue forward and the glow changes to a bright orange. This is the domain of the **Cherubim**, guardians of heavenly wisdom. Their energy opens your mind, allowing you to access knowledge that transcends logical thinking. Feel how their presence activates clarity and understanding within you.

7. Now, the path is tinged with golden yellow. You have entered the sphere of the **Thrones**, the angels of divine will. Their light envelops you with strength and determination, aligning you with your highest purpose. Let their energy propel you to act with certainty and confidence.

8. Further on, the path glows with a radiant emerald green. This is the domain of the **Dominions**, who bring balance and divine organization. Feel how

their presence strengthens your ability to manifest your goals, guiding you with discipline and order.

9. The color transforms into a deep sky blue. You are in the realm of the **Virtues**, the angels of grace. Their vibration fills your being with faith and courage, dispelling any fear or doubt. Allow their light to sustain you, giving you the confidence that everything is unfolding perfectly.

10. Now, the path turns to an intense indigo. You have reached the sphere of the **Powers**, guardians of spiritual protection. Feel their energy forming a shield of light around you, freeing you from negative influences and strengthening your energy field.

11. As you move forward, a violet glow envelops you. You have entered the realm of the **Principalities**, the angels who guide the transformation of humanity. Their energy awakens in you compassion and the ability to positively influence your environment. Feel their love spreading through you into the world.

12. A vibrant magenta appears around you. You are in the sphere of the **Archangels**, the great divine messengers. Their presence raises your vibration, connecting you to higher planes of consciousness. Listen to their messages, for they may come to you as thoughts, feelings, or images.

13. Finally, a pure white light envelops you. You have reached the realm of the **Angels**, the close companions of humanity. Their loving energy surrounds you in an embrace of light. Feel their protection

and unconditional support, reminding you that you never walk alone.

14. Gradually, the path begins to fade and you feel yourself gently returning to your body. The white light above your head dims, but the connection with the angels remains alive within you.

15. Calmly move your fingers and take a deep breath. When you are ready, open your eyes and return with the certainty that angelic energy is always present in your life.

4. The Seven Major Archangels: Profiles and Functions

Michael: Protection and Courage

The archangel Michael, whose name means "Who is like God?", is the guardian of protection and courage. His role goes beyond simple physical defense: he works to configure the energy fields that surround beings, creating vibrational shields that block negative influences. You can imagine his presence as a luminous bubble surrounding you, reinforcing itself against any energetic disturbance.

From a metaphysical perspective, he is associated with the manipulation of light plasmas in the aura, organizing vibrational patterns that strengthen the spirit and provide security. It is like the dance of lights in the northern lights: each flash synchronizes to form a protective barrier that maintains internal balance. In this sense, Michael combats "spiritual entropy," that is, the disorder or depletion of the sacred energy that keeps us aligned with our purpose.

Beyond his protective role, Miguel also embodies courage. It is not just about facing external dangers, but about transforming fear into an active force that drives firm and courageous decisions. His energy helps you turn insecurity into determination, allowing you to overcome internal blocks. In psychological terms, this relates to the integration of the personal shadow: the process of recognizing and accepting those aspects of yourself that you have repressed or ignored in the past.

Michael's presence manifests itself at key moments in life through synchronicities: meaningful coincidences that occur when you need to reaffirm your confidence in your chosen path. Traditionally, he is depicted with a flaming sword, a symbol of discernment. This sword not only cuts through darkness, but also through illusions and emotional ties that prevent you from moving forward. His power does not lie in imposition, but in empowerment: Michael does not protect through fear, but by teaching you to find your own inner strength.

Gabriel: Communication and Annunciation

Gabriel, whose name means "Strength of God," is the great heavenly messenger, the one who connects dimensions and facilitates the flow of information between the material and spiritual worlds. His energy acts as a bridge between the visible and the invisible, helping to translate intuitive messages and revelations into understandable thoughts.

When Gabriel is present, his influence is felt in dreams, meditations, or moments of sudden clarity. His work is not only to transmit knowledge, but also to unlock the capacity for expression. He is a guide for artists, writers, and communicators, helping to transform abstract ideas into words and images that resonate with the soul.

From a metaphysical perspective, his vibration is compared to quantum entanglement: the instantaneous connection between particles regardless of distance. In the same way, Gabriel facilitates communication that transcends space and time, allowing guidance to be received from higher planes of consciousness.

His symbolic trumpet represents the primordial vibration that shapes reality. In esoteric language, it is said that its sound harmonizes matter with divine intention, manifesting new beginnings. For this reason, Gabriel is the archangel of annunciation and creation: his presence is a call to give shape to projects, reveal hidden truths, and express one's purpose with authenticity.

When you feel blocked in your communication or creativity, invoking Gabriel helps you restore fluidity. From a neuroscientific perspective, his action is associated with the synchronization of the brain hemispheres, allowing intuition and logic to work together. In essence, Gabriel reminds us that every word, every idea, and every vision has the power to transform the world.

Raphael: Healing and Science

Raphael, whose name means "Medicine of God," is the divine healer. His presence not only restores the physical body, but also heals emotions and energy patterns that create imbalances. His work extends beyond healing symptoms: he gets to the root of the problem to bring about real transformation.

Spiritual traditions affirm that his energy activates cellular self-repair mechanisms, helping the body to regenerate naturally. This finds parallels with studies in epigenetics, which suggest that our cells respond not only to biological factors, but also to intention and emotional vibration.

Raphael is also the guardian of medical and scientific knowledge. In the Hermetic tradition, he is associated with the caduceus: a staff with two intertwined snakes, symbolizing the balance between body and spirit. His influence drives ethical research and the discovery of new forms of healing that respect universal harmony.

Beyond traditional medicine, Raphael guides processes of emotional and spiritual healing. His energy helps release trauma, cut ties with the past, and restore inner peace. He does not impose healing, but rather illuminates the path for each person to find their own inner medicine.

If you seek clarity on issues of health, well-being, or emotional balance, invoking Raphael helps you receive answers and solutions aligned with your growth. His presence reminds us that true healing is not just about eliminating pain, but restoring harmony at all levels of being.

Uriel: Wisdom and Creativity

Uriel, whose name means "Fire of God," is the archangel of revealed wisdom. His energy illuminates the mind, allowing us to see hidden connections and understand deeper realities. Unlike Gabriel, who facilitates external communication, Uriel works on internal knowledge, guiding processes of introspection and transformation.

His influence awakens creativity and intuition. In moments of doubt, his light brings clarity, revealing unexpected solutions. In transpersonal psychology, he is associated with states of creative flow, those moments when ideas flow effortlessly and time seems to stand still.

Uriel is also the guardian of esoteric mysteries. His energy manifests itself in symbols, sacred geometries, and ancestral archetypes. His presence can cause an image, a book, or an everyday experience to take on a deeper meaning, as if a universal truth were suddenly revealed to you.

Neuroscience has shown that the appreciation of beauty and art stimulates regions of the brain related to perception and memory. In this sense, Uriel not only inspires artists, but also helps us recognize harmony and order in all things.

His sacred fire does not destroy, but transforms. In times of crisis, his energy helps burn old beliefs and make way for a new vision of reality. His presence reminds us that knowledge is not just about accumulating information, but about integrating wisdom into everyday life.

Jofiel: Beauty and Enlightenment

Jofiel, whose name means "Beauty of God," is the guardian of light and harmony, revealing the divine balance present in all creation. His energy transforms ordinary perception into a deep and contemplative gaze, allowing the sacred geometry underlying nature to become evident. From the symmetry of a flower to the rhythm of the ocean waves, Jofiel helps us recognize that beauty is not only an aesthetic quality, but a subtle language of the universe. It is as if, through his presence, the everyday acquires a special glow, awakening wonder and gratitude for the perfection of existence.

His influence also extends to the mental and spiritual planes. Quantum physics posits that the act of observing can modify what is observed, and Jofiel embodies this principle: by changing the way we look at the world, we transform reality itself. As the archangel of enlightenment, he facilitates moments of deep understanding, those moments of clarity in which everything seems to fit together with a greater purpose. Furthermore, in the realm of spiritual ecology, his presence helps to restore the connection between humanity and nature, reminding us that beauty is not something external, but a reflection of the universal harmony that also dwells within us.

Chamuel: Love and Relationships

Chamuel, whose name means "He who sees God," represents the essence of unconditional love, an invisible bond that unites souls beyond time and space. His energy flows like a healing balm in the realm of human relationships, restoring damaged connections and strengthening bonds with those around us. Just as glue binds the pieces of a broken vase, Chamuel repairs the emotional cracks that may have formed throughout life. From family relationships to bonds of friendship or love, his influence balances and harmonizes, promoting interactions based on understanding and empathy.

Beyond romantic love, Chamuel guides us toward a deeper relationship with our own being, helping us recognize our value and build authentic relationships from a place of self-love. Studies on cardiac coherence have shown that the rhythm of the heart influences our emotional state, and Chamuel's vibration helps stabilize these patterns, fostering peace and balance even in the midst of conflict. His energy is said to harmonize the "quantum social field," that subtle network of interactions that connects people, facilitating meaningful encounters and synchronicities that drive mutual growth. His presence dissolves the illusions of the ego and allows us to see the divinity in every being, reminding us that love is the force that sustains all creation.

Zadkiel: Freedom and Transmutation

Zadkiel, whose name means "Justice of God," is the archangel of transmutation, the one who helps us free ourselves from the burdens of the past and transform experiences into wisdom. His energy acts as an inner alchemist, dissolving limiting thought patterns and beliefs that keep us anchored to suffering. His vibration is said to resonate with violet fire, an energy of purification and change that allows us to release old wounds and give way to a new way of being. Imagine his influence as a brush that delicately erases the marks of time with , leaving in its place a blank surface ready to be rewritten with a new story.

But his work is not limited to personal liberation. Zadkiel also inspires collective change, driving processes of justice and social evolution. Throughout history, his energy has been invoked in times of profound transformation, in movements that have sought to balance power with compassion. As the bearer of the violet sword of light, he symbolizes the discernment that cuts the chains of illusion without destroying the divine essence in each experience. His presence reminds us that true freedom is not only about breaking bonds, but also about taking responsibility for our own destiny and walking courageously toward a life of greater awareness and fulfillment.

Colors, days, and crystals associated with each archangel

Each archangel vibrates at a unique frequency that is reflected in specific colors, days, and crystals, which amplify their energy and facilitate their connection with those who seek their guidance.

Michael, protector and heavenly guardian, resonates with electric blue, a shade that embodies strength, determination, and spiritual power. His energy peaks on Sundays, a solar day linked to vitality and enlightenment . To tune into his protection, it is recommended to use sodalite and lapis lazuli, crystals that promote mental clarity and spiritual connection, reinforcing courage and confidence.

Gabriel, divine messenger, vibrates with silvery white, a color that represents purity and revelation. His influence intensifies on Mondays, the day ruled by the Moon and its cycles, promoting intuition and communication. Clear quartz and selenite are his related crystals, as they act as energy conductors that order the flow of information and promote spiritual perception.

Raphael, universal healer, radiates emerald green, a symbol of renewal and balance. His energy is strengthened on Wednesdays, the day ruled by Mercury, planet of communication and medicine. Malachite and green aventurine reinforce his influence, facilitating healing processes in the body, mind, and soul. His vibration resonates at a frequency of 528 Hz, associated with cellular repair and harmonization.

Uriel, guardian of wisdom and enlightenment, emits a ruby gold glow, a color that evokes ancestral knowledge and creativity. His day is Thursday, linked to Jupiter, the planet of expansion and growth. His affinity crystals are tiger's eye, which strengthens intuition and courage, and amber, a stone of wisdom that safeguards memories and activates mental clarity.

Jofiel, the archangel of beauty and inspiration, vibrates in a diamond yellow, a tone that reflects enlightenment and earthly manifestation. His energy is most intense on Fridays, the day dedicated to Venus, symbol of love and harmony. Crystals such as citrine, which promotes creativity and joy, and imperial topaz, which stimulates mental clarity, enhance his presence on the physical plane.

Chamuel, the embodiment of unconditional love, resonates with a deep pink, a vibration that envelops the heart with tenderness and understanding. His influence is strongest on Tuesdays, ruled by Mars, the planet of action and determination, balancing passion with empathy. Rhodochrosite and rose quartz, crystals that promote emotional healing and self-love, are his energetic allies.

Zadkiel, master of transmutation, radiates a platinum violet, a tone that symbolizes transformation and spiritual freedom. His day is Saturday, under the regency of Saturn, planet of discipline and inner growth. Amethyst, stone of intuition and purification, and sugilite, crystal that promotes the release of limiting patterns, facilitate his work in the process of energetic transmutation.

Specific invocations for each archangel

Each archangel responds to a particular vibration that can be activated through sacred sounds and specific mantras.

Michael, symbol of protection and courage, responds to the invocation of **Mikha'el**, pronounced firmly to activate his shield of light. His mantra **MI-CHI-EL**, intoned at 936 Hz, strengthens the body of light, dissolving discordant energies and establishing a vibrational barrier of protection.

Gabriel, the archangel of revelation, responds to the call **Gavri'el**, whose ascending pronunciation represents the elevation of knowledge. The key syllable **GAB** activates the throat chakra, unblocking authentic expression, while the bija mantra **GAM** facilitates the reception of divine messages.

Raphael, bearer of universal healing, is invoked through **Rapha'el**, emphasizing **RAH**, a vibration that stimulates cellular regeneration and harmonization. His mantra, resonating at **741 Hz**, aligns the energy field, promoting physical and emotional well-being.

Uriel, guardian of wisdom, connects through the intonation **Uri'el**, in a low tone that deepens intuitive knowledge. The syllable **UR** opens channels of heightened perception, while **RI** stimulates the pineal gland[25], facilitating the understanding of universal truths.

Jofiel, illuminator of hidden beauty, responds to **Yofiel**, in high tones that expand aesthetic perception. His mantra **YOF**, intoned at **639 Hz**, synchronizes consciousness with cosmic harmony, awakening the ability to contemplate beauty in all its forms.

Chamuel, ambassador of love, vibrates with the intonation **Khamu'el**, pronounced from the heart to activate the heart chakra. The syllable **KHA** opens the doors to compassion, while **MUEL** synchronizes personal vibration with the energy of unconditional love, resonating at **528 Hz**, the frequency of emotional healing.

Zadkiel, the archangel of transmutation, responds to the sound **Tzadqiel**, intoned in a descending scale that represents the dissolution of karmic blockages. The syllable **TZAD** promotes the release of old mental structures, while **KIEL** stabilizes the process of transformation. His mantra **TZA**, resonating at **852 Hz**,

---

[25] The pineal gland regulates circadian cycles and is associated with the spiritual; in mystical traditions it is called the "third eye." René Descartes called the pineal gland "the seat of the soul" because of its role in spiritual perception according to ancient philosophies.

promotes inner renewal and access to higher states of consciousness.

How to work with the archangels in daily life

Incorporating the energy of the archangels into your daily routine does not require complex rituals, but rather a conscious attunement to their presence. From the moment you wake up, you can harmonize with the vibration of each archangel, starting by visualizing the color associated with the one who rules the day. For example, on Mondays, evoking Gabriel's silvery white can enhance your communication and receptivity, helping you express yourself more clearly in conversations and daily tasks.

Everyday objects can also become points of connection with their energy. You can consecrate a ring with Michael's seal to carry his protection with you, program your keys with an archangelic sigil, or even place a small symbol of Raphael on your desk to promote healing and well-being. By giving these objects a specific intention, you transform them into vibrational anchors that remind you of the presence and assistance of these beings of light throughout the day.

Even food can be a form of archangelic connection. Dedicating each food to a spiritual purpose strengthens communion with its energy: visualizing Raphael's green light while nourishing your body reinforces regeneration and balance, while consciously savoring a bite under Jophiel's inspiration allows you to appreciate the sensory beauty in each experience. Turning the act of eating into one of gratitude and intention elevates its impact and transforms it into a channel for spiritual harmonization.

In the professional sphere, the influence of the archangels can be a great ally. If you need creativity and inspiration, invoking Uriel can open you up to new ideas and solutions. For important negotiations or presentations, Gabriel helps you communicate with clarity and persuasion. You can also tune into their vibration using technological tools: setting wallpapers with colors associated with each archangel or programming ringtones with specific frequencies, such as 639 Hz for Michael, can be a vibrational reminder of their presence. Some even integrate numerical sequences, such as 444 for Chamuel, into documents or passwords, reinforcing their influence in everyday life.

Rest is another space conducive to archangelic connection. Before going to sleep, you can set specific intentions, such as asking Zadkiel to help you release energy blockages during the REM phase or Raphael to promote cell regeneration in the delta phase of sleep. During these stages, the subconscious mind is more receptive to healing and spiritual guidance, allowing angelic energy to flow more freely.

Finally, gratitude is an essential pillar in this connection. Consciously thanking Michael for the security you feel,

Chamuel for the harmony in your relationships, or Jofiel for the beauty you discover in every moment creates an energetic circuit that strengthens their presence in your life. This small, simple but powerful gesture keeps the interaction with the archangels alive and allows their light to be integrated into every aspect of your existence.

Specific Invocation Prayers for the Seven Main Archangels

1. Michael: Protection and Courage

Invocation:

"Archangel Michael, I call upon you to envelop me in your protective light and dispel all shadows. Surround me with your shield of strength and guide me with your sword of light in every challenge I face. Give me the courage to act with determination and the wisdom to choose what is right. Thank you for your constant protection and guidance."

Daily Work:

Each morning, before beginning your day, invoke Michael and visualize his blue light enveloping you like an energetic armor that protects you from negative influences. If you face a challenging situation or need to make an important decision, call upon his presence and feel his strength instilling confidence within you.

2. Gabriel: Communication and Annunciation

Invocation:

"Archangel Gabriel, messenger of light, help me to communicate with clarity and truth. Let my words reflect love and understanding, and let my voice inspire those around me. Awaken my intuition to receive messages from the universe. Thank you for your constant guidance."

Daily Work:

Before important meetings, sensitive conversations, or any creative activity, call upon Gabriel to help communication flow and your truth be expressed clearly. Visualize his silvery white light clearing any mental blocks and allowing you to speak from the heart with confidence and gentleness.

3. Raphael: Healing and Science

Invocation:

"Archangel Raphael, divine healer, I ask you to envelop my body, mind, and spirit with your emerald light. Restore my energy, remove all imbalances, and guide my path to wholeness and well-being. Help me make decisions that strengthen my health and inner harmony. Thank you for your healing love."

Daily Work:

When you feel physically or emotionally exhausted, visualize Raphael's green light enveloping every cell in your body, regenerating and harmonizing your energy. If you practice yoga, meditation, or alternative therapies, invoke his presence to enhance their benefits and receive his assistance in the healing process.

4. Uriel: Wisdom and Creativity

Invocation:

"Archangel Uriel, flame of wisdom, enlighten my mind with your divine knowledge. Help me find answers, expand my creativity, and solve every challenge with clarity and ingenuity. Inspire me to discover opportunities where others see obstacles. Thank you for your transformative light."

Daily Work:

If you need clarity in decision-making or inspiration for creative projects, invoke Uriel. Visualize his golden light activating your mind, illuminating ideas, and revealing paths that previously seemed invisible. His energy is especially useful in learning, studying, and intellectual development.

5. Jofiel: Beauty and Enlightenment

Invocation:

"Archangel Jofiel, mirror of divine beauty, help me see harmony and perfection in all things. Enlighten my mind so that my vision is clear and my spirit reflects light. Guide me to discover beauty in simplicity and to radiate peace in all I do. Thank you for your loving inspiration."

Daily Work:

When you need to renew your surroundings or find beauty in everyday life, call on Jofiel. Visualize his golden yellow light expanding around you, elevating your perception and awakening your sense of wonder. His presence will help you find light even in the darkest moments.

6. Chamuel: Love and Relationships

Invocation:

"Archangel Chamuel, infinite source of love, teach me to love without fear or barriers. Heal the wounds of my heart and help me build relationships based on understanding and tenderness. Allow me to see the divinity in every being I encounter on my path. Thank you for your unconditional love."

Daily Work:

Whenever you feel emotional conflict or need to strengthen your relationships, call upon Chamuel. Visualize his pink light enveloping your heart, dissolving resentments and filling you with compassion. His energy will help you cultivate harmonious bonds and heal any fractures in your self-love.

7. Zadkiel: Freedom and Transmutation

Invocation:

"Archangel Zadkiel, master of transmutation, help me release the bonds of the past and embrace transformation with gratitude. Fill my being with violet light to dissolve all burdens and be reborn into a higher version of myself. Thank you for your guidance on my path of evolution."

Daily Work:

If you wish to free yourself from negative habits, dense emotions, or energetic burdens, invoke Zadkiel. Visualize his violet fire consuming what you no longer need, leaving room for new energy. You can call on him especially during meditation practices, energy work, or inner healing processes.

5. Guardian Angels: How to Identify and Connect with Yours

Concept of guardian angels

Since ancient times, various cultures have shared a belief in spiritual beings whose mission is to watch over the protection and well-being of people. This idea is reflected in millennial traditions which, although different in form, agree on the existence of guardian entities that accompany human beings on their journey through life.

In Persian Zoroastrianism, one of the oldest religions, there is mention of fravashi, protective spirits that not only care for individuals but also embody the ideals and essence of the community, ensuring order and harmony. In ancient Egypt, the Ka[26] represented a life force that coexisted with each person, functioning as a spiritual double that ensured their protection and continuity beyond earthly life. This notion of an energy that transcends physical existence and guides human destiny is present in multiple traditions.

---

[26] In Egyptian mythology, the Ka was a spiritual double that preserved individual identity after death, linked to the concept of the eternal soul.

[27]Judaism, for its part, introduced the malakhim—divine messengers—as beings who intervene at crucial moments to guide and assist humans. An example of this is found in the Book of Tobit, where the archangel Raphael accompanies and protects Tobit throughout his journey, guiding him toward healing and personal growth.

With the spread of Christianity, the idea of guardian angels became even more structured. Figures such as Pseudo-Dionysius the Areopagite, a 5th-century mystic, proposed that each person is assigned an angel at birth, a concept that gained strength in medieval spirituality. During the Renaissance, angelology became intertwined with Hermeticism—an esoteric movement that explores the connection between the microcosm and the macrocosm—and Kabbalah, encouraging practices of communication with these beings. In the modern era, movements such as the Golden Dawn[28], a 19th-century esoteric society, explored rituals to invoke and connect with angels. Today, a more universal and transreligious view conceives guardian angels not only as protectors, but also as catalysts for the spiritual evolution of each individual.

---

[27] The Book of Tobit (2nd century BC) is a deuterocanonical text that shows angelic intervention in human affairs through healing and practical guidance.

[28] The Golden Dawn (1888-1903) was a hermetic order that revitalized the study of angelology through Kabbalistic rituals and angelic tarot. It was known in Spanish as La Orden del Amanecer Dorado (The Order of the Golden Dawn) and was popularized by figures such as Aleister Crowley.

Do we all have a guardian angel?

Spiritual traditions from various cultures maintain that angelic protection is a universal principle. In the Bible, Psalm 91:11 proclaims, "He will command his angels concerning you," reaffirming the belief that each person has the assistance of these heavenly beings. In Matthew 18:10, reference is made to the special presence of angels in the lives of children, suggesting that their protection accompanies us from childhood.

Islam also recognizes the malaikah, entities that record human actions and ensure divine balance in each person's life. In Hinduism, the devas—luminous beings linked to nature and the cosmos—act as spiritual guides and guardians, promoting harmony in the universe.

From a more esoteric perspective, theosophy[29] , a 19th-century philosophical movement, maintains that each soul has multiple guardians, assigned according to its karmic evolution . This implies that certain angels and guides may have accompanied the individual in past lives, adapting to their spiritual growth. In the psychological realm, Carl Jung described the guardian angel as an archetype[30] of the collective unconscious, that is, a symbolic image that

---

[29] A movement founded by Helena Blavatsky (1875) that synthesizes Eastern and Western occultism, including angelic hierarchies.
[30] Jung considered angels to be manifestations of the Self, bridges between the conscious and the collective unconscious.

reflects the human need for guidance and protection in times of uncertainty.

Neurotheology—the discipline that studies the relationship between spiritual experiences and brain activity—has identified that belief in heavenly guardians activates regions such as the medial prefrontal cortex, an area of the brain linked to decision-making and feelings of support. This suggests that, beyond their objective existence, the idea of guardian angels positively influences human psychology, generating a perception of accompaniment and guidance at key moments.

How to identify the signs of your guardian angel

Guardian angels often manifest themselves in subtle ways, through meaningful coincidences or events that seem designed to catch our attention. Among the most common signs are:

- White feathers in unexpected places: many traditions interpret these as a message of protection and confirmation of their presence.
- Repetitive number sequences: combinations such as 11:11, 333, or 444 are considered by some to be angelic codes that reinforce their closeness.
- Sudden changes in temperature: sensations of heat or cold with no apparent explanation may indicate energetic contact with these beings.

- Symbolic dreams: Angels may appear in dreams as luminous figures delivering messages or symbols, such as keys (access to hidden knowledge) or mirrors (invitations to introspection).
- Unexplained aromas: The sudden perception of fragrances such as incense, flowers, or perfumes without a recognizable physical source is one of the most commonly reported manifestations.

Parapsychology—the discipline that studies phenomena that cannot be explained by conventional science—has documented that many of these experiences arise at times of important decisions, suggesting that they could be responses to states of spiritual openness or deep intuition.

Techniques for communicating with your guardian angel

Connecting with your guardian angel does not require complex rituals, but rather a willingness to listen and perceive subtle signs. Some effective practices include:

- Moments of introspection: set aside daily breaks to quiet your mind and be attentive to spontaneous thoughts or feelings.
- Recording synchronicities: Keep a journal where you note coincidences or signs that, when viewed together, reveal meaningful patterns.
- Artistic expression: Music, writing, or painting can be tools for channeling symbolic messages and strengthening your connection with angels.

- Prayer or conscious intention: establishing clear communication through thoughts or words directed with gratitude and openness.

Some concepts from quantum physics have been used metaphorically to explain this interaction. Quantum entanglement, a phenomenon in which two particles affect each other regardless of distance, has been used to illustrate the idea that human consciousness can resonate with spiritual entities without the need for physical contact. In simple terms, it is as if there were an invisible link that allows thought and intention to generate responses at subtle levels of reality.

It is important, however, to discern between authentic intuitions and projections of the mind. Spiritual semiology—the study of symbols in the mystical realm—warns that not all signs come from external entities, but that some may be internal reflections of the subconscious. The key lies in consistency and repetition: if a sign persists over time and occurs at relevant moments, it is more likely to be a genuine manifestation of your guardian angel.

Difference between guardian angel and spirit guide

In the exploration of the spiritual, the distinction between guardian angels and spirit guides may seem subtle, but their natures and purposes are profoundly different. Guardian angels belong to immutable celestial orders, beings of light who operate within a universal divine plan and whose presence transcends time and space. Their manifestation is often expressed through archetypal symbols such as bright light, wings, or an enveloping sense of protection and unconditional love. Their work is not conditioned by previous human experiences, but responds to the cosmic vibration of the divine order.

On the other hand, spiritual guides are souls who have passed through human existence and, after reaching a high level of consciousness, choose to accompany and guide those who continue on their earthly path. Their help is more personalized and h , based on empathy and knowledge acquired through their own past lives. While guardian angels convey their message through intuitive impulses and universal energy patterns, spiritual guides may present themselves in more familiar forms, evoking ancestors, teachers, or even historical figures that resonate with the purpose of those who receive them.

The perception of these beings has been studied from different approaches, including in the field of neuroscience. Neuroimaging research has shown that the sensation of angelic presence activates regions of the right parietal lobe, an area linked to spatial orientation and the perception of an external protective presence. In contrast, interaction with spiritual guides involves the left temporal lobe, which is related to memory and the evocation of past experiences, reinforcing the idea that your guide often presents itself in the form of memories, images, or narratives with personal meaning.

How to strengthen the connection with your guardian angel

Deepening your connection with your guardian angel is a process of conscious alignment based on three essential principles: vibrational purity, focused intention, and active gratitude. Vibrational purity implies a state of internal and external harmony, avoiding the accumulation of dense energies on the physical, emotional, and levels. Focused intention is the act of consciously tuning in to the angelic presence, establishing a clear purpose in each request or communication. Finally, active gratitude strengthens the bond with the divine, recognizing and appreciating the signs that the angel sends, such as the unexpected appearance of feathers, lights, or synchronicities that confirm their closeness.

To strengthen this connection, there are specific practices that can enhance spiritual receptivity. The use of quartz crystals, considered energy amplifiers, allows for a clearer channel for angelic interaction. The vibration of certain sound frequencies, such as 528 Hz, has also been used in meditations and energy harmonization techniques, as it is associated with opening the heart chakra and tuning into higher frequencies of love and healing.

From an energetic perspective, the constant repetition of these practices generates what some call "morphogenetic fields," vibrational structures that facilitate connection with subtle planes. The key is continuity and intention: establishing frequent dialogue with your guardian angel, assigning them specific tasks—such as protection during a trip or inspiration in moments of doubt—and being attentive to the responses that manifest in your environment. Although these signs cannot always be measured with scientific parameters, their impact on daily life is perceived in the form of greater clarity, serenity, and a deep sense of accompaniment and guidance.

The name of your guardian angel: importance and how to discover it

While knowing the name of your guardian angel is not a requirement for receiving their guidance and protection, many people find that doing so strengthens their connection and facilitates communication with this heavenly presence. It is important to remember that your angel's name is unique to you and is not part of any predefined or generalized list.

Beyond a specific name, what really matters is the intention and feeling with which you call them. Just as in everyday life we can use an affectionate nickname for someone close to us without it affecting the bond, your angel will respond with love to any name you choose from the heart. Their connection with you is vibrational, beyond words.

Below, I share an exercise to discover the name of your guardian angel through your intuition, dreams, and synchronicities. This process does not seek to force an immediate answer, but rather to open the channel for the revelation to come naturally.

Exercise to discover the name of your guardian angel

1. **Prepare the space and your intention**

    Before going to sleep, find a quiet place and get into a comfortable position. Breathe deeply several times until you feel relaxed. Visualize a white light enveloping you with warmth and protection, as if you were inside a sacred space.

2. **Perform the invocation**

    With an open heart, express a request mentally or aloud, such as:

    "Beloved guardian angel, I invite you to make yourself present in my consciousness. Show me your name or a symbol that represents our connection. I am open and receptive to your guidance."

3. **Surrender and trust**

    As you drift off to sleep, maintain an attitude of openness. Do not cling to receiving an immediate answer or try to control the process. Allow the information to come at the perfect moment.

4. **Record your dreams**

Upon waking, remain still for a few moments before moving. Try to remember any words, images, or feelings that stood out in your dream. Write them down in a journal, even if they seem unclear or meaningless at first.

5. **Watch for signs during the day**

Pay attention to names or words that repeat themselves throughout the day. They may appear in a conversation, in a book, in a song, or even on a street sign. Repetition is a key sign that your angel is trying to communicate.

6. **Continue the process for several days**

Do this exercise for at least a week, recording your observations both in your sleep and while awake. At the end of this period, review your notes and look for patterns or coincidences.

7. **Recognize the answer**

If a name or symbol has come up repeatedly, use it with confidence in your invocations and meditations. If instead of a name you have received an image, emotion, or feeling, take this as a reference point for connecting with your angel.

8. **Cultivate your relationship with your angel**

Beyond the name, the essential thing is to strengthen the bond through meditation, prayer, and attention to the subtle signs you receive every day. Remember that your angel communicates with you constantly, in ways that go beyond words.

Trust that the information will come at the right time and in the most harmonious way for you. The connection with your guardian angel is not based on rigid formulas, but on opening your heart and the certainty that their presence is always with you.

6. The language of angels: Symbols, numbers, and synchronicities

Angelic communication is not expressed in conventional words, but in a vibrational language that manifests through symbols, number sequences, and synchronicities. These messages act as bridges between the material world and the subtle dimensions, activating resonances in consciousness and allowing the invisible to become perceptibly present. In many spiritual traditions, these codes are considered keys that open portals to higher realities, facilitating connection with the angelic planes.

To capture these messages, it is necessary to develop a state of attunement that allows the signals to be perceived clearly. Just as a musical instrument must be tuned to produce a harmonious sound, the mind and spirit of the receiver must be aligned with the frequencies at which angels operate. This capacity for perception has even been studied in the field of neurotheology, where it has been observed that spiritual experiences activate areas of the brain related to intuition and connection with expanded states of consciousness. Thus, angelic communication is not an external imposition, but an invitation to raise one's internal vibration in order to correctly interpret the messages sent to us.

Common angelic symbols and their meanings

Angelic symbols have appeared in different cultures and historical moments as archetypal representations of the divine. They are not mere decorative figures, but condensations of energy and meaning that transmit information directly to the consciousness.

- **Wings:** Beyond their iconic image, wings represent the ability to transcend human limitations and access higher states of understanding. They are symbols of freedom, spiritual elevation, and protection.
- **Swords**: Associated with the archangel Michael, swords symbolize the power of discernment, the ability to cut through illusion and confusion to access truth. They also represent the strength to face challenges with courage.
- **Halos of light**: These luminous spheres indicate a state of expanded consciousness and connection with the divine. In many artistic representations, halos surround the heads of enlightened beings as a sign of their elevated vibration.
- **Feathers**: Finding feathers at key moments in life is one of the most common angelic signs. It is considered a message of encouragement, a confirmation that we are being guided and protected.
- Luminous **orbs**: Sometimes captured in photographs or perceived in meditative states, these flashes of light are associated with the angelic presence manifesting itself in subtle ways in physical reality.

- **Sacred geometry**: Figures such as the icosahedron or dodecahedron have been used since ancient times as structures connecting to higher dimensions. These geometric patterns reflect the divine order in the universe and can serve as tools for meditating and aligning consciousness with higher planes.

These symbols do not appear randomly, but emerge at specific moments as answers to questions, confirmations of decisions, or reminders that we are not alone on our spiritual path.

Angelic numerology: number sequences and their messages

Numbers are also a universal language through which angels convey messages. Each number vibrates at a specific frequency, and when it appears repeatedly, it signals a communication directed toward the person who perceives it.

- **111**: Indicates the opening of an energy portal. It is an invitation to maintain positive thoughts and focus your intention on manifesting desires aligned with your life purpose.
- **222**: Represents balance and harmony. It is a message of confidence, assuring that everything is aligning for the best, even if it is not immediately evident.
- **333**: Symbolizes the presence of spiritual guides and the activation of body, mind, and spirit in the

same purpose. It is a sign of support to move forward with confidence.

- **444**: Connection with angelic protection. When this number appears frequently, it is considered a reminder that we are surrounded by spiritual assistance.
- **555**: Indicates imminent changes. It may appear when a major transformation in life is approaching, encouraging us to accept the flow of events with confidence.
- **666**: Beyond misinterpretations, this number represents a call to balance the material and the spiritual. It appears when it is necessary to readjust priorities and reconnect with one's inner essence.
- **777**: Related to introspection and mystical wisdom. It is a number of alignment with higher knowledge and the revelation of profound spiritual truths.
- **888**: A symbol of abundance and prosperity. It indicates that doors are opening for the manifestation of resources on all levels.
- *999*: Represents the closing of cycles and preparation for new beginnings. It is a sign that it is time to leave behind what no longer serves you and move forward with a new perspective.
- **11:11**: Considered a code of spiritual activation, this number is associated with alignment with destiny and connection to higher planes of consciousness.

These numerical codes can appear on clocks, license plates, receipts, or in any other everyday context. Their repetition is not a coincidence, but an invitation to pay attention to the messages of the universe.

You will find an entire appendix dedicated to delving deeper into angelic numerology at the end of this book.

Synchronicities as a form of angelic communication

Synchronicities are seemingly random events that, when viewed together, reveal a meaningful pattern. From an angelic perspective, these coincidences are not random, but manifestations of a higher intelligence that adjusts circumstances to guide us on our path.

- **Chance encounters**: Reuniting with people from the past or meeting someone important at a decisive moment can be a message that we are on the right path.
- **Repeated messages**: When the same word, image, or phrase appears repeatedly in different media, it is a sign that there is an important message waiting to be understood.
- **Access to accurate information**: Sometimes, just when you need clarity on an issue, a book, a video, or an unexpected conversation provides exactly the answer you were looking for.
- **Synchronization of events**: Situations that seem to be impeccably aligned, as if the universe were conspiring to smooth the way, are a clear sign of angelic intervention.

In quantum physics, the theory of entanglement suggests that everything in the universe is interconnected beyond time and space. This principle can be applied to synchronicity, where distant and seemingly unconnected events align to deliver a message or facilitate a transformative experience.

Synchronicities are often most evident during times of change or crucial decisions. When experienced frequently, it is a sign that consciousness is aligning with the natural flow of the universe and spiritual guidance is becoming more present.

The language of angels is neither arbitrary nor chaotic. Each symbol, number, or synchronized event acts as a point of contact between dimensions, reminding us that reality is much vaster and more complex than what we perceive with our ordinary senses. Developing the sensitivity to recognize these signs is to open oneself to a form of communication that transcends the intellect and allows for direct interaction with the divine.

Feathers, rainbows, and other angelic messages

Nature acts as a vast canvas on which subtle messages from angels are displayed. These signs can manifest in unexpected ways, and when we learn to recognize them, we strengthen our connection to the spiritual realm.

One of the most common signs is feathers, which can appear in unusual places, such as inside a home with no open windows or in spaces where there are no birds nearby. When you find a feather in your path without a logical explanation, it is interpreted as a reminder that angels are near, supporting and guiding you. The color of the feather can also give clues about its message: white feathers are often associated with peace and protection, blue feathers with communication and truth, while gold or yellow feathers symbolize enlightenment and joy.

Rainbows, meanwhile, are a universal symbol of connection between heaven and earth, between the visible and the invisible. If a rainbow appears at a key moment in your life—for example, when you say a prayer or think about a situation that concerns you—it is confirmation that the answers you seek are on their way. In some cases, these rainbows may appear in unusual forms, such as a halo of light around the sun or a reflection in the water , reinforcing their message of hope and divine guidance.

Clouds can also serve as vehicles for angelic communication. Some people have observed formations that take on the silhouette of wings, hearts, or celestial figures. These ephemeral images invite introspection and openness to the loving presence of our spiritual guides.

Another common sign is the repetitive appearance of certain animals, such as white butterflies or hummingbirds, especially in times of doubt or transition. From a spiritual perspective, these beings are messengers who bring vibrations of joy, transformation, and protection. Their appearances are linked to synchronicity and reflect the presence of subtle energies at work.

Each of these signs functions as a reflection of the principle of correspondence: the meaning of the sign depends on the perception and inner state of the observer. The most important thing is that, when you notice these messages in nature, you take a moment to connect with their meaning and trust the guidance that the angels are sending.

Dreams and visions: decoding angelic messages

Angels often use the dream world to communicate, as in the dream state the conscious mind relaxes and is more receptive to symbolic messages. These dreams are characterized by being vivid and having an intense sense of reality, as if they belong to another dimension.

In angelic dreams, it is common to experience the presence of luminous beings, landscapes of light, or harmonious sounds that convey peace and clarity. They can also appear through symbols such as keys (representing new opportunities), mirrors (self-knowledge and truth), or ladders (spiritual progression). The feeling upon waking is usually one of deep calm or certainty, as if you had received a silent revelation.

From a neurological perspective, it has been observed that dreams with high emotional intensity activate areas of the brain linked to symbolic processing, suggesting that our subconscious interprets these experiences with a deeper meaning. If you dream about angels or receive messages during sleep, it is advisable to write them down upon waking to analyze them more clearly.

Waking visions are another type of angelic manifestation. These can occur during moments of deep meditation, in crisis situations, or in moments of intense introspection. They appear as flashes of light, geometric figures, words that seem to float in the air, or even the impression of having glimpsed an ethereal silhouette. These visions, although fleeting, often leave a lasting emotional impact and may contain key messages for your spiritual evolution.

To interpret these messages, it is helpful to observe the details and patterns that recur in your experiences. Are there recurring symbols in your dreams? Do the visions occur at specific times? The key is to connect these events to your life and the questions you have at the moment. Angels speak through the language of intuition, and the more attention you pay to their signs, the clearer their communication will be.

Developing intuition to interpret angelic messages

Refining your intuition is essential for receiving and understanding angelic messages. This process involves sensitizing the connection between the heart and the mind, establishing a balance between reason and subtle perception.

One of the most effective ways to strengthen this ability is through heart-centered meditation. Science has shown that there is a synchronization between heart rate and brain activity that enhances intuition. By entering a state of deep calm, this coherence facilitates the reception of intuitive information and amplifies the perception of subtle energies.

Another powerful technique is attuning to the Schumann frequency, a natural electromagnetic vibration of the Earth that resonates at approximately 7.83 Hz. This frequency is believed to help balance the energetic body and connect with higher planes of consciousness. There are sounds and meditations specifically designed to induce this state and enhance extrasensory perception.

The use of crystals such as clear quartz or selenite can also act as an amplifier of angelic messages. These crystals have piezoelectric properties, which means they can transform and amplify subtle energies, helping to tune into the celestial vibration. Keeping them nearby during meditation or while sleeping can facilitate experiences of angelic contact.

The daily practice of recording your intuitions, messages, or visions strengthens the neural connections associated with extrasensory perception. This process, known as neuroplasticity, allows the brain to adapt and refine the ability to receive subtle information with greater clarity.

Even diet influences intuitive openness. It has been observed that a balanced diet that promotes states of mental clarity—such as moderate consumption of healthy fats and natural foods—can enhance sensory acuity and improve connection with spiritual messages.

Developing intuition is a progressive journey. As you pay more attention to signs and practice symbolic interpretation, communication with angels becomes more fluid and spontaneous.

Practical exercise: Angelic Communication Journal

A journal dedicated to recording angelic messages and signs is an invaluable tool for strengthening your spiritual connection. This exercise will allow you to recognize patterns, analyze recurring symbols, and deepen your understanding of angelic language.

Steps to create your Angelic Communication Journal:

1. **Choose a special notebook** that inspires you and resonates with your intention to connect with the angels.
2. **Write a dedication** on the first page, expressing your desire to receive and understand divine messages.
3. **Divide your journal into sections**, for example:

- **Symbols:** Record any meaningful signs in nature (feathers, rainbows, animals).
- **Numbers:** Write down repeating number sequences (111, 444, 12:12) and their possible meanings.
- **Synchronicities:** Write down surprising coincidences or events that seem to be guided by a higher power.
- **Dreams:** Describe your angelic dreams and analyze their symbols.
- **Intuitions:** Write down thoughts or feelings that seem like internal messages or spontaneous revelations.

4. **Carry your journal with you** or keep it in an accessible place so you can record any experiences as they happen.

5. **Review your journal regularly** and look for patterns in the messages you receive.

6. **Express gratitude** for angelic guidance. Gratitude strengthens the bond with angels and increases the frequency of communication.

7. Spiritual Preparation for Angelic Work: Cleansing and Protection

Preparing your body and environment before any spiritual work is essential to establishing a clear connection with the angels. On an energetic level, dense vibrations can act as interference, hindering communication with these entities of light. This is not a matter of moral judgment, but rather the need to generate a vibrational state that is compatible with their frequency. Just as in music certain notes must harmonize to create a pleasant melody, in interacting with angels it is necessary to tune into their energy to facilitate their presence.

A good example of this is found in quantum physics: in many experiments, scientists create a controlled vacuum to eliminate any external particles that could distort the results. Similarly, angels operate on higher planes where energetic purity is key. Without a clean and orderly space, communication becomes diffuse, as if we were trying to pick up a radio signal in the middle of a thunderstorm. Purification is the process that allows us to clear away energetic "noise" and facilitate a meeting point between our dimension and theirs.

The oldest spiritual traditions understood this need well. In Egypt and Sumeria, for example, cleansing rituals were performed before contacting the gods and their messengers[31], using herbs, oils, and ceremonial baths. The Hermetic tradition expresses this principle with the famous phrase "As above, so below," reminding us that if we want to attract higher energies, we must reflect that same purity within ourselves and our environment.

Personal energy cleansing techniques

Energy purification operates on three levels: physical, emotional, and mental. On a physical level, the use of sea salt baths is an ancient practice based on the ability of minerals to absorb and neutralize discordant energies. Water, long recognized as a purifying element[32], acts as a channel of release, especially when combined with clear and conscious intention. Transforming a daily bath into an energy cleansing ritual can make a big difference in the quality of your connection with the angels.

On an emotional level, conscious breathing helps release accumulated blockages and tensions. Prolonged exhalation has been shown to activate the parasympathetic nervous system, inducing a state of deep calm. This balance is

---

[31] In Egypt, priests performed ritual ablutions and used incense such as kyphi, while in Sumeria, baths and prayers were used to purify temples and people.
[32] In numerous traditions, such as Christianity (baptism) and Hinduism (bathing in the Ganges), water symbolizes spiritual cleansing and renewal.

essential for subtle energies to flow without resistance. Visualizing a white or golden light surrounding the body during this process further enhances its effect, aligning our frequency with that of angelic beings.

Even modern science finds parallels with these practices. Studies in bioelectromagnetism[33] have shown that states of psychophysiological coherence, in which body and mind are in balance, improve the body's ability to interact with subtle energy fields. This harmonization facilitates communication with the transcendental and allows energy to flow without obstruction.

Creating a sacred space for angelic communication

[34]Since ancient times, human beings have understood the importance of sacred spaces in connecting with the divine. Architectural structures such as Mesopotamian ziggurats and Gothic cathedrals were designed with the intention of elevating the mind toward the celestial, using forms and symbols that promote attunement with higher energies. This same logic can be applied in everyday life by consecrating a personal space for angelic work.

---

[33] Bioelectromagnetism studies how the electric and magnetic fields generated by the human body influence health and energetic interaction.
[34] Ziggurats were stepped temples dedicated to the gods in Mesopotamia, while Gothic cathedrals sought to symbolize spiritual ascension through their high arches.

Mesopotamian ziggurat

From an energetic point of view, spaces that are repeatedly used for spiritual purposes acquire their own vibration. This is because the repetition of prayers, meditations, and rituals leaves a kind of energetic imprint on the environment, facilitating the opening of an increasingly stable channel of connection. It is like a string that, when tuned frequently, acquires the ability to vibrate in perfect harmony with the correct note.

In addition to the energetic impact, environmental psychology has shown that spaces with symbolic elements can induce altered states of consciousness. The selection of specific colors, scents, and materials is not a mere decorative detail, but a tool to predispose the mind to spiritual openness. When entering a space designed for contact with angels, the mind and heart respond by activating states of peace and receptivity, thus facilitating communication with these celestial presences.

Use of incense, candles, and essential oils in preparation

Ritual elements such as incense, candles, and essential oils not only beautify the ceremonial space, but also function as activators of higher states of consciousness. Their aromatic and symbolic properties have been used for millennia in various spiritual traditions, as their action transcends the physical realm and impacts the practitioner's psyche and energy field.

Incense and essential oils contain aromatic compounds capable of stimulating the limbic system, the region of the brain associated with emotions and memory. This interaction allows certain aromas, such as sandalwood or myrrh—a sacred resin used in ancient temples—to induce states of deep relaxation and spiritual receptivity. Neuroscience studies have revealed that these aromas can enhance the activity of alpha brain waves, those linked to meditation and the expansion of consciousness.

Candles, for their part, represent the principle of energetic transmutation. Solid wax is converted into light through fire, symbolizing the elevation of matter to its purest essence. In alchemical terms, this process reflects the spiritual transformation that the practitioner seeks to achieve. The choice of candle color responds to the principles of chromotherapy, as each shade emits a specific frequency that can influence the emotional state and energetic vibration of the environment.

Since ancient times, the combination of these elements has been considered an advanced spiritual technology. In Solomon's Temple, for example, frankincense incense was prepared using a precise formula designed to generate specific effects on the collective consciousness, demonstrating a deep understanding of the relationship between aroma, light, and energy . Far from being mere accessories, these components act as keys that attune the practitioner to higher planes of existence.

Meditations for protection and grounding

Meditative practices aimed at energetic protection are based on the premise that thought and intention shape reality. By visualizing luminous structures or sacred geometric patterns, the practitioner generates a vibrational shield that not only strengthens their auric field but also establishes a resonance with the harmonic structures of the universe.

Energetic anchoring is another fundamental pillar within spiritual practice, as it allows for psychic and emotional stability during transcendental experiences. One of the most effective techniques involves imagining roots of light extending from the body to the Earth's core, creating a balance between celestial energy and earthly solidity. This exercise not only helps to keep one's feet grounded in everyday reality, but also prevents the energetic fragmentation that can occur after intense meditation or practices of connection with higher planes.

From a scientific perspective, these visualizations can be interpreted as the creation of interference patterns in the quantum field. Experiments on the observer effect have shown that conscious attention is capable of modifying reality at subatomic levels, suggesting that directed intention in meditation has a real impact on the configuration of the personal energy field. Thus, protection and grounding are not just symbolic acts, but processes that directly affect the way the individual interacts with their energetic environment.

The importance of intention in angelic work

Intention is the central axis of all interaction with the angelic realm. According to the holographic model of the universe[35], every thought and emotion projects specific patterns into the matrix of reality, which means that a clear and focused intention can attract vibrationally related experiences and entities.

Quantum physics has postulated that observation modifies what is observed, supporting the idea that consciousness

---

[35] This model, proposed by physicists such as David Bohm, suggests that every part of the universe contains information about the whole, similar to a hologram.

influences spiritual experience. If we apply this principle to angelic work, we understand that the quality of intention determines the nature of the response received. The more aligned the intention is with frequencies of love and clarity, the more powerful the connection established will be.

Mystical traditions such as Kabbalah maintain that angels are manifestations of specific divine principles, and that intention functions as a mechanism for spiritual attunement. Just as a radio station only picks up certain frequencies depending on its setting, personal vibration and clarity of purpose act as filters and amplifiers that allow contact to be established with like-minded angelic entities. In this way, intention not only facilitates communication with angels, but also creates a field of resonance that enhances the effectiveness of any spiritual practice.

Mantras and affirmations to raise your vibration

The power of mantras lies in their ability to modify vibrational patterns on a subtle level, reconfiguring the practitioner's energy through sound and rhythmic repetition. Cymatics, a discipline that studies how sound waves affect matter, has shown that certain frequencies can generate harmonic geometric patterns, suggesting that chanting mantras can reorganize an individual's energy structure.

Affirmations, on the other hand, function as decrees that reconfigure the perception of reality and reinforce higher states of consciousness. When spoken with conviction and in harmony with angelic energies, they become powerful tools for spiritual empowerment. Ancient languages such as Sanskrit and Hebrew have been used for centuries in spiritual practices due to the vibratory structure of their sounds, which have been identified as carriers of high frequencies.

Incorporating mantras and affirmations into angelic work allows us to establish a bridge between our personal vibration and the frequency of the higher planes. Their constant use not only helps to raise consciousness, but also strengthens the auric field and facilitates a deeper connection with celestial guidance. Thus, sound and word become instruments of transformation, resonating through the very fabric of reality and opening paths to spiritual expansion.

Mantras and affirmations to raise your vibration

Words have power. Every sound, every thought, and every intentional statement generates a vibration that resonates in our energy field and in the universe. Mantras and affirmations not only reprogram our subconscious mind, but also align our frequency with higher energies, facilitating connection with angels and higher planes.

Below, you will find 50 mantras and affirmations designed to raise your vibration and harmonize you with the angelic presence. You can repeat them aloud, whisper them in meditation, write them in a journal, or integrate them into your daily spiritual practices.

50 Powerful Mantras and Affirmations

1. I am a radiant channel of light and divine love.
2. The angelic presence surrounds, guides, and protects me.
3. I fully trust in the wisdom and guidance of my angels.
4. My heart opens to receive heavenly guidance with gratitude.
5. I breathe in peace, breathe out light, and connect with the divine.
6. I deserve the love, healing, and abundance of the universe.
7. I walk with the certainty that I am always accompanied by beings of light.
8. I release fear and surrender with faith to divine purpose.
9. My thoughts vibrate in harmony with truth and clarity.
10. The healing light of Archangel Raphael restores my body, mind, and spirit.

11. I radiate love and compassion in every word, thought, and action.

12. Archangel Michael extends his shield of protection over me.

13. My entire being resonates with the frequency of unconditional love.

14. I gratefully receive all the blessings the universe has for me.

15. I honor the constant presence of my angels and their unconditional love.

16. I am a channel of healing, peace, and harmony for the world.

17. Archangel Gabriel illuminates my voice and my words with clarity and love.

18. I release the past with gratitude and open myself to a new dawn.

19. Divine wisdom flows through me with ease and confidence.

20. Everything in my life happens in perfect synchronicity with the divine plan.

21. The magic of miracles manifests itself in my path every day.

22. The golden light of Archangel Uriel illuminates my mind with deep understanding.

23. I envelop myself in the transmuting violet light of Archangel Zadkiel.

24. I listen to my intuition with confidence and follow the voice of my soul.

25. I am in perfect harmony with the infinite abundance of the universe.

26. I breathe light, release burdens, and rise to my highest potential.

27. My thoughts, words, and actions are guided by pure love.

28. I vibrate with gratitude and allow love to fill every corner of my life.

29. I am aligned with the energy of the highest good.

30. I bless my path and surrender with confidence to the flow of existence.

31. I am a beacon of light, expansion, and divine wisdom.

32. I am grateful for the transformation and healing that blossoms within me each day.

33. Every challenge I face propels me to grow and evolve.

34. The beauty and grace of Archangel Jofiel beautify my mind and heart.

35. I let go of control and surrender to the perfect order of the universe.

36. My intuition is clear, and I trust the guidance I receive from above.

37. I choose joy and allow lightness to dwell in my heart.

38. The energy of Archangel Metatron activates my gifts and my sacred mission.

39. I am the reflection of divine light on this earthly plane.

40. I am grateful for every visible and invisible blessing that comes into my life.

41. I cultivate thoughts that lift my soul and nourish my spirit.

42. Angels walk with me and surround me with their love and protection.

43. I release judgment and embrace compassion for myself and others.

44. I trust that everything in my life is aligned with the highest good.

45. My inner light shines brightly and ignites hearts in its path.

46. I connect with the healing and nurturing essence of Mother Earth.

47. In the silence within, I hear the loving voice of the universe.

48. I appreciate every moment as a divine gift on my life journey.

49. I am a being of light experiencing the greatness of infinite love.

50. I surrender completely to the divine grace that dwells within me.

These mantras and affirmations can be used in various spiritual practices. Recite them with intention, integrate them into your daily life, and observe how your vibration rises, allowing you to connect with the angelic presence more clearly and deeply.

If you want to enhance their effect, accompany your practice with meditation, conscious breathing, or visualizing the light of angels surrounding you. Over time, these affirmations will not only raise your energy, but also transform your perception and open paths of love, clarity, and healing in your life.

Preparation Ritual for Angelic Work

To connect with angels in a clear and profound way, it is essential to create a sacred space and prepare your body, mind, and spirit. This ritual will allow you to raise your vibration, harmonize your energy, and establish a pure connection with beings of light.

Begin by purifying the space where you will perform your practice. Light incense, palo santo, or white sage, and as the sacred smoke fills the room, visualize how a bright white light dissolves any dense or stagnant energy. With each movement of the smoke, imagine the place becoming radiant and vibrant, ready to receive the celestial presence. Affirm aloud with conviction:

"This space is now a sanctuary of light and love. Only the divine presence and angelic energy dwell here."

Now, create a sacred altar. Its size is not important, but rather the intention with which you prepare it. Place a cloth in a color that inspires peace, such as white, sky blue, or lavender. On top of it, arrange items that resonate with the energy of angels: white or blue candles, crystals such as clear quartz or amethyst, white feathers, images of angels, or sacred symbols. As you place each object, take a moment to bless it, infusing it with love and gratitude, visualizing each element becoming an anchor point for the celestial vibration.

To cleanse your own energy field, immerse yourself in a purifying bath with sea salt or Epsom salts. If you prefer, you can simply wash your face and hands with water to which you have added a few drops of lavender, rose, or incense essential oil. As the water touches your skin, visualize any tension, worry, or discordant energy dissolving away. Feel how the purity of the water cleanses not only your body but also your aura, leaving you light and receptive . When you get out of the water, wrap yourself in bright white light, feeling its protection and warmth.

Choose comfortable clothing in soft colors, preferably shades associated with purity and spiritual connection. If you wish, you can sprinkle a little rose water on your clothing or rub a few drops of essence on your wrists, consecrating it as sacred clothing for your encounter with the angels.

Sit in front of your altar with your back straight and your eyes closed. Breathe deeply, inhaling through your nose and allowing the light to fill your inner being. Hold your breath for a few seconds and then exhale slowly through your mouth, letting go of any tension. Repeat this process until you feel your mind clear and your heart calm.

When you are ready, invoke the angels with love and respect. You can do this silently or aloud, with words that come from your heart, or by using this prayer:

"Beloved angels, archangels, and beings of light, I call upon you with devotion and humility. Come to this sacred space, surround me with your love and protection. Create a shield of light around me where only the purest energies can enter. Thank you for your presence and your loving guidance."

Feel how the energy in the room rises, how the atmosphere fills with a warm and comforting feeling. You may perceive a change in the air, a subtle glow, or simply a deep peace that envelops you.

At this moment, set your intention for this practice. Ask yourself: What do I wish to receive or understand in this encounter with the angels? Am I seeking guidance, healing, clarity, or simply their loving presence? Formulate your intention in simple words, such as:

"I open myself to angelic guidance and healing with gratitude and love."

Now, remain silent, in a state of receptivity. You can choose to do a guided meditation, chant a mantra, work with an angelic oracle, or simply remain still, allowing the angelic energy to flow through you. Do not hold on to any expectations; simply feel, observe, and receive. You may perceive images, words, sensations, or simply a feeling of infinite love and peace. Trust whatever comes to you.

When you feel the process is complete, express your gratitude to the angels for their presence and unconditional love. You can say aloud:

"Thank you, beloved angels, for enlightening me with your light. I appreciate your guidance and eternal love. May your presence continue to accompany me every step of the way. Thank you, thank you, thank you."

To close the ritual and anchor the energy you have received, perform a small gesture of integration. You can touch the ground with your hands to connect with the Earth, write down any messages or feelings you have received in a journal, drink a glass of water with the intention of absorbing the angelic light, or simply remain still for a few minutes, feeling the elevated vibration settle into your being.

At any time of the day, you can return to this state of attunement by simply closing your eyes, taking a deep breath, and feeling their love enveloping you.

8. Meditation techniques for tuning into angelic frequencies

Fundamentals of Angelic Meditation

Angelic meditation is based on the principle that human consciousness can tune into celestial energies, establishing a vibrational link with more subtle planes. Research in neurotheology—the discipline that studies the relationship between spirituality and brain activity—has shown that deep meditative states activate specific areas of the brain associated with experiences of transcendence. This suggests that meditation generates a "neurochemical bridge," a state in which the electrical and chemical activity of the brain facilitates access to higher dimensions, allowing a direct connection with higher intelligences.

This process does not involve a disconnection from reality, but quite the opposite: it is a state of hyperconsciousness in which the mind is freed from the usual filters that limit perception. From the perspective of quantum physics[36] , ,

---

[36] In quantum physics, phenomena such as entanglement and interference patterns suggest that consciousness could influence subatomic systems.

meditation can be compared to a particle collider at the conscious level, generating interference patterns that, in some way, can be perceived by angelic entities. It is a phenomenon reminiscent of the way subatomic particles interact in quantum mechanics experiments, revealing hidden information in the universe.

Different spiritual traditions have developed similar methods of angelic meditation throughout history. From contemplative practices in Tibet[37] to the shamanic rituals of Mesoamerican civilizations, three essential elements are repeated: a clear intention focused on the divine, the suspension of rational judgment to allow for deeper perception, and the activation of internal energy centers, known in many cultures as chakras.

Conscious Breathing to Raise Vibrational Frequency

Breathing is the most powerful biological tool for inducing higher states of consciousness. Techniques such as 4-7-8 breathing[38] —inhaling for four seconds, holding the breath for seven, and exhaling for eight—have been extensively studied in neurophysiology, demonstrating their ability to

---

[37] In Tibet, monks use mantras and visualizations to reach elevated states; Mesoamerican shamans used sacred plants and chants to connect with the divine.

[38] The 4-7-8 technique, popularized by Dr. Andrew Weil, calms the nervous system by activating the vagus nerve, reducing stress and anxiety.

induce gamma brain waves. These waves are associated with multisensory integration and states of expanded perception.

[39]In angelic meditation, breathing functions as a tuning fork that harmonizes the body's vibrational frequency with celestial energies. This phenomenon is mentioned in hermetic texts such as the *Kybalion*, where it is explained that the correspondence between the human microcosm and the universal macrocosm allows for synchronization with higher planes.

From a biochemical point of view, proper oxygenation increases the body's electrical conductivity, transforming it into a kind of antenna capable of picking up and transmitting subtle vibrations. For this reason, many spiritual traditions insist on breath control before performing practices of connection with higher entities.

Visualization of Light and Color in Angelic Meditation

The human brain does not completely distinguish between what it sees with the eyes and what it imagines with the mind. Studies in cognitive psychology have shown that visualizing images activates the same areas of the brain as

---

[39] The Kybalion* is a 20th-century Hermetic text that synthesizes universal principles attributed to Hermes Trismegistus, such as correspondence and vibration.

actual perception. In angelic meditation, this principle is used to project light and colors that act as codes of communication with celestial intelligences.

Each color has a specific frequency and is linked to different angelic energies. Chromotherapy—therapy based on the use of colors to influence physical and emotional well-being—has shown that indigo blue light, for example, stimulates the pineal gland, a brain structure related to intuition and spiritual perception. In terms of quantum physics, photons—particles of light—carry information encoded in their vibration, which could explain how the conscious visualization of certain colors facilitates attunement with higher planes.

This knowledge is not new. Alchemical texts such as *De Radiis Stellarum*, attributed to the sage Al-Kindi[40] in the 9th century, detail the relationship between colors, celestial bodies , and spiritual entities, establishing a basis for understanding light as a bridge between worlds.

Light Ladder Technique: Ascending to Angelic Realms

The image of the ladder as a symbol of spiritual ascension is found in many traditions. A classic example is *Jacob's*

---

[40] Al-Kindi was an Arab philosopher who explored how the rays of the stars influence earthly objects, laying the foundations for scientific astrology.

Ladder, mentioned in the Bible as the bridge between Earth and heaven. In shamanic cultures, this concept is expressed in the *axis mundi*, the axis that connects different dimensions of existence.

From a psychological perspective, Carl Jung described this archetype as part of the collective unconscious, a universal symbol reflecting the human longing to reach the divine. In modern physics, the idea of the ladder can be compared to Calabi-Yau spaces, mathematical structures used in string theory to describe hidden dimensions of the universe. According to this interpretation, each step represents a level of vibration, and by raising our consciousness, we ascend in this multidimensional structure toward higher states of perception.

The ladder of light technique in angelic meditation consists of imagining a luminous path extending upward, where each step represents an expansion in the connection with the divine. As the mind rises , the vibratory resonance adjusts, facilitating contact with the celestial planes. This practice not only promotes states of peace and clarity, but also strengthens the perception of the angelic presence in everyday life.

Exercise: Ascending to Angelic Realms (Guided Astral Journey)

1. **Prepare your sacred space**

Find a quiet place where you can lie down without interruptions. It can be your bed or a yoga mat with a light blanket. Make sure the temperature is comfortable and that nothing distracts you. This is your moment to connect with the subtle.

2. **Breathe in golden light**

   Close your eyes and breathe deeply. With each inhalation, imagine absorbing radiant golden light, infusing every cell of your body with its pure vibration. With each exhalation, let go of any tension, worry, or heavy thoughts. Feel yourself sinking into an expansive serenity.

3. **Release the density of the physical body**

   As your breathing becomes slower, feel your body becoming heavy, as if melting into the surface beneath you. Meanwhile, your consciousness becomes lighter, becoming ethereal, ready to rise.

4. **Visualize the stairway of light**

   In front of you, a majestic staircase of luminous energy appears, rising endlessly, submerged in a misty golden glow. Each step vibrates at a higher frequency than the one before.

5. **Receive guidance from your guardian angel**

   At the foot of the staircase, your guardian angel awaits you. Their presence radiates unconditional love and absolute security. Take a moment to feel their energetic embrace and allow their vibration to envelop you, harmonizing you with the frequency of the higher planes.

6. **Begin the ascent**

    Take the first step on the staircase alongside your angel. With each step you climb, notice how you become lighter, more luminous. Imagine your physical body falling into a deep rest, while your true essence—your energetic being—rises effortlessly.

7. **Pass through different dimensions**

    As you ascend, you pass through levels of different vibrations and colors. Each one emits a unique frequency, a distinct sensation. Some may feel like spaces of infinite calm, others like vast oceans of pulsating light. Do not stop, just observe and continue climbing.

8. **Enter the angelic realm**

    Eventually, the staircase dissolves into a dazzling white glow. Your guardian angel guides you through this light, and as you cross it, you emerge into a realm of luminous purity. Here, the vibration is so high that everything emanates love, peace, and wisdom.

9. **Explore and perceive**

    Observe your surroundings without expectations. How does this space feel? Are there other beings? Do you hear sounds or messages within yourself? Allow yourself to receive the experience intuitively, without needing to rationalize it.

10. **Interaction with angelic beings**

    You may perceive the presence of angels or spiritual guides offering you their knowledge, healing, or simply their company. Receive their love and allow their energy to raise your consciousness.

11. **The return**

    When you feel it is time to leave, thank the beings you have connected with for their presence. Your guardian angel accompanies you back to the stairway of light.

12. **Conscious descent**

    Descend each step gently, noticing how your vibration becomes denser again as you approach the physical plane. Each step is a conscious anchor, allowing you to integrate the energy received into your body and mind.

13. **Return to the physical body**

    When you reach the bottom of the staircase, visualize your energetic being merging back into your physical body. Feel the texture of the surface beneath you, slowly move your fingers and toes, and when you are ready, calmly open your eyes.

14. **Recording the experience**

    Before sitting up, take a few minutes to write about your journey. What images, sensations, or messages did you receive? How do you feel now? It doesn't matter if the experience was vivid or subtle; trust that you have received what you need for this moment.

An Alchemical Perspective

Hermetic texts describe this ascension as a process of purification, where human consciousness is refined to interact with each hierarchical angelic level. In contemporary terms, this phenomenon could be compared to Richard Dawkins' theory of "memes": just as ideas are transmitted and evolve in culture, spiritual information spreads and refines as consciousness ascends, facilitating connection with the divine.

Meditation with angelic music and sounds

Since ancient times, music has served as a bridge to higher states of consciousness. In esoteric musicology, it is recognized that certain scales, such as the Dorian in ancient Greece or the raga in Hindu music, possess harmonic qualities that induce a deep spiritual connection. These scales generate resonance patterns that help synchronize the brain hemispheres, promoting a more integrated meditative experience that is receptive to the angelic presence.

Research in cymatics—the study of how sound organizes matter—has revealed that specific frequencies, especially in the range of 432 Hz to 528 Hz, create harmonious geometric patterns in liquid media. This suggests that sound not only affects the emotional state, but also influences the energetic structure of the body. It is no coincidence that ancient cultures used Tibetan bells and quartz bowls in their spiritual practices, as their vibrations facilitate the opening of the energy field and prepare the consciousness for attunement with the divine.

From a neurological perspective, the power of sound has been extensively studied. It has been proven that Gregorian chants, characterized by their prolonged and biphasic tones, can induce brain states associated with deep meditation, such as theta and gamma waves. Modern technologies, such as "binaural beats," have taken advantage of this principle to induce altered states of consciousness, facilitating access to subtle dimensions and enhancing the perception of higher energies.

Using crystals in meditation to amplify the connection

The use of crystals in meditation is not only an esoteric practice, but also has foundations in physics. Certain minerals have piezoelectric properties, which means they generate small electromagnetic fields when subjected to pressure. This phenomenon explains why holding a crystal during meditation can influence the human biofield, helping to tune into higher spiritual frequencies.

Studies in geobiology have shown that minerals such as smoky quartz—known for its ability to transmute dense energies—and angelite—associated with celestial connection—have molecular structures that resonate with frequencies in the range of 40 to 70 Hz. These oscillations coincide with the brain's gamma states, which are activated in moments of intense clarity and spiritual connection. This suggests that the resonance of certain crystals can act as a channel between different planes of existence.

Since ancient times, the relationship between crystals and angelic hierarchies has been documented in mystical texts such as the *Picatrix*, a medieval compendium of astrological and alchemical knowledge. Today, this tradition is echoed in studies on "crystalline memory," a theory that posits that crystals can store and transmit energy patterns, functioning as transmitters of subtle information. Thus, beyond their beauty, crystals become powerful allies in intensifying our connection with the sacred.

Mindfulness practice for perceiving angelic presences

1. **Find a moment in the day** for this mindfulness practice. It can be during a walk in nature, sitting in a park, or even while going about your daily activities.

2. **Focus your attention on your breathing.** Don't change it, just observe it. Feeling the natural rhythm of your inhalation and exhalation will help you focus on the present.

3. **Expand your awareness** by keeping your attention on your breathing while perceiving what is happening around you.

4. **Use all your senses.** Observe colors, shapes, and movements. Listen to sounds near and far, perceive aromas, feel the touch of air on your skin.

5. **Mentally ask the angels for a sign of their presence.** Ask them to show you their energy through small synchronicities.

6. **Remain alert** to unusual events or patterns: a bird that appears unexpectedly, a butterfly fluttering around you, a sudden breeze, an object that falls for no apparent reason.

7. **When something catches your attention, reflect.** What emotions or thoughts emerge when you notice this synchronicity? Is there an implicit message in what you have observed?

8. **Keep an open mind and free of expectations.** Don't attach yourself to any immediate interpretation; allow the meaning to reveal itself over time.

9. **If you don't perceive any signs at the moment, don't be frustrated.** Sometimes the greatest connection lies in simply being present and contemplating the moment.

10. **End with gratitude.** Thank the angels for their guidance and life itself for the opportunity to experience this conscious connection.

Psychologist Carl Jung described synchronicities as meaningful coincidences that seem designed by a higher intelligence. For him, these events were expressions of the hidden order that governs the universe, small clues that remind us that we are in constant dialogue with the divine. By adopting this perspective, every moment can become an opportunity to perceive the subtlety of the angelic presence in our daily lives.

9. The Art of Angelic Invocation: Effective Rituals and Prayers

Angelic invocation is based on the vibrational resonance between planes of existence, which implies that human energy can be synchronized with the frequencies of angels through conscious intention. Quantum physics has explored the possibility that celestial entities exist in specific frequency states, and that these can be tuned into by modifying one's own electromagnetic field, that is, the vital energy that emanates from each person and interacts with the invisible structures of the universe.

Hermetic tradition states that all invocation requires three fundamental elements: purity of intention, which implies a sincere and selfless desire; knowledge of energetic correspondences, which relate vibrational elements of the universe; and mastery of sacred language, which acts as a bridge for dimensional transduction.

From a metaphysical perspective, angels are understood as organized patterns of energy-light, which means that their nature is not material, but vibrational and luminous. Kabbalah teaches that each invocation activates a circuit in the Tree of Life, establishing connections with sefirotic forces through specific phonetic codes. Research in sacred linguistics[41] has shown that certain syllables in Hebrew and Aramaic contain frequencies capable of altering perception and affecting the structure of space-time at the quantum level, suggesting that sound plays a role in modulating reality.

Structure of an effective invocation

Every functional invocation follows a four-phase pattern:

1. **Preparation:** This involves energetic cleansing, which can be achieved through purification baths, harmonic sounds, or the use of incense and consecrated elements.

2. **Opening:** Contact is established with the invoked energy through visualizations, keywords, or ritual gestures.

3. **Formulation:** The request is expressed clearly and precisely, using language aligned with the vibration of the entity to be invoked.

4. **Closure:** The invocation is sealed with words of gratitude and a conscious reintegration into the ordinary state is performed.

---

[41] Sacred linguistics analyzes how the sounds of ancient languages, such as Hebrew, can have energetic or spiritual properties.

Neurotheology has identified that this process activates regions of the brain responsible for concentration, memory, and emotional experience, suggesting that invocation induces a state of receptive hyperconsciousness.

Ancient traditions incorporate three essential phases into their invocations:

- **Kavanah:** Focused intention that aligns mind and emotion.
- **Devotion:** Sincere surrender that allows connection with the invoked entity.
- **Hitbodedut:** Contemplative isolation that facilitates clear perception of the angelic response.

These phases correspond to alchemical principles in which the process of dissolution, concentration, and expansion of energy is reflected in the way the practitioner opens themselves to the experience of invocation.

Use of the sacred name in invocations

Angelic names have a specific vibration that acts as an interdimensional access key. Studies in cymatics have shown that certain sounds generate precise geometric patterns in elements such as water, suggesting that the pronunciation of sacred names may have effects on the energetic structure of the environment.

Jewish esoteric tradition holds that each angelic name contains a vibrational activation code that resonates with higher spheres. The proper pronunciation of these names follows principles of sacred bioacoustics, where breath modulation, nasal resonance, and glottal articulation ensure the purity of the sound emitted. Research in ancestral phonetics suggests that certain tones can stimulate the pineal gland, enhancing extrasensory perception.

The Sefer Yetzirah[42] states that the combination of Hebrew letters in specific sequences generates energy structures that can interact with human consciousness and higher planes. These principles find parallels in the theory of morphogenetic fields, where vibrational patterns can influence the manifestation of specific realities.

Specific invocations according to purpose

Each invocation responds to the principle of correspondence, which implies that different entities vibrate in tune with different functions:

- **Michael:** Protection, strength, and defense.

---

[42] The Sefer Yetzirah is one of the oldest texts of Kabbalah, detailing the creation of the universe through Hebrew letters and numbers.

- **Raphael:** Physical, emotional, and spiritual healing.
- **Gabriel:** Communication, revelation, and clairvoyance.
- **Uriel:** Wisdom, enlightenment, and conflict resolution.

From the perspective of modern physics, these attributes can be understood through the theory of scalar fields, which posits that each entity acts as a node within an interconnected energy network.

Sufism developed the concept of muraqaba, which consists of active spiritual vigilance, where specific invocations generate resonance patterns in the human auric field. Studies in transpersonal psychology have identified that these states of concentration can induce synchronization between the brain hemispheres and increase cardiac coherence, favoring connection with higher dimensions.

Medieval Christian angelology established a classification of invocations based on the seven gifts of the Holy Spirit, associating them with specific angelic hierarchies and processes of consciousness expansion in the mystical tradition.

The power of repetition in angelic prayers

Repetition in invocation rituals operates as a technique of vibrational imprinting on the energy matrix of space, allowing the energy of intention to anchor more deeply. This principle, studied in neuroscience, has shown that the repetition of angelic mantras can strengthen neural connectivity in the prefrontal cortex, the region of the brain associated with decision-making and concentration. This suggests that ritual repetition not only reinforces the practitioner's state of consciousness, but also establishes optimal mental circuits for the reception of higher energies.

In the Kabbalistic tradition, this practice is known as kavanot, which consists of repeating sacred phrases with a focused intention to modify the vibrational structure of the practitioner and their environment. From a hermetic perspective, each repetition generates what is called an akashic echo ( ), an energetic imprint that reinforces the channel of communication with the divine and leaves a record in the universal vibrational field.

Quantum mechanics has explored the possibility that the repetition of sacred formulas generates resonance patterns in the quantum vacuum, stabilizing energy structures that could be compared to Einstein-Rosen bridges, theorized as connections between distant points in space-time. In Eastern traditions, practices such as japa yoga, which consists of repeating mantras, have been used to transform sound into a means of connecting with higher planes.

Creating your own personalized invocation ritual

Designing a personalized invocation ritual requires the application of dynamic symbolism, a principle that establishes that each ritual element—colors, sounds, geometric shapes, and gestures—must be in tune with the vibration of the invoked angel. The selection of these elements must be based on precise energetic correspondences, as their function is to amplify the connection with the celestial entity.

From Carl Jung's analytical psychology, this process can be understood as the activation of collective archetypes, universal images, and symbols that reside in the unconscious and, when used consciously, facilitate communication with more subtle realities.

In the field of modern physics, string theory posits that the universe is composed of microscopic vibrations that generate the structure of reality. Applying this view, rituals can be seen as sequences of vibrational commands that interact with these fundamental energies.

Research in sacred geometry has revealed that certain shapes, such as the merkaba—an energy field with a tetrahedral structure—or the flower of life, act as resonance amplifiers, enhancing the transmission of energy during invocations. Esoteric texts such as the Sefer Ha Razim explain that the right combination of symbols generates an energetic hologram, a three-dimensional vibrational structure that is recognized by angelic intelligences and facilitates their manifestation on the human plane.

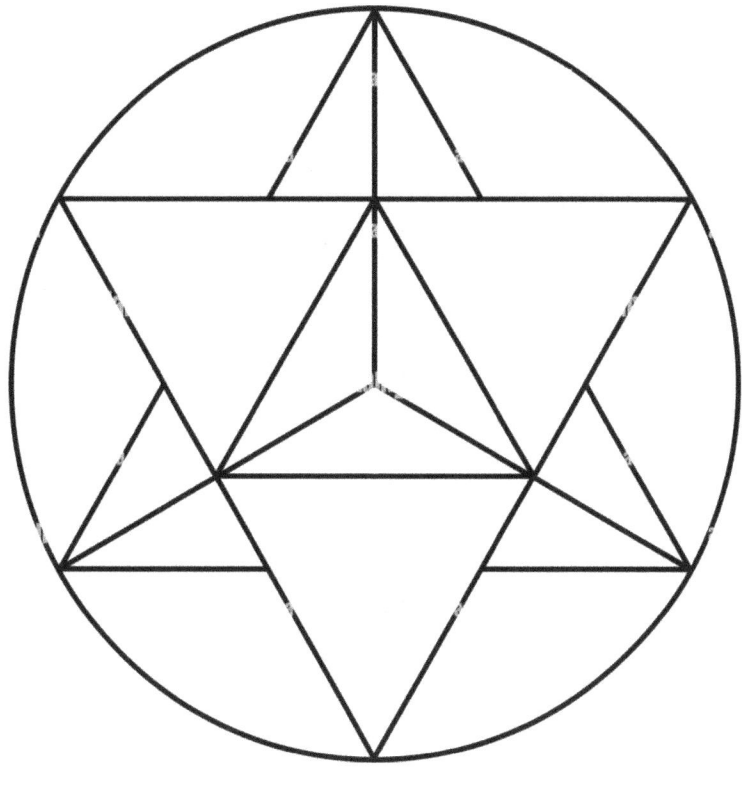

Merkabah

Use of gestures and movements in invocation

Ritual gestures and body movements in invocation are part of what is known as sacred kinesics, the discipline that studies how the body can channel energies through postures and dynamic symbols. Each gesture, known in various traditions as a mudra, generates a specific pattern in the human bioelectr y field, functioning as an antenna that focuses and directs the invocative energy.

Studies in energy kinesiology have shown that certain gestures can modify the conductivity of acupuncture meridians, facilitating the circulation of vital energy in the body and allowing greater attunement to higher frequencies. In the Taoist tradition, these movements are considered a form of writing in the air, as they trace invisible geometric codes that reconfigure the energy of the practitioner and the environment.

Research in plasma physics has found that certain repetitive movements can generate energy vortices, whirlwind-like structures that can be detected with instruments such as the Kirlian camera, which records the bioenergetic radiation of living beings.

The mystical text Ma'aseh Merkavah, based on the visions of the prophet Ezekiel, describes specific gestural sequences designed to activate and move celestial chariots, energetic structures that allow access to higher planes. These techniques, combined with conscious intention and the recitation of sacred formulas, facilitate more direct interaction with the angelic hierarchy.

Precautions and ethical considerations in angelic invocation

Every invocation mobilizes energies that generate repercussions at different levels of reality, so its practice requires careful observance of ethical principles. The Law of Three, a concept present in various esoteric traditions, holds that any ritual act affects three levels simultaneously: the physical, the astral, and the causal. This means that an invocation not only influences the person performing it, but also their energetic environment and karmic development.

Research into complex systems dynamics has found that improper manipulation of energy patterns can generate distortions in the morphogenetic field, which is the subtle structure that organizes the form and function of living beings. In esoteric terms, this implies that an invocation performed with a selfish or misaligned intention can cause disordered effects or unexpected results.

The Rosicrucian tradition has established four fundamental principles for the practice of invocation:

- **Purity of motive:** Act with a clear intention free of ego.
- **Respect for free will:** Do not influence or manipulate the will of others.

- **Alignment with the greater good:** Seek universal harmony in every action.
- **Vibrational discernment:** Ensure that the energy invoked comes from a higher source.

Studies in esoteric psychology have revealed that ritual practices performed from the ego can activate negative karmic feedback mechanisms, attracting adverse experiences as a consequence of misaligned intention.

The mystical text Pirkei Heikhalot, which describes access to the heavenly palaces, warns of the need to properly seal rituals to avoid dimensional interference. This involves closing the channel of invocation with specific formulas that ensure the reintegration of the mobilized energy into cosmic balance.

Example of an Angelic Invocation Ritual

The following ritual is a guide for performing an angelic invocation, integrating symbolic and energetic elements that favor connection with these beings of light. You can adapt it according to your personal preferences and needs, making sure to keep your intention clear and aligned with the vibration of the angel invoked.

Suggested elements:
- **Incense or aromatic herbs** (myrrh, sandalwood, lavender, or jasmine) to purify the space.

- **A candle** as a representation of divine light.
- **A crystal or stone** that resonates with your intention.
- **Consecrated oil** to anoint the candle and enhance the energy.
- **A symbol or image of the angel** to focus the connection.
- **An offering** (flowers, fruit, or a glass of pure water) as a sign of gratitude and harmonization.

Ritual steps:

1. **Prepare the space:**

   Choose a quiet place where you can perform the ritual without interruptions. Light the incense and pass it around the area while visualizing how any dense energy dissolves, leaving the space clean and harmonized.

2. **Create the altar:**

   Place the candle in the center and arrange the other elements around it. Anoint the candle with the oil, gently touching the wick and sliding it toward the base while focusing on your purpose.

3. **Enter a meditative state:**

   Sit comfortably in front of the altar, close your eyes, and breathe deeply. Visualize a radiant white light enveloping you, filling you with calm and receptivity. Feel your mind quiet and your heart open to the angelic connection.

4. **Invoke the angel:**

Once you feel centered, say the angel's name and attributes, calling upon them with respect and clarity. For example:

"Archangel Raphael, great healer and heavenly guide, I invoke you in this sacred space. Surround this place with your emerald light and allow me to feel your presence."

5. **Express your request:**

From your heart, state your request clearly and sincerely. You can do this aloud or silently, feeling the vibration of each word. For example:

"Archangel Raphael, help me release the emotional blocks that prevent me from moving forward. Guide me toward healing, inner peace, and balance."

6. **Meditate on the angel's presence:**

Remain in a state of receptivity, allowing the angelic energy to envelop you. Observe any sensations, images, or thoughts that arise without judging or forcing them. Trust that the connection has been established and that the message will come at the right time.

7. **Give thanks and close the ritual:**

   When you feel the process is complete, express gratitude to the angel for their presence and assistance. You can say:

   "Thank you, Archangel Raphael, for your love and guidance. I open myself to receive your blessings in my life."

   Respectfully extinguish the candle, without blowing it out, and remain silent for a few moments, integrating the energy before resuming your daily routine.

10. Angelic decrees: Formulation and power of words

What are decrees and how do they work?

Angelic decrees are affirmations of power spoken with conscious intent to activate universal principles through collaboration with angelic forces. Unlike traditional prayer, which often takes on a tone of supplication, the decree is based on the certainty that reality responds to vibrational commands aligned with divine will. This principle is grounded in the Hermetic teaching "as above, so below," which suggests that the same laws governing the higher planes are reflected in the material world. Thus, when words are uttered in attunement with higher energies, they can influence the very fabric of existence.

From a metaphysical perspective, each decree acts as an energetic template that angels can use to materialize changes on the physical plane. The Akashic records, conceived as a cosmic memory that stores information about all souls and events, record these decrees as long as they meet three key conditions: clarity of purpose, purity of intention, and alignment with the greater good. When a decree is formulated with precision and from the heart, the angels, guardians of universal laws, accelerate the processes necessary to transform those words into tangible realities.

The power of decrees lies in their ability to generate a vibrational bridge between human consciousness and the angelic planes. Each word emits a unique energetic frequency, attracting those angels whose vibration matches the expressed intention. For example, a decree of healing will resonate with the presence of Archangel Raphael, recognized in esoteric tradition as the divine healer, while a decree of protection will tune into the energy of Archangel Michael, the defender of light. These entities are not only mythical figures, but embody universal archetypes that channel specific energies for transformation.

The science behind the power of words

Quantum physics has shown that sound can modify the structure of matter, a phenomenon illustrated in **cymatics**, the study of how sound vibrations generate visible patterns in materials such as water or sand. This discovery reinforces the idea that sound is not just an auditory experience, but a force capable of reorganizing matter at subtle levels. As words are structured sound patterns, they generate vibrational waves that impact energy fields, creating what some call "energy signatures."

Neuroscience has proven that the use of affirmative language stimulates the formation of new neural connections, which means that repeating affirmations with conviction helps to reconfigure the perception of reality in a more positive way. In turn, esoteric linguistics suggests that certain sounds have an ancestral vibrational charge, such as those found in sacred languages like Sanskrit or Hebrew, used in ancient spiritual texts. Angelic decrees, although formulated in modern languages, follow this principle by using phonetic combinations that activate specific energy centers.

Transpersonal psychology has studied how repeated affirmations can influence the auric field, the subtle energy surrounding the human body. By combining these affirmations with visualization practices, the limbic brain—responsible for emotions—interprets the imagined experience as if it were real, thus creating a "bridge of manifestation" that allows angels to transform intention into tangible action.

Structure of an effective angelic decree

A powerful angelic decree must contain four essential elements:

1. **Invocation**: The connection with angelic forces is established through specific names and attributes, for example: "Archangel Michael, defender of di-

vine light." This call not only names the being, but also activates its essence and power.

2. **Declaration of power**: The intention is formulated with verbs in the present continuous tense, reinforcing the certainty of change. Example: "I decree the immediate dissolution of...". The choice of the present tense is crucial, as it indicates an ongoing action.

3. **Specification of the result**: The desire is expressed clearly but flexibly, avoiding limitations that interfere with angelic action. Instead of saying "I cure my illness," it is more effective to declare: "I manifest harmony and balance in my body, in alignment with the divine plan," allowing the solution to come in the best possible way.

4. **Affirmation of gratitude**: The decree is closed with an expression of gratitude, reinforcing the certainty of its fulfillment. Phrases such as "I thank the angels for materializing this decree" consolidate the energy flow and strengthen the manifestation.

The language used should always be positive and in the present tense. That is, it is more effective to say "I decree that my energy field reflects only divine light" rather than "I decree protection against harmful energies," since the former affirms the desired reality rather than reinforcing the presence of what one wants to avoid.

Finally, a well-structured decree should have between three and seven concise sentences, allowing for rhythmic repetition that reinforces its vibration without dispersing the intention.

Decrees for different aspects of life: Health, Abundance, and Love

Angelic decrees can be applied to multiple areas of life, acting as vibrational keys that open paths of transformation. Their effectiveness lies in the power of intention and alignment with the universal principles that govern reality. When spoken with conviction and clarity, they become powerful tools of manifestation, guided by angels to facilitate harmony and balance in different aspects of existence.

Health: Healing from the energetic plane

Health is not only a physical state, but a manifestation of the energetic balance that sustains the body. In this sense, healing decrees operate directly on the etheric body, the subtle structure that precedes matter and acts as a bridge between the spirit and the tangible. When a decree focused on "perfect cellular harmony according to the divine plan" is used, a channel is opened for the angels of healing to act on the vibrational root of the imbalance, correcting energy patterns that may be manifesting as ailments or diseases.

It is essential to avoid decrees focused on specific diagnoses, as expressions such as "I cure my diabetes" can limit angelic action to the purely physical realm. Instead, by decreeing states of harmony and integral well-being, healing is allowed to occur on multiple levels: emotional, mental, spiritual, and physical. Angelic energy does not work with concepts of illness, but with the restoration of the original perfection inscribed in each being. Therefore, decrees that reinforce the divine order in the body generate a synergy with the healing forces of the universe, allowing for complete recovery and transcending any medical label imposed from a limited perspective.

Abundance: Activating the Flow of Prosperity

Abundance is a state of flow, not accumulation. Decrees intended to strengthen prosperity must reflect this universal truth, moving away from the narrow view that wealth is reduced solely to money. In this context, a powerful affirmation is "I decree that I channel and distribute divine abundance in service to the cosmic plan." This formulation establishes a connection with the energy of universal provision, allowing resources to arrive in the measure necessary for each individual's life purpose.

The angels of prosperity operate under laws of energy circulation, not static possession. True abundance lies in the ability to give and receive in balance, so decrees that reinforce this dynamic are more effective than those based on the mere acquisition of goods. Expressions such as "I open my life to the infinite provision of the universe" or "I manifest opportunities and resources in perfect synchronicity with my evolution" allow prosperity to manifest organically, opening unexpected doors and generating synchronicities that multiply available resources.

The fundamental principle behind these decrees is trust in divine provision. It is not about attracting money for its own sake, but about aligning one's energy with the natural flow of the universe, where every need is met at the precise moment. The vibration of gratitude is key in this process, as recognizing the abundance that is already present reinforces attunement to new opportunities and blessings.

Love: Attracting authentic connections

Love, in its purest essence, is a frequency that transcends the personal and the relational, being a universal energy that permeates everything. Decrees related to this aspect should focus on expanding self-love and attracting relationships that reflect the highest vibration of the self. A powerful decree is "I decree to magnetize relationships that reflect my divine essence," as this affirmation allows the connections that come into life to be consistent with the evolution of the soul.

The angels of love work by harmonizing emotional patterns and removing blockages that may be interfering with the manifestation of authentic relationships. Therefore, it is essential to avoid decrees directed at specific people, as these can fall into attempts at energetic manipulation that create imbalances. Instead, focusing on qualities such as "I manifest unconditional love in my life" or "I attract bonds based on respect, growth, and spiritual connection" helps to tune into fuller and higher relationships.

Furthermore, love should not be viewed solely from a romantic perspective. A well-formulated decree can open doors to the healing of family ties, friendships, and, above all, the most important relationship of all: the one you have with yourself. By strengthening self-love and decreeing from a space of inner fulfillment, the energy of love radiates and becomes a beacon that attracts those who resonate with the same vibration.

The role of emotion and visualization in decrees

The effectiveness of a decree depends not only on the words used, but also on the emotion with which it is issued. Emotions are the vibrational fuel that enhances the resonance of the decree on the subtle planes. Research by the HeartMath Institute has shown that states of gratitude and love generate measurable electromagnetic fields that interact with the environment. When decreeing from a high emotion, a clear signal is emitted that angels recognize as alignment with the divine order.

Visualization reinforces the process by adding a multisensory component. By clearly imagining the desired outcome, energetic scaffolding is created that functions as blueprints for manifestation. These stimuli activate neural networks in the brain, sending chemical signals that predispose the body to receive the invoked transformation. Angels use these images as a reference to organize the necessary energies and bring the decree into tangible reality.

When emotion and visualization reach a sufficient level of intensity, a perceptual quantum leap occurs, a fusion of faith and certainty that opens the door to the materialization of profound changes.

Techniques to empower your decrees

Conscious repetition of decrees strengthens their impact, functioning as a personalized mantra that reconfigures the mind and reinforces intention. Studies on neuroplasticity have shown that sustained repetition of affirmations generates new neural connections that transform an individual's perception and inner reality. However, the key is not in the number of times a decree is repeated, but in the attention and emotion that is put into it each time.

Synchronization with natural cycles also enhances the effectiveness of decrees. The energy of dawn is ideal for decrees of beginning, while that of dusk favors the integration of changes. The phases of the moon offer different impulses: the crescent moon favors attraction, the full moon enhances manifestation, and the waning moon facilitates release.

The use of crystals and angelic symbols can serve as an energetic anchor to focus intention. Clear quartz amplifies the vibration of the decree, fire agate reinforces determination, and sacred symbols can act as energetic catalysts.

The combination of these elements with a clear and sustained intention allows decrees to become authentic channels of transformation, facilitating angelic intervention in the manifestation process.

Creating personalized decrees

Formulating a personalized decree is a process of deep self-knowledge, as each person has a unique energetic signature. Tools such as numerological name analysis—which reveals the relationship between certain numbers and personal traits—or the study of the Tree of Life in Kabbalah, which breaks down the structure of the universe into interconnected levels, allow us to identify our own vibrational patterns. When a decree is aligned with the expression number or life path of the person issuing it, its effect is enhanced, as it resonates with personal energy points that facilitate connection with angelic forces.

Language is key in this process. The words and metaphors used should reflect the way each person r individual perceives the divine. Those who associate the celestial presence with light will use resplendent images; those who feel it as an ocean of love will lean toward affectionate expressions. This coherence between what is felt and what is said is essential for the decree to have a real and vibrant impact, avoiding contradictions that can disperse its energy.

It is important to remember that decrees are not static. They grow and evolve along with the person. Reviewing them periodically—for example, at the beginning of each season—allows them to be adapted to new circumstances and aligned with the energy being experienced in the present moment. In this process, angels can offer guidance through intuitions, dreams, or synchronicities, pointing out necessary adjustments so that the decree remains a living and dynamic tool for transformation.

Decrees assisted by the power of the Angels

Decrees of Love
- Archangel Chamuel, I invoke your presence to guide me on the path to my soul mate, helping me to cultivate a relationship full of love and harmony.
- Angels of divine love, I decree that unconditional love flows freely in my life, attracting healthy and happy relationships.

- I decree that my heart will open and remain receptive to love, allowing the angels to help me give and receive affection without fear or barriers.

- Archangel Haniel, I ask for your assistance in healing my heart and releasing any blockages that prevent me from experiencing love in its purest form.

- Angels of union, I decree that my current relationship be strengthened and flourish under your loving guidance.

Decrees of Health

- Archangel Raphael, I decree that your healing light surround me, restoring harmony to my body, mind, and spirit.

- Healing angels, I invoke your assistance so that every cell in my body vibrates with the energy of health and divine vitality.

- I decree that any health challenge be transformed into an opportunity for growth and well-being, with the loving guidance of the angels.

- Angels of regeneration, I decree that my body align with its perfect design, manifesting complete and lasting balance.

- I decree that my mind be freed from thoughts or beliefs that affect my health, allowing peace and serenity to be my natural state.

Work Decrees

- Archangel Uriel, I decree that you illuminate my professional path, guiding me toward opportunities aligned with my life purpose.

- Angels of success, I decree that my work be a joyful expression of my talents, serving the world with love and dedication.

- I decree that abundance will flow through my vocation, allowing the angels to facilitate all my needs and aspirations.

- Angels of harmony, I decree that my work environment be filled with collaboration, creativity, and well-being.

- I decree that every challenge in my work be an opportunity for learning and expansion, with the luminous guidance of the angels.

Family Decrees

- Archangel Jofiel, I decree that your light bring beauty, understanding, and unity to my family relationships.

- Guardian angels of the home, I invoke your presence so that my home may be a sanctuary of peace, love, and harmony.

- I decree that any conflict in my family be resolved with compassion and understanding, with the assistance of the angels.

- Angels of ancestral healing, I decree that my lineage be blessed, liberated, and strengthened in love.

- I decree that my family will always be protected and guided by our guardian angels, feeling their love and companionship at every step.

Problem-Solving Decrees

- Archangel Zadkiel, I decree that you assist me in resolving this challenge, enlightening me with clarity and creative solutions.
- Angels of wisdom, I decree that you guide me toward the best decisions, facilitating access to divine truth.
- I decree that all the people and resources necessary to resolve this situation arrive at the perfect moment, with the support of the angels.
- Angels of transformation, I decree that all obstacles dissolve in the light of divine love.
- I decree that I emerge from this challenge with greater strength, wisdom, and alignment with my higher purpose.

Decrees to Leave Something Behind

- Archangel Michael, I decree that you cut with your sword of light all ties or attachments that no longer serve me, freeing me with love.
- Angels of transformation, I decree that you help me let go of fear and resistance, trusting that the best is yet to come.
- I decree that I forgive and free myself from any resentment or guilt, with the assistance of the angels.

- Angels of evolution, I decree that I integrate the lessons of this experience and move forward with gratitude.

- I decree that my path is cleared of all limitations, allowing the angels to guide me toward new opportunities.

Decrees of Prosperity

- Angels of abundance, I decree that I become a magnet for wealth in all its forms.

- I decree that my relationship with money be healed and harmonized, allowing it to flow naturally.

- Angels of sustenance, I decree that all my needs will always be met and that I will have more than enough to share and enjoy.

- I decree that new doors of prosperity open for me, with the loving guidance of the angels.

- Angels of fulfillment, I decree that my life be filled with opportunities and blessings.

Decrees of Protection

- Archangel Michael, I decree that your shield of blue light protect me from all discordant energy.

- Guardian angels, I decree that you always keep me safe and guided in every step I take.

- I decree that my home and my family be enveloped in the protective light of the angels.

- Angels of strength, I decree that my aura be strengthened and made immune to all negative influences.

- I decree that my actions and decisions are always aligned with my highest good, under the guidance of the angels.

Decrees of Divine Guidance

- Angels of enlightenment, I decree that my intuition be opened and strengthened, clearly receiving divine guidance.

- I decree that each of my decisions be in harmony with my higher purpose.

- Messenger angels, I decree that you help me interpret the signs and signals of the universe.

- I decree that I will always be in the right place at the perfect time, with the loving guidance of the angels.

Decrees of Inner Peace

- I decree that I am a being of peace and harmony, radiating calm around me.

- Angels of serenity, I decree that my mind be still and my heart be filled with light.

- I decree that forgiveness and compassion be my guides, freeing me from judgment and resentment.

- Angels of trust, I decree that I rest in the certainty that everything works for my highest good.

- I decree that I live in the grace of the present moment, accompanied by the loving presence of the angels.

11. Manifestation with Angelic Assistance: Principles and Practices

Universal Laws of Manifestation

Angelic manifestation follows metaphysical principles that have been recognized and passed down through various spiritual traditions. Over the centuries, different cultures have expressed these same laws in belief systems that converge on one essential point: reality is not static, but malleable through intention and vibration. A clear example of this is the Law of Attraction[43], which holds that like energies attract each other, establishing that thoughts and emotions can influence the surrounding reality. Although this concept has been popularized in New Age movements, its essence is much older and deeper. In this context, angels can be understood as mediators between human consciousness and the potentialities of the universe, operating as amplifiers of vibration that facilitate alignment between the desires of the individual and the possibilities that exist in the quantum field.

---

[43] The Law of Attraction was popularized by the book The Secret (2006), but it has roots in ancient philosophies such as Hermeticism and New Thought.

Another fundamental principle is the Law of Correspondence, whose axiom "as above, so below" suggests that everything that occurs on the subtle planes is reflected in the physical world. This idea has been explored since ancient times through sacred geometry, where structures such as the spiral, the cube, and the flower of life are considered archetypal patterns that organize matter and energy. In this framework, angels can be seen as beings who operate through these same patterns, modulating the energetic configuration of the universe to facilitate manifestation on the material plane.

Quantum physics, for its part, has discovered that the simple observation of a phenomenon can alter its outcome[44]. This finding, far from being an isolated piece of data, has been interpreted by some scholars of spirituality as evidence that human consciousness plays an active role in the transformation of reality. If our perception influences the subatomic world, why couldn't it do so in broader spheres of existence? This principle is linked to the Law of Vibration, which teaches that everything in the universe emits a measurable frequency. Just as a radio must be tuned to the right frequency to pick up a signal, human beings can adjust their internal energy to attract experiences aligned with their intention. In this sense, angels not only respond to emotional or verbal calls, but also interact with these vibrations, amplifying them so that manifestation accelerates and takes concrete form.

---

[44] This phenomenon is known as the observer effect and is related to the double-slit experiment, a pillar of quantum mechanics.

However, these laws do not act in isolation, but in a delicate interdependent balance. The Law of Cause and Effect, for example, manifests itself in synchronicities: coincidences that seem charged with higher meaning and can be interpreted as angelic signs. When human actions align with universal principles, effects are generated that facilitate the materialization of desires. In this sense, neuroscience has identified that cardiac coherence—a state in which the heart and brain work in harmony—increases the capacity for subtle perception. Techniques such as conscious breathing and meditation allow people to reach this state, which in turn facilitates connection with angels and access to creative energies of manifestation.

The role of angels as catalysts for desires

From a mystical perspective, angels can be understood as active interfaces between human consciousness and the vast quantum fields of possibility. They are said to operate in non-local dimensions, meaning they can influence multiple events simultaneously, without the limitations of space and time. Their work is not to arbitrarily intervene in people's lives, but to empower those intentions that are aligned with spiritual growth and soul purpose.

Various studies in parapsychology have documented cases in which individuals have experienced remarkable accelerations in the resolution of vital conflicts after invoking angelic assistance. In some testimonies, people have reported unexpected turns in legal, financial, or even medical situations, where heavenly help seems to have tipped the scales in their favor. Within these interventions, certain angelic figures stand out for their specific roles: Archangel Michael is frequently invoked in situations of protection and conflict resolution, while Archangel Raphael is recognized for his influence in processes of healing and regeneration. In both cases, these beings act as energy focalizers, directing vibrational currents that facilitate the manifestation process in a more effective and orderly manner.

The functioning of this intervention is better understood in light of the concept of the Akashic field, described in various esoteric traditions as an energetic record where all the possibilities of the universe are stored. Angels are said to have the ability to interact with this field, activating timelines and potential paths that might otherwise remain dormant. From this perspective, what is often perceived as a miracle is nothing more than the accelerated materialization of a potential possibility that already existed in potency but was catalyzed by angelic intervention.

Aligning personal will with angelic guidance

For angelic manifestation to be effective, there must be congruence between the individual's desires and their evolutionary purpose. Various studies in transpersonal psychology have shown that internal conflicts—such as the tension between selfish motivations and higher aspirations—can generate energetic interference that hinders the materialization of intentions. From an esoteric point of view, it is said that these contradictions affect the auric field, generating blockages that prevent the proper circulation of creative energy.

Angels, in their role as guides, use synchronistic signs to guide people toward choices more aligned with their essence. These signs can manifest in multiple forms: recurring numerical patterns such as 11:11, chance encounters with key people, or dreams containing relevant symbolic information. In many traditions, numbers and symbols have been considered vehicles of coded knowledge, which explains why those who work with angels often develop a special sensitivity for interpreting these messages.

Science has shed light on this phenomenon through studies such as those conducted by the HeartMath Institute, which have shown that when a person is in a state of psychophysiological coherence—that is, when their thoughts, emotions, and bodily responses are in harmony—their ability to perceive intuitive information increases significantly. This suggests that openness to angelic guidance is not simply a matter of faith, but has measurable correlates in the functioning of the nervous system and the electromagnetic field of the heart.

To achieve true alignment with these forces, it is essential to develop spiritual discernment, the ability to distinguish between desires that emerge from the soul and those that are the product of the conditioned mind. Traditions such as numerology or Kabbalah have offered tools for this purpose, providing symbolic maps that allow us to identify our individual mission within a broader framework. Applying these tools not only helps to clarify the right direction, but also allows us to identify key moments when angelic assistance can be most effectively harnessed.

Creative visualization techniques with angels

Angelic visualization is a powerful practice that activates neural circuits linked to emotion and spiritual perception . Studies have shown that the brain reacts to mental images with a response similar to that which it would have to a real experience. In other words, when you visualize the presence of an angel, your mind and body respond as if you were truly in contact with that energy. Research using advanced brain imaging techniques, such as functional magnetic resonance imaging (fMRI), has identified that imagining encounters with angelic beings stimulates the superior parietal lobe, a region linked to transcendental experiences and states of expanded consciousness.

When you visualize angels with intention and clarity, you create energy patterns in your "mental body," something like subtle maps that allow their energy to flow into your reality. These mental images can act as vibrational blueprints that help manifest what you want to attract, aligning your energy with that of the beings of light. To enhance this practice, you can incorporate principles of cymatics, the science that studies how sound and vibration shape matter. Geometric figures such as the "flower of life" or "Metatron's cube" are considered especially powerful because they resonate with the energetic structure of the universe, amplifying the impact of visualization.

Metatron's Cube

To make the experience even more profound, you can engage multiple senses in the visualization. In addition to imagining the image of the angel, you can incorporate sacred scents such as sandalwood incense for Michael or the fragrance of roses for Chamuel. You can also add sounds, such as the ringing of bells that evokes the presence of Gabriel or the thermal sensation of enveloping warmth that suggests the protection of Uriel. It has been proven that when we activate several senses simultaneously, the brain increases its activity in the prefrontal cortex, the region that enhances concentration and intention, thus strengthening the connection with the angelic plane.

Creating angelic vision boards

Vision boards are an effective tool for materializing intentions and attracting specific energies. When we incorporate angelic elements into them, they function as energetic antennas, focusing consciousness on higher goals and creating a vibrational resonance with the higher dimensions. The human mind responds deeply to visual stimuli: studies in cognitive psychology have revealed that frequent exposure to images with symbolic meaning can improve the perception of opportunities and strengthen the capacity for manifestation.

To design an angelic vision board, you can include sacred images and symbols that strengthen your spiritual connection. Elements such as the "eye of providence," which represents divine vigilance, spheres of light that evoke heavenly purity, or angelic seals from the Kabbalistic tradition can act as powerful energy activators. Some research suggests that certain symbols influence the emission of biophotons, particles of light emitted by living beings, which could indicate greater energetic activity in boards containing these elements.

In addition, the location of the board can enhance its effectiveness if you follow the principles of geomancy, the art of harmonizing spaces according to their orientation. Placing it facing north can promote professional stability, while placing it facing east can enhance the energy of health and well-being. Those who have tried these techniques have reported that intentionally aligned boards generate faster and more tangible results than those placed without a specific purpose.

Angelic Manifestation Exercise: Anticipatory Gratitude

This exercise uses the power of gratitude and visualization to align your energy with your desires, allowing angels to facilitate them in your life. The key is to experience your dreams as if they were already a reality and, from that state of fulfillment and gratitude, allow them to manifest on the physical plane.

Metaphysical Foundation

This method is based on fundamental principles of manifestation. First, the idea that our thoughts and emotions directly influence our reality. By focusing on what we desire with clarity and positive emotion, we send a powerful signal to the universe.

This principle is aligned with the Law of Attraction, which holds that we attract what we focus on. By visualizing and feeling our desires as already fulfilled, we adjust our vibration to that frequency, bringing us closer to their materialization.

Spiritual teacher Neville Goddard taught about the power of imagination and assumption, stating that when we assume the feeling that something is already real, we plant the seed for its manifestation. His teaching is summed up in the biblical phrase:

"Whatever you ask for in prayer, believe that you have received it, and it will be yours" (Mark 11:24).

In this exercise, we apply these principles with the assistance of angels, who, as divine messengers and agents of change, can accelerate and facilitate the process of manifestation. Gratitude, being one of the highest vibrational frequencies, opens us up to receiving abundance and well-being.

Step-by-Step Instructions

1. **Find a quiet place**

   Spend 15 to 20 minutes in a space where there will be no interruptions. You can sit comfortably or lie down, whichever helps you relax completely.

2. **Relax your body and mind**

   Take several deep breaths. Inhale through your nose, allowing the air to fill your abdomen, and exhale slowly through your mouth. Feel how, with each exhalation, any tension or worry disappears.

3. **Define your intention**

   Think of a specific desire you would like to manifest. It can be related to your health, relationships, career, abundance, or any aspect of your life.

4. **Visualize your desire as a fulfilled reality**

   Imagine that your desire has already materialized. Use all your senses to make it as vivid as possible:

   - What do you see around you?
   - What sounds surround you?
   - What physical sensations do you experience?
   - How does it feel emotionally to have achieved this?

5. **Immerse yourself in the emotion of achievement**

   Let joy, gratitude, excitement, or peace wash over you. Smile naturally, allowing the happiness of the manifestation already fulfilled to flow through your entire being.

6. **Express gratitude to the angels**

7. Say it out loud or mentally:

   "Thank you, beloved angels, for bringing this blessing into my life. I am deeply grateful for [insert your desire here]. It is even better than I imagined."

8. **Detail your gratitude**

   Continue expressing gratitude for the details:

   - *"Thank you for all the incredible opportunities that are appearing."*
   - *"Thank you for the loving relationship I am enjoying."*
   - *"Thank you for the harmony and fulfillment in my life."*
   - Feel each word with complete certainty.

9. **Feel the presence of the angels.**

   Visualize them surrounding you in a halo of loving light. You may feel them as flashes of energy, gentle warm currents, or a comforting presence. Let their energy raise your vibration and reinforce the certainty that your desire is already on its way.

10. **Remain in this state of gratitude.**

   Enjoy this moment for as long as you wish, allowing every cell in your body to absorb this frequency of fulfillment.

11. **Slowly return to the present**

   When you feel the exercise is complete, begin to become aware of your breathing. Gently move your fingers and toes, and slowly open your eyes.

12. **Surrender the outcome and trust**

   Give one last "thank you" to the angels and the universe. Then, let go of any attachment to "how" or "when" your desire will manifest. Trust that it is on its way at the divinely perfect moment.

13. **Act in alignment with your intention**

   Stay alert for any inspiration or signs that prompt you to take action. Remember that manifestation is a dance between intention and action.

Tips for Enhancing the Exercise

- **Do it daily** to strengthen your connection and accelerate manifestation.

- **Write it down in a journal** as if it has already happened.
- **Recreate the emotion throughout the day** whenever you think about your desire.
- **Listen to uplifting music or high-frequency sounds** before practicing.
- **Let go of expectations about time** and allow it to flow naturally.

The more you live *"as if"* your desire were already a reality, the faster it will be reflected in your physical world. Trust in the magic of the universe and the unconditional love of the angels, who are always ready to guide and support you on your path.

Successful manifestations with angelic help

Various reports and testimonials have documented experiences in which angelic manifestation has proven to be an effective tool. A 2019 study by a prestigious institute dedicated to the expansion of consciousness revealed that 72% of participants in retreats focused on angelic manifestation achieved tangible results in less than three months. In comparison, only 22% of a control group that did not use these techniques experienced significant changes, suggesting a positive influence on those who applied practices of connecting with angels.

On the other hand, research conducted at a renowned university in Arizona analyzed the impact of these practices on 154 terminally ill patients. The findings showed that 38% of patients who integrated angelic techniques into their treatment experienced unexpected clinical improvements, in contrast to only 9% of those who received only conventional medical care. These results have sparked interest in the scientific community about the possible relationship between spiritual healing and physical health.

In addition, a recent report from a center specializing in global consciousness identified a significant correlation between the activation of archangels and an increase in favorable synchronicities in legal and commercial processes. The cases analyzed coincided in certain key factors, such as the constant use of specific invocations, alignment with service purposes, and the daily integration of principles inspired by hermetic teachings. These studies suggest that angelic manifestation reaches its maximum potential when combined with concrete actions on the physical plane, confirming that the key to success lies in the collaboration between the spiritual and the material.

12. Angels and Chakras: Energetic Alignment for Celestial Communication

Chakras are energy centers that act as links between the physical body and spiritual dimensions. In Eastern traditions, such as Hinduism and Buddhism, they are described as wheels of light that regulate the flow of prana, or vital energy. From the perspective of angelology, these centers function as natural antennas capable of tuning into the celestial frequencies emanating from higher planes, where light entities reside. Each chakra vibrates at a particular frequency and is linked to specific aspects of the being, forming a vibrational ladder that connects the earthly plane with the angelic realms.

To strengthen this connection, you can perform the following visualization and breathing exercise:

1. Adopt a comfortable posture with your spine straight and your feet firmly planted on the ground.

2. Inhale deeply and imagine a radiant white light entering through the crown of your head and descending to the base of your spine.

3. As you exhale, visualize that light expanding, filling each of your chakras from root to crown.

4. With each inhalation, feel the angelic energy flowing through these centers, cleansing and balancing them.

5. As you exhale, let go of any accumulated blockages or density, allowing the light to dissolve them completely.

6. Maintain this conscious breathing for several minutes, sensing how your chakras harmonize with the celestial frequencies.

These energy vortexes act as dimensional keys: when they are in balance, they facilitate the reception and understanding of angelic messages with greater clarity. For example, the root chakra, located at the base of the spine, provides the stability necessary to anchor celestial protection, channeling energy that forms shields of light against negative influences.

To unblock and strengthen your root chakra, try this grounding exercise:

1. Standing, visualize roots sprouting from the soles of your feet and sinking deep into the earth.

2. With each inhalation, feel the energy of the earth rising through those roots and filling your root chakra with a bright red glow.

3. As you exhale, release any fears or insecurities, allowing the earth to transform them into strength and stability.

4. Repeat this breathing cycle, feeling yourself become more grounded and rooted with each inhale.

5. Imagine Archangel Uriel beside you, enveloping you with his energy of solidity and security.

At the opposite end of the body, the crown chakra, located at the top of the head, acts as a portal that facilitates the reception of inspiration and divine messages. It is the ultimate receiver of wisdom from higher dimensions. When all the chakras are harmonized, a pure channel is formed through which angelic energies can flow freely, allowing for clearer communication with beings of light.

To activate and tune into your crown chakra, perform this guided meditation:

1. Sit in a comfortable position with your eyes closed and your hands resting gently on your legs.

2. Imagine a golden, shining light descending from above and entering through your crown chakra.

3. Notice how this light fills your head, dispelling any heavy thoughts or worries.

4. Inhale, drawing in more of this light, and exhale, allowing it to spread throughout your body.

5. Visualize Archangel Metatron at your side, adjusting the vibration of your crown chakra to align it with the frequency of celestial wisdom.

6. Remain in this meditative state for as long as you wish, open to receiving inspiration and guidance.

Each angelic order resonates with a specific chakra following a principle of vibrational correspondence. That is, both angels and the energy centers of human beings share related frequencies and qualities. For example, the Seraphim, guardians of divine fire, are linked to the crown chakra because of their ability to transmit transcendental truths and expand consciousness. Cherubim, protectors of occult knowledge, are associated with the third eye, promoting intuitive perception and prophetic visions.

Activation of the Third Eye with Cherubim

Cherubim, guardians of sacred knowledge, are closely linked to the third eye, the center of inner vision and deep intuition. Through this chakra, perception expands beyond the obvious, allowing subtle messages and hidden truths to be grasped. To strengthen this connection, try the following inner vision practice:

1. Sit in a quiet place and close your eyes.

2. Direct your attention to the space between your eyebrows, where your third eye resides.

3. Inhale, imagining an indigo glow lighting up in this energy center, and as you exhale, allow any tension to dissipate.

4. As you breathe, visualize the presence of a Cherub in front of you, radiating a light of wisdom and clarity.

5. Ask it to strengthen your psychic perception and help you accurately interpret the signs you receive.

6. Remain receptive to any images, symbols, or sensations that arise, trusting that they are angelic guidance manifesting in your consciousness.

Harmonizing the Throat Chakra with the Thrones

The Thrones, responsible for sustaining the divine structure of the universe, resonate with the throat chakra, the center of communication and authentic expression. Their influence strengthens the ability to convey essential truths to th through language, music, or any form of artistic creation. To balance this center and connect with the vibration of the Thrones, perform the following light chanting exercise:

1. Adopt a comfortable posture, sitting or standing, and bring your attention to your throat.

2. Inhale, visualizing a sky blue light expanding in your throat chakra, and as you exhale, allow any blockages or fears related to expression to dissolve.

3. Begin to intone a primordial sound, such as "OM" or "AH," feeling the vibration resonate in your throat and expand throughout your being.

4. As you sing, visualize an Angelic Throne beside you, harmonizing your energy with the frequencies of truth and sincere communication.

5. Allow your voice to flow with confidence, without restriction, feeling your chakra align with the celestial vibration.

6. When you feel it is enough, stop chanting and remain silent for a few moments, feeling the energetic activation in your throat.

Opening the Heart Chakra with the Dominations

The heart chakra is the gateway to the energy of unconditional love and compassion. Its balance is essential for establishing harmonious relationships and experiencing life from a higher perspective. Dominations, responsible for radiating vibrations of pure love, can help you release emotional blocks and heal deep wounds through this conscious breathing meditation:

1. Place both hands on your heart and close your eyes.

2. Inhale deeply, imagining a pink or emerald green light filling your heart chakra, and as you exhale, allow any pain or resentment to dissolve.

3. With each inhalation, feel your heart expand and fill with unconditional love.

4. As you exhale, project this energy toward yourself, your loved ones, and finally, the entire world.

5. Visualize the presence of an angel of Domination enveloping your chest with its healing vibration, releasing any emotional ties.

6. Remain in this flow of love, feeling its restorative energy, until your heart feels light and radiant.

Purification of the Chakras with Diamond Light

Angels purify the chakras through streams of diamond light, a high-frequency energy that gently and precisely dissolves any blockages. This cleansing process takes place in three fundamental phases:

1. Transmutation phase: Angels linked to fire, such as Verchiel, act as catalysts, consuming the energetic densities accumulated in the chakras and restoring their natural flow.

2. Restructuring phase: Thrones reorganize the energy patterns in the subtle body, restoring internal harmony so that energy can flow without interference.

3. Stabilization phase: Cherubim intervene by consolidating the new configuration through the implementation of sacred geometries, which fix the restored frequencies in the auric field.

Unlike conventional healing methods, which focus on visible symptoms, angelic cleansing operates simultaneously in all dimensions of being, addressing karmic, ancestral, and emotional blockages at their root. Its influence is comprehensive, balancing not only the chakras but also the subtle bodies that connect matter with spirit.

Angelic Cleansing of the Chakras

The archangels can assist in a deep cleansing of the chakras, releasing energy blockages and restoring inner harmony. To experience this process, perform the following visualization:

1. Lie down in a quiet place and close your eyes.

2. Visualize Archangel Michael standing at your feet, holding a sword of bright blue light.

3. Imagine Michael gently sliding his sword over your body, from your feet to your head.

4. As the sword passes through each chakra, feel it cutting and dissolving any blockages, cords, or stagnant energy.

5. Now, observe Archangel Raphael at your side, pouring a cascade of emerald light over your chakras.

6. Feel how this light fills and balances each energy center, bringing you freshness and vitality.

7. Finally, Archangel Uriel appears before you, projecting sacred geometries of golden light onto your chakras.

8. Allow these shapes to anchor and stabilize the new energy, creating a harmonious flow within your being.

9. When you feel that the process is complete, thank the archangels and slowly return to your usual state of consciousness.

Activation of the Crown Chakra with the Lotus of Light

The crown chakra is the gateway to heavenly guidance. When activated, it acts as a vortex that receives messages in the form of images, intuitions, or deep certainties. However, opening it requires stability in the lower chakras to prevent the heavenly energy from overwhelming the nervous system. To awaken this center and connect with the angels, practice the following meditation:

1. Sit in a meditative posture and close your eyes.

2. Visualize a thousand-petaled white and gold lotus floating above your head.

3. With each inhalation, imagine the lotus slowly opening, radiating pure light from its center.

4. As you exhale, feel this light descend through your crown chakra, filling you with clarity and peace.

5. Sense the presence of Archangel Metatron at your side, facilitating the opening of your consciousness to the angelic realms.

6. Remain receptive to any messages, visions, or sensations that arise, knowing that they come from heavenly guidance.

7. When you feel it is time to conclude, visualize the lotus gently closing, keeping your spiritual connection active.

Opening the Heart Chakra with Gratitude

The heart chakra is the bridge between human consciousness and angelic frequencies. When it expands, it generates a vibrational field that attracts guardian angels, who operate in the fourth dimension, where the primordial language is love. To strengthen this connection, try this gratitude practice:

1. Place one hand on your heart and close your eyes.

2. Bring to mind a person, situation, or memory for which you feel deep gratitude.

3. Inhale, allowing this feeling of appreciation to expand your heart chakra, and exhale, sending that energy out into the universe.

4. Continue breathing gratitude for a few minutes, feeling your vibration rise.

5. Mentally invite your guardian angel to join you in this state of love and harmony.

6. Remain alert to any subtle signs of their presence: a sudden emotion, a feeling of warmth, or an intuitive message.

7. When you feel it is time to finish, open your eyes and carry this loving connection with you throughout your day.

Solar Plexus Balance for Manifesting Angelic Guidance

The solar plexus is the center of will and manifestation. Here, heavenly inspirations take shape and translate into concrete actions. When this chakra is balanced, it allows you to receive angelic visions without them becoming illusions disconnected from reality. To enhance its energy, perform this personal power exercise:

1. Standing, place both hands on your solar plexus, just above your navel.

2. Inhale, visualizing a golden light igniting this center, and exhale, dissolving any doubts or feelings of helplessness.

3. With each breath, feel your confidence and inner clarity grow stronger.

4. Bring to mind a project or desire you long to manifest and visualize it in detail.

5. Repeat mentally or aloud: "I am a co-creator with the Divine. Everything I imagine manifests in perfect harmony."

6. Imagine Archangel Jofiel at your side, illuminating your solar plexus with his golden energy of creativity and expansion.

7. Feel how this radiant force takes root in your being, strengthening your connection to your higher purpose.

Chakra Harmonization Meditation with Angelic Vibration

When the chakras are aligned, the energetic body tunes into cosmic rhythms that transcend human logic. Angels use sound frequencies and sacred geometries to readjust these centers, returning them to their natural state of balance. During this meditation, entities such as Hathor emit harmonic tones that resonate with the energy patterns of the subtle body. To experience this vibrational alignment:

1. Sit or lie down in a quiet space.

2. Inhale deeply and allow your body to relax completely.

3. Visualize a sphere of golden light enveloping your entire being, stabilizing your energy field.

4. Feel each chakra begin to vibrate in its unique tone, like a note in a celestial symphony.

5. Sense the presence of angels emitting healing frequencies, tuning each center with their vibrational sound.

6. Allow these vibrations to flow through your being, adjusting and elevating your energy.

7. When you feel that the harmonization is complete, breathe deeply, feeling the fullness of your body and spirit in balance.

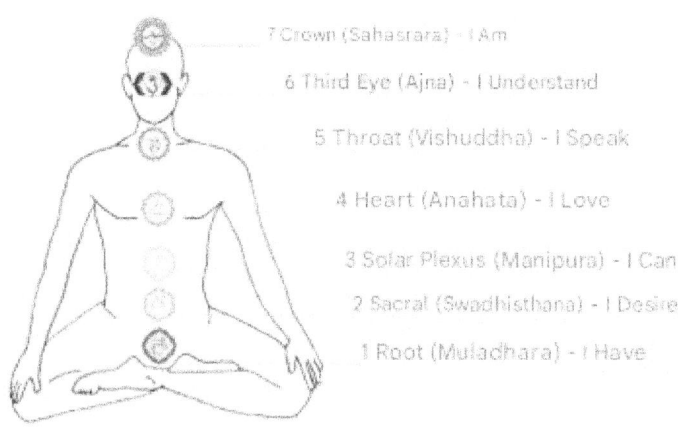

Chakras

13. Angelology and astrology: Cosmic connections and planetary influences

Ruling angels of the zodiac signs

Each zodiac sign resonates with angelic entities that modulate its essential attributes, amplifying its virtues and balancing its challenges. Below are the links between each sign and its ruling angel, along with a brief description of their influence.

Aries – Archangel Samael

Strength and transformation

Samael, whose name translates as "severity of God," embodies impetus, courage, and pure energy of action. His influence on Aries enhances determination and leadership, but also teaches self-control and the conscious channeling of personal power to avoid excessive impulsiveness.

Taurus – Angel Anael

Harmony and Earthly Love

Anael, angel of love and beauty, helps Taurus balance their connection to the pleasures of material life, encouraging gratitude and conscious enjoyment. His guidance softens rigidity and reinforces emotional stability, reminding us that security also resides in spiritual confidence.

Gemini – Archangel Raphael

Communication and mental clarity

Raphael, whose name means "God heals," facilitates the fluid expression of thoughts and emotions. For Gemini, his presence stimulates curiosity, intelligence, and connection with inner truth, helping to avoid distraction and excessive superficiality in their interactions.

Cancer – Archangel Gabriel

Protection and intuitive sensitivity

Gabriel, divine messenger and guardian of emotions, guides Cancer on their journey toward understanding their own feelings and those of the people around them. His influence strengthens intuition and connection with family, providing security in times of change.

Leo – Archangel Michael

Leadership and purpose

Michael, the great heavenly protector, reinforces Leo's courage and authenticity, helping them to manifest their light with integrity. His energy promotes the expansion of leadership with nobility and purpose, avoiding pride or the need for external validation.

Virgo – Angel Metatron

Order and spiritual perfection

Metatron, known as the celestial scribe, channels his energy into structuring and analysis. For Virgo, his presence inspires organization and precision, helping to transform meticulousness into meaningful service, without falling into excessive self-criticism.

Libra – Angel Jofiel

Beauty and divine wisdom

Jofiel, the illuminator of harmony, drives Libra to seek balance and justice in their relationships. Their energy inspires appreciation for beauty in all its forms, promoting art, diplomacy, and conscious love based on respect and understanding.

Scorpio – Angel Azrael

Transformation and rebirth

Azrael, guardian of the cycles of life and death, accompanies Scorpio in its processes of internal transformation. Its energy helps Scorpio let go of what no longer serves it, embrace regeneration, and understand that every ending is the threshold of a new beginning.

Sagittarius – Angel Zadkiel

Expansion and spiritual freedom

Zadkiel, angel of mercy and knowledge, guides Sagittarius in their search for truth. Their energy promotes wisdom, learning, and openness to new perspectives, helping to integrate spirituality into everyday life.

Capricorn – Angel Cassiel

Discipline and karmic evolution

Cassiel, angel of patience and structure, helps Capricorn navigate the path of maturity and responsibility. His influence strengthens perseverance, teaching that true success comes from consistency and inner growth.

Aquarius – Angel Uriel

Innovation and transcendental vision

Uriel, bearer of the divine fire of knowledge, inspires Aquarius to challenge established paradigms and work for the collective good. His energy drives creativity, social awareness, and the search for ideas that transform humanity.

Pisces – Angel Sandalphon

Intuition and spiritual connection

Sandalphon, angel of music and prayer, guides Pisces in their mystical sensitivity and connection to the universe. His energy strengthens subtle perception, facilitating artistic inspiration, emotional healing, and universal compassion.

Planetary influences and their associated angels

In classical astrology, each planet reflects an aspect of the psyche and reality. Archangels oversee these influences, helping to harmonize their energies.

Sun – Archangel Michael

Strengthens leadership, confidence, and life purpose.

Moon – Archangel Gabriel

Modulates emotions and intuition, facilitating connection with internal cycles.

Mercury – Archangel Raphael

Stimulates intelligence, communication, and mental clarity.

Venus – Angel Anael

Harmonizes love, beauty, and artistic sensitivity.

Mars – Archangel Samael

Channels action and courage in a positive direction.

Jupiter – Angel Sachiel

Expands abundance, wisdom, and optimism.

Saturn – Angel Cassiel

Promotes discipline, karmic learning, and maturity.

For transpersonal planets:

Uranus – Angel Uriel

Promotes evolution, innovation, and the breaking down of obsolete structures.

Neptune – Angel Asariel

Encourages connection with the divine, intuition, and visionary art.

Pluto – Angel Azrael

Facilitates profound transformation and spiritual rebirth.

Angelic work during planetary retrogrades

Retrograde periods represent moments of review and energetic readjustment. Angelic intervention helps navigate these phases with greater awareness:

- Mercury retrograde: Raphael helps clarify communication and avoid misunderstandings.
- Venus retrograde: Anael guides the review of relationships and emotional values.
- Mars retrograde: Samael teaches how to redirect energy constructively.
- Jupiter retrograde: Sachiel encourages introspection and inner growth.

- Saturn retrograde: Cassiel assists in the integration of karmic lessons.

Angels of the astrological houses

The astrological houses represent specific areas of life, each with a guardian angel who facilitates its development:

- 1st House (Identity): Metatron – Helps manifest your authentic essence.
- 2nd House (Resources): Mammon – Teaches the ethical management of abundance.
- 3rd House (Communication): Raphael – Encourages expression and learning.
- 4th House (Roots): Gabriel – Connects with ancestral memory and home.
- 5th House (Creativity): Jophiel – Inspires artistic expression and joy.
- 6th House (Health and Service): Michael – Organizes and strengthens personal discipline.
- 7th House (Relationships): Chamuel – Harmonizes emotional bonds and agreements.
- 8th House (Transformation): Azrael – Guides processes of profound change.
- 9th House (Philosophy and Expansion): Zadkiel – Promotes exploration and knowledge.
- 10th House (Vocation): Cassiel – Provides structure and purpose in one's career.
- 11th House (Collective): Uriel – Stimulates social vision and innovation.

- 12th House (Unconscious): Sandalphon – Facilitates connection with the divine and introspection.

Angelic rituals to enhance favorable astrological transits

Angelic energy can be enhanced when synchronized with astrological cycles, as these open key moments for working on different aspects of life. For example, when Jupiter forms harmonious angles with the natal Sun, ideal opportunities are created to connect with Sachiel and focus energy on expansion, the materialization of projects, and the opening of new paths. Similarly, the lunar phases— nd especially the new moon and full moon—activate energy portals in which Gabriel guides the sowing of intentions at the beginning of a cycle and facilitates the realization of achievements when the Moon reaches its fullness.

Solar eclipses, considered in many traditions as moments of profound transformation, can be used for inner renewal with the assistance of Metatron, who helps reorganize internal structures and readjust the course of life. In the case of the most intense lunar phases, Sandalphon acts as a channel for emotional healing, facilitating the purification of stagnant memories or emotions. In addition, the Sun's entry into each zodiac sign marks a new energy cycle that can be accompanied by the ruling angel of the sign in question, allowing you to begin the stage with clarity and purpose.

When challenging aspects appear in the sky, such as the square between Saturn and Uranus—symbolizing the clash between the established and the innovative—the intervention of Cassiel and Uriel is recommended to find the balance between responsibility and necessary change. On the other hand, planetary conjunctions, by uniting the energies of two or more celestial bodies, can enhance the combined action of kindred angels. An example of this is the conjunction of Venus and Neptune, whose fusion with the energy of Anael and Asariel favors artistic inspiration, spiritual sensitivity, and the manifestation of visionary projects.

Karmic healing with angels according to the natal chart

The natal chart is a tool that allows us to understand inherited karmic patterns and how they influence our current life. Through angelic guidance, it is possible to transform blockages or pending lessons. One of the most significant points in this analysis is the lunar nodes: the South Node represents previous lessons that may be limiting the present, and their release can be facilitated with the intervention of Zadkiel, who helps dissolve repetitive emotional ties. In contrast, the North Node points to one's life purpose and the direction to follow, a path in which Metatron acts as a guide to align personal will with spiritual evolution.

When Saturn is in the twelfth house or forms tense aspects in the chart, it can indicate unconscious karmic debts that require resolution. In these cases, Cassiel is the right ally to maturely take on these lessons and transform the burden into wisdom. If Pluto creates tensions with the Moon, Azrael's energy can facilitate the release of deep-rooted emotions and promote transformation through deep healing. On the other hand, when several planets are grouped together in the same sector of the chart, forming a stellium, an energetic emphasis is produced that may require the assistance of different angels to balance its effects.

A particular case is the square of Chiron with the Sun, which represents wounds in identity and the way a person perceives themselves. In this context, Raphael can help transform pain into learning, strengthening self-concept and guiding toward inner healing. Likewise, Grand Cross configurations, which involve tensions in four directions of the chart, indicate karmic challenges that require the collaboration of several angels to restore balance and facilitate personal growth.

Angels and lunar nodes: life purpose and karmic lessons

The lunar nodal axis, composed of the South Node and the North Node, is a map of each person's spiritual evolution. Its position in the natal chart indicates the lessons accumulated in previous lives and the areas in which progress is needed to achieve greater harmony. For example, if the South Node is in Aries, there may be a tendency toward extreme independence or impulsiveness, aspects that can be worked on with Samael's guidance to balance these impulses. In this case, the North Node in Libra invites you to develop harmonious relationships and encourage cooperation, with Jofiel's assistance in cultivating balance and empathy.

When the South Node is in Capricorn, it often reflects an excessive attachment to structure, control, or the " r materialism. Cassiel helps to release these restrictions, while the North Node in Cancer, guided by Gabriel, promotes emotional connection and the development of sensitivity. In the case of nodes located on the axis of the third and ninth houses, the teaching focuses on integrating rational knowledge with intuition, a process in which Raphael and Zadkiel can assist in achieving balanced learning that combines logic and spiritual wisdom.

The positions of the nodes in angular houses—related to identity, relationships, and service—often indicate missions of public impact, where the presence of Michael and Chamuel is key to aligning personal goals with collective responsibility. On the other hand, when the nodes are in fixed signs, difficulties in accepting change may arise, making Azrael's intervention essential to break rigid structures and facilitate evolution.

Each of these interactions between angelology and astrology shows how celestial movements and angelic energies can work together to offer guidance, healing, and opportunities for transformation. Consciously integrating this knowledge allows us not only to interpret astrological transits, but also to connect with the subtle vibration of angels, creating a bridge between heaven and everyday life. In this way, every experience can become a path of spiritual growth and personal fulfillment.

14. Angels in dreams: Interpretation and angelic dream work

Types of angelic dreams: messages, visits, teachings

Dream encounters with angels can be classified according to their purpose and symbolic depth. Message dreams function as warnings or precise guides, expressing themselves through recurring symbols such as white feathers, spheres of light, or numerical sequences. These elements are not simply random images, but carriers of a specific vibration that has been interpreted by different mystical traditions as signs of spiritual communication. Dream visits, on the other hand, involve direct interaction with the angel, who manifests with recognizable attributes. It is common for them to appear with characteristic signs, such as Michael's flaming sword, a symbol of protection and spiritual strength; Gabriel's trumpet, associated with announcements and transcendental revelations; or Raphael's healing staff, an emblem of both physical and emotional healing in various esoteric currents and sacred texts.

Teaching dreams, on the other hand, unfold complex scenarios laden with symbolism, such as journeys through celestial labyrinths or lessons on sacred geometry. The latter concept is linked to universal patterns present in nature and mystical structures, considered reflections of the divine order. Those who experience this type of dream often wake up with a feeling of mental expansion, as if they had received fragments of knowledge that need to be integrated over time. The intensity of light, the sharpness of details, and sensory clarity are aspects that distinguish them from ordinary dreams, revealing access to higher planes of consciousness.

Techniques for inducing angelic dreams

Preparation for receiving angelic dreams is based on tuning the mind and body to an appropriate vibrational frequency, especially during the REM phase of sleep, when brain activity intensifies and access to subtle planes of perception becomes more accessible. Research in parapsychology has pointed out that the hypnagogic state[45] —that transition between wakefulness and deep sleep— acts as a natural gateway to spiritual experiences, since at

---

[45] The hypnagogic state is studied in neuroscience for its ability to generate vivid images due to the activity of the parietal lobe.

that moment the barrier between the conscious and the unconscious weakens, allowing the manifestation of unusual images, sounds, and sensations.

One of the most effective tools for inducing these encounters is sleep programming through affirmations prior to rest. Repeating a specific intention before sleeping facilitates the opening of the mind to these messages. However, the effectiveness of this practice is closely related to the activation of the pineal gland, considered in many esoteric traditions as the "third eye," capable of capturing subtle energy frequencies. Diet also plays a fundamental role in the quality of dreams. For example, an excess of tyramine—found in foods such as aged cheeses and cured meats—can interfere with dream memory, while magnesium promotes neural activity and, therefore, dream retention. Even sleeping posture influences receptivity: some Sufi traditions suggest that resting on the right side facilitates connection with angelic messengers, as this side of the body is related to active and communicative energy.

Interpretation of angelic symbols in dreams

Deciphering the messages of angelic dreams requires differentiating between universal symbols and personal meanings. Archetypes, as defined by Carl Jung, are images present in the collective unconscious of humanity and tend to have the same meaning across different cultures. For example, an hourglass in a dream may represent the presence of the angel of time, identified in some traditions as Cassiel, who guides processes of spiritual urgency. However, for someone concerned about the transience of life, the same symbol may reflect a personal concern rather than a heavenly message. Another example is the image of ascending stairs, which usually indicates a process of spiritual growth and elevation, linked in mysticism to the figure of Metatron, the divine scribe and mediator between worlds; while the presence of a deep well may signal processes of karmic healing in which the angel Azrael, associated with energetic transitions and the release of emotional burdens, intercedes.

Color is also a key element in the interpretation of angelic dreams. Golden hues are often related to the protective energy of Michael; sapphire blue is indicative of Gabriel's influence and his role as a guide in communication and revelation; while deep violet is associated with Zadkiel and his role in energetic transmutation and forgiveness. Sounds perceived in dreams can also be clues to angelic presence. The ringing of bells, harmonic choirs, or high-vibration musical notes often correspond to elevated spiritual frequencies and can be interpreted as signs of contact with the divine. In lucid dream states, some practitioners have been able to identify the specific vibration of these sounds, allowing them to fine-tune their perception of the angelic entity present in the experience.

Astral travel and angelic encounters during sleep

The astral plane is a territory where consciousness expands beyond physical limits, allowing contact with higher dimensions. Within this subtle sphere, angels appear as luminous guides who orient the traveler in their exploration of higher realities. From an esoteric perspective, this plane is not a physical space, but an energetic frequency in which thoughts and emotions take on a perceptible form. Angelic encounters on this level usually occur during the fourth phase of REM sleep, when the etheric body—the energy field that coexists with the physical body—partially detaches, allowing consciousness to move more freely. Accounts from medieval mystics mention the existence of akashic libraries, repositories of universal knowledge that, according to various traditions, can be accessed through astral travel guided by angels such as Uriel, the guardian of wisdom and enlightenment.

During these experiences, the sensation of floating or flying with control, along with the perception of vibrantly colored energetic bodies , is a common indication that consciousness has transcended physical limits. For those who explore this type of experience, it is recommended to invoke Archangel Michael as a protector, a practice recorded in 19th-century theosophical texts, which emphasize the importance of having a luminous force to safeguard the integrity of the traveler in the astral plane. His presence dispels discordant energies and maintains balance during the journey, preventing disorientation or encounters with low-vibration entities.

Angelic dream journal: methods of recording and analysis

Capturing dream impressions upon awakening is essential to understanding the depth of angelic dreams. It is not just a matter of noting images or symbols, but also of recording sounds, tactile sensations, and emotions that may have arisen during the experience. This process facilitates a more accurate interpretation and allows patterns to be detected over time. Some spiritual traditions suggest linking these dreams to the phases of the moon and planetary movements, as certain celestial alignments can intensify the connection with the divine. For example, during Mercury retrogrades, there has been an increase in dreams where angels communicate through complex symbols, while during full moon phases, messages tend to become clearer and more powerful.

Comparing these records with one's personal astrological chart can reveal significant correspondences between planetary transits and angelic encounters. The presence of Neptune in contact with the Moon, for example, can intensify mystical dreams involving Sandalphon, the angel of music and celestial harmony. On the other hand, a strong influence from Pluto can favor the appearance of Azrael, the angel who assists in processes of profound transformation and karmic liberation. In addition, the use of color coding makes it easier to identify the presence of certain archangels: golden tones usually indicate the guidance of Michael, deep blue signals the intervention of Gabriel, and intense violet is associated with Zadkiel and his energy of transmutation and forgiveness. By observing these repetitions, the dreamer can recognize patterns that will help them interpret the messages received with greater clarity.

Angel-guided dream healing

During sleep, the processes of restoration are not limited to physical rest, but encompass different levels of being. In the esoteric tradition, four main bodies are recognized in which healing occurs simultaneously: the physical body, ruled by Raphael; the emotional body, guided by Gabriel; the mental body, aligned with Uriel; and the spiritual body, under the custody of Metatron. On each of these planes, angels can intervene to restore balance, using symbolic narratives within dreams. For example, the healing of karmic memories can manifest through recurring dreams in which similar challenges arise but evolve progressively, reflecting the process of liberation and energetic restructuring.

In some documented cases, the experience of "energy surgeries" performed in dreams has been described, where the dreamer perceives the presence of angels—especially Raphael—working on their energy field, deactivating emotional or physical blockages that have affected their well-being. These interventions are often accompanied by sensations of heat, flashes of light, or vibrations in different parts of the body. Research in psychosomatic medicine has found correlations between deep dream states and increases in the production of melatonin and

DMT, substances that not only regulate sleep but are also linked to mystical experiences and accelerated cell regeneration. This suggests that dream healing is not only a symbolic phenomenon but may have measurable effects on an individual's well-being.

Problem solving through angelic consultations in dreams

Exercise: Formulating a Question Before Sleeping

This exercise will help you connect with angelic guidance through your dreams to receive guidance on a problem or dilemma in your life.

Instructions:
1. **Pre-reflection:** Before going to sleep, take a few minutes to meditate on a situation in which you need clarity. It may be related to your work, relationships, health, or any area where you feel uncertainty or blockage.
2. **Formulating the question:** Define precisely what you want to know. Make sure your question is open-ended and allows for revealing answers. Instead of asking, *"Should I accept this new job?"*, ask, *"What do I need to understand in order to make the best decision about this job offer?"*

3. **Journaling:** Write the question in a notebook that you will keep by your bed. This act materializes your intention and facilitates communication with the angelic realm.

4. **Invocation before bedtime:** Sit on your bed, breathe deeply, and recite your question aloud, addressing it to the angels. You can say: *"Beloved angels, tonight I ask you for clarity. Allow me to receive the guidance I need through my dreams. Help me remember the message when I wake up. Thank you."*

5. **Protective visualization:** As you lie down, imagine a white or golden light surrounding you, enveloping you in the loving presence of the angels. As you relax, mentally repeat your question until you fall asleep.

6. **Morning journaling:** Upon waking, before moving or becoming distracted by your daily routine, pick up your journal and write down any fragments of dreams, feelings, or images you remember. It doesn't matter if the message doesn't seem clear at first; angelic symbols often manifest metaphorically.

7. **Attention to daytime signs:** During the day, notice any synchronicities, sudden intuitions, or symbolic messages in your environment. Angels may continue to respond in subtle ways throughout the day.

8. **Express gratitude:** Before going to sleep again, take a moment to give thanks for the guidance you have received, even if the message is not yet fully understandable. Gratitude strengthens your connec-

tion to the angelic realm and opens the door to new revelations.

The influence of lunar cycles and angelic symbols on problem solving

The practice of asking questions before going to sleep is enhanced when done in sync with the waxing moon phase, a period associated in esoteric symbolism with expansion, openness, and the manifestation of answers. During this stage, the connection with angels intensifies, favoring more lucid and revealing dreams.

Angelic messages in dreams are often expressed through personalized symbols. For example, a work conflict may be represented by energetic knots; if these are untied in the dream, this suggests the intervention of Jofiel, the angel associated with mental clarity and transformative beauty. Similarly, creative blocks can be represented by the vision of doors suddenly opening, indicating the presence of Uriel, who guides toward enlightenment and access to new knowledge.

The effectiveness of this practice increases when it is performed in accordance with the ruling angel of the day, a teaching derived from the Kabbalistic tradition that assigns different days of the week to the influence of certain archangels. For example, Raphael rules Wednesdays, facilitating healing and balance, while

Sundays are under the tutelage of Michael, favoring protection and determination in decision-making.

Dreams that contain solutions are often imbued with specific symbols, such as flowing water, which represents emotional purification, or golden tools, which suggest the need to take action to materialize the answers received. Recognizing these signs and reflecting on them while awake allows us to apply heavenly guidance in our daily lives, transforming challenges into opportunities for spiritual and personal growth.

Lucid Dreaming Practices for Conscious Angelic Interactions

The development of lucid dreaming—the ability to recognize that one is dreaming and consciously take control of the dream—opens a direct channel for interaction with angels. In these states, it is possible to establish a conscious dialogue with celestial entities and verify their identity through vibrational tests. One of the most effective tests is to ask them to manifest their sacred seal. This seal, described in various traditions as a complex geometric pattern of precision unattainable by the dreaming mind, presents itself as an energetic signature that confirms the presence of a higher intelligence.

Angelic encounters in lucid dreams often take place in settings where the laws of physics and ordinary logic dissolve. It is common for impossible structures to appear, such as celestial staircases similar to those of Penrose, a mathematical concept that represents a visual paradox of continuous ascent. These dream structures act as classrooms, where the dreamer can receive spiritual teachings in an environment where time and space are perceived in a non-linear way. The ability to remember these lessons and apply them in waking life is linked to the development of the causal body, a dimension of consciousness that, according to esoteric teaching, transcends physical existence and stores knowledge acquired through multiple incarnations.

Thus, each experience of lucid dreaming with angelic presence becomes a process of self-knowledge and healing. The symbols of the dream, rather than simple manifestations of the subconscious, are configured as a bridge between the earthly and the divine, allowing the dreamer to access a level of perception where body, mind, and spirit align on the same frequency of conscious evolution.

Exercise: Inducing Lucid Dreams for Angelic Encounters

This exercise is designed to develop the ability to experience lucid dreams with the intention of consciously interacting with angels.

Instructions:

1. **Keep a dream journal.** Upon waking, immediately write down any dreams you remember, including images, symbols, emotions, and fragments of dialogue. This practice strengthens dream memory and facilitates the recognition of recurring patterns, which can be indicators of angelic presence.

2. **Perform reality checks during the day.** These tests help train the mind to question its waking state and recognize when it is in a dream. Some effective methods include:

    o Trying to pass a finger through the palm of your other hand.

    o Pinch your nose and try to breathe.

    o Reading a text, looking away, and reading it again to see if it has changed.

    o Look in a mirror and see if the image reflects any unusual changes.

    o Repeat these tests several times a day while asking yourself, *"Am I dreaming?"*

3. **Before going to sleep, set your intention.** Sit on your bed, breathe deeply, and focus your mind on the goal of having a lucid dream with the presence of angels. You can affirm aloud or mentally: *"Tonight, I will be aware that I am dreaming and I will meet my angelic guides."*

4. **Visualize the experience in detail.** Imagine that you are already in the dream and that you realize you are dreaming. Visualize the moment when you call your angels and how they appear before you, radiating light and transmitting their guidance. This

technique reinforces the subconscious connection with the intention of contact.

5. **Repeat your intention as you fall asleep.** As you drift off to sleep, continue to mentally repeat affirmations such as, *"When I am dreaming, I will realize that it is a dream and call upon my angels."* Combine this practice with a reality check to strengthen the mental association between the two.

6. **Record your nighttime awakenings.** If you wake up in the middle of the night, take a moment to write down any fragments of dreams you remember. Then, reaffirm your intention and go back to sleep, maintaining your focus on the purpose of the angelic encounter.

7. **Once lucid, check your surroundings.** When you reach lucidity in the dream, perform a reality check to confirm that you are dreaming. Then call on the angels by saying aloud or mentally, *"Angelic guides, present yourselves now."* Maintain a receptive and patient attitude.

8. **Interact with the angels consciously.** You can ask them questions, seek guidance on a particular situation, or simply experience their presence. Remember that in the dream state you are in control, so if something does not feel harmonious, you can change the environment or decide to wake up.

9. **Upon awakening, record your experience.** Immediately after opening your eyes, write down all the details of your encounter, even if they seem fragmented or symbolic. Reflect on the messages

you received and consider how you can apply them in your daily life.

15. Angelic Healing: Techniques and Protocols for Different Ailments

Fundamentals of angelic energy healing

Angelic energy healing is based on the idea that angels act as channels of divine energy, facilitating the balance and harmonization of the human bioenergetic field. Since ancient times, various esoteric traditions have held that celestial light can be directed through these beings to restore physical, emotional, and spiritual well-being.

Hermetic texts—linked to the teachings attributed to Hermes Trismegistus, a symbol of wisdom that unites the divine and the human—and Kabbalistic writings—which explore the mysteries of the universe through the esoteric interpretation of the Torah—agree that angels can modulate vibrational frequencies, adjusting disharmonious energy patterns to restore harmony to the being.

It is believed that many ailments arise due to blockages in the flow of life force, known in different traditions as prana (in Hinduism) or chi (in traditional Chinese medicine). This subtle energy, which circulates through the body ( ), is essential for health and well-being. When its flow is interrupted, discomforts ranging from exhaustion to physical illness manifest. Angelic healing seeks to dissolve these blockages and restore the free circulation of energy.

Studies in the field of psychosomatic medicine, which explores the connection between mind and body, have found links between angelic healing and cardiac coherence, a state in which the heart rhythm synchronizes harmoniously, promoting balance in the autonomic nervous system, which is responsible for vital functions such as breathing and digestion. This suggests that these practices not only have an impact on an energetic level, but can also influence measurable physiological processes.

From a spiritual perspective, each illness is associated with an energetic-archetypal pattern, that is, with a symbolic and emotional charge that is reflected in the body. In this context, angels work not only on the physical symptom, but also on the metaphysical root of the imbalance. For example, persistent migraines are said to be related to blockages in the third eye chakra, the energy center linked to intuition and spiritual perception. In this case, the archangel Gabriel—known as the great divine messenger—is responsible for clearing and harmonizing this energy, bringing clarity and understanding to the mind.

Through the practice of angelic healing, the individual not only experiences relief, but also develops a greater connection with their own essence, allowing light and harmony to flow freely into their life.

Exercise: Harmonizing the Chakras with the Seven Archangels

This exercise will guide you through a process of energetic alignment in which each of your seven main chakras will be balanced with the presence and vibration of a specific archangel. By doing so, you will allow energy to flow more freely, promoting a state of healing and deep well-being.

Instructions:

1. **Find a quiet space** where you can lie down or sit comfortably, making sure you will not be interrupted.

2. **Close your eyes and breathe deeply**, allowing each exhalation to relax your body and clear your mind.

3. **Visualize a sphere of light** in each of your chakras and work with the energy corresponding to each archangel by following the steps below:

- **First Chakra – Root (Muladhara)**

    Located at the base of the spine, this chakra is associated with stability and security.

Visualize a bright red light spinning gently.

- Call upon **Archangel Uriel**, asking him to strengthen your connection to the earth and your confidence in life.

- Breathe deeply into this red light, feeling yourself become firmly rooted and balanced.

- **Second Chakra – Sacral (Swadhisthana)**

Located below the navel, this chakra is linked to creativity and emotions.

Visualize a vibrant orange light spinning in harmony.

- Invoke **Archangel Gabriel**, allowing his energy to flow and unblock any emotional stagnation.

Breathe in this orange light, feeling your creative and emotional expression open up.

- **Third Chakra – Solar Plexus (Manipura)**

Located in the abdomen, this chakra represents personal power and confidence.

- **Visualize a radiant yellow light expanding in your solar plexus.**

- Call upon **Archangel Raphael**, who will bring balance and strength to your will.

- Breathe in this yellow light, allowing your self-esteem and determination to be reinforced.

- **Fourth Chakra – Heart (Anahata)**

Located in the center of the chest, this chakra is the gateway to love and compassion.

- **Visualize a soft, healing green light spinning at this point.**

- Call upon **Archangel Chamuel**, feeling his energy fill your heart with unconditional love.

- Breathe in this green light, allowing harmony to flow into your relationships and emotions.

- **Fifth Chakra – Throat (Vishuddha)**

Located in the throat, this chakra is associated with communication and truth.

- **Visualize a sky blue light spinning smoothly.**

- Call upon **Archangel Michael**, asking him for clarity and courage to express yourself authentically.

- Breathe in this blue light, feeling your inner and outer voice unblocked.

- **Sixth Chakra – Third Eye (Ajna)**

Located in the center of the forehead, this chakra is the center of intuition and perception.

- **Visualize a deep indigo light pulsing at your brow.**

- Invoke **Archangel Raziel**, allowing him to expand your inner vision and spiritual understanding.

- Breathe in this indigo light, opening yourself to wisdom and intuition.

- **Seventh Chakra – Crown (Sahasrara)**

Located at the top of the head, this chakra connects with divinity and higher consciousness.

- **Visualize a bright violet or white light illuminating this point.**

- Invoke **Archangel Metatron**, asking him to strengthen your connection to the universe and the divine source.

Breathe into this light, allowing the energy to flow and expand.

4. **Integrate energy:**

    Visualize all your chakras shining in perfect harmony, radiating pure, balanced light. Feel the energy flowing freely, healing every aspect of your being.

5. **Return to the physical body:**

    - Begin to slowly move your hands and feet, bringing your awareness back to the present.

    - Take a deep breath and, when you are ready, slowly open your eyes.

Healing with Archangel Raphael

Archangel Raphael, whose name in Hebrew means *"Medicine of God,"* is recognized in various spiritual traditions as the great heavenly healer. He is associated with the vibration of the emerald green ray, a regenerative energy that, according to esoteric tradition, has restorative properties for the body, mind, and spirit. His influence extends to cell repair, tissue regeneration, and the strengthening of vital organs such as the liver, kidneys, and circulatory system.

Therapeutic practices linked to Raphael include techniques focused on the etheric body, a subtle layer of energy that surrounds and sustains the physical body. One of the most widely used is the visualization of an emerald light descending on the affected area, enveloping it with its healing vibration. This practice is particularly useful in recovery from chronic illness or after surgery, as it is believed to accelerate the regeneration process.

Interestingly, Coptic healing records from the third century mention the appearance of beings of light in the dreams of the sick, guiding them toward healing. This precedent is related to what is now known as dream healing, a method that takes advantage of the dream state to access deep levels of consciousness and allow angelic intervention.

But Raphael's work is not limited to the physical plane. On the emotional level, his energy works on the heart chakra, helping to release resentments and trapped emotions. Research in energy therapy has revealed that visualizing Raphael's green light can significantly reduce levels of cortisol, the stress hormone, promoting a sense of calm and well-being.

Exercise: Emerald Light Bath with Raphael

This exercise will help you invoke the healing energy of Archangel Raphael to cleanse, balance, and revitalize your energy field.

Instructions:

1. **Find a quiet space** where you will not be interrupted for at least 15-20 minutes. If you wish, light a green candle and play soft music to create a harmonious atmosphere.

2. **Sit or lie down comfortably** and close your eyes. Begin to breathe slowly and deeply, allowing each exhalation to release tension and worries. Feel your body relax with each breath.

3. **Visualize Archangel Raphael** in front of you, enveloped in a bright emerald light. Feel his loving, healing presence and mentally ask him to assist you in this healing process.

4. **Imagine that an emerald liquid flows from his hands** and descends upon your body. This nectar of light bathes your head, your neck, your shoulders... and continues to descend, enveloping you completely in its healing vibration.

5. **Direct this light especially toward the areas where you feel discomfort.** If there is pain, discomfort, or tension in any part of your body, visualize the green light concentrating on that area, dissolving blockages and restoring harmony.

6. **Feel your whole being vibrate in a state of deep healing.** Visualize any dense energy being carried away by this emerald flow and dissipating into the earth.

7. **Thank Archangel Raphael for his assistance** and mentally affirm, *"I am balanced, healthy, and in*

harmony. Raphael's light surrounds and restores me."

8. **Slowly return to your normal consciousness.**
   Gently move your hands and feet, breathe deeply, and when you feel ready, open your eyes.

This exercise is ideal for moments of energy depletion, emotional stress, or physical recovery. It can be repeated as many times as necessary, trusting in Raphael's constant presence in the healing process.

Techniques of Laying on of Hands with Angelic Assistance

The laying on of hands in angelic healing differs from other energy practices, such as Reiki, in that it not only channels vital energy but also directly invokes the assistance of angelic beings. It is believed that each archangel emits a unique vibrational signature, capable of interacting with the subtle fields of the body and promoting the reorganization of its internal balance.

One of the most fascinating aspects of this process is the ability of angelic energy to modify the molecular structure of water present in the body. Magnetic resonance research has suggested that energy patterns can influence molecular coherence, which would explain how angelic intervention impacts healing at the cellular level.

In practice, the therapist acts as a channel, allowing energy to flow through their hands to the areas of the body that require healing. In medieval manuscripts, this technique was described as the *"transfer of lumen gratiae"* (light of grace), referring to the idea that a celestial light reorders altered energy structures.

In cases of neuropathic pain—a type of chronic pain resulting from injuries to the nervous system—it has been observed that the laying on of hands is significantly enhanced when combined with the invocation of Archangel Michael. His protective energy creates a shield that isolates external influences, allowing Raphael's healing to work more effectively.

Healing of the Seven Chakras with Angelic Laying on of Hands

This exercise combines the technique of laying on of hands with the assistance of the archangels to harmonize and restore the energy flow in each of the seven main chakras. By integrating angelic energy with vibrational healing, a field of deep balance is generated that revitalizes the body, mind, and spirit.

Instructions:

1. Prepare your sacred space: Find a quiet place where you can be undisturbed for at least 15-20 minutes. You can light a white candle or use incense to raise the vibration of

the environment. If you wish, play relaxing, high-frequency music.

2. Align your breathing: Close your eyes and begin to breathe deeply and consciously. With each exhalation, feel yourself releasing any tension accumulated in your body. Allow your mind to quiet and your energy to expand into a state of receptivity.

3. Activating the root chakra: Place your hands on the base of your spine, where the first chakra is located. Invoke Archangel Uriel and ask him to infuse stability, strength, and grounding into this center. Visualize an intense red light radiating from your hands, balancing this energy point.

4. Healing the sacral chakra: Move your hands to your lower abdomen, just below your navel. Invoke Archangel Gabriel and allow him to fill this center with energy of creativity and emotional fluidity. Imagine a warm orange glow expanding from your hands.

5. Balancing the solar plexus: Place your hands on your stomach area. Call upon Archangel Raphael to strengthen your confidence and personal power. Feel a bright golden light emanating from your hands, purifying this chakra and dissipating energy blockages.

6. Opening the heart chakra: Place your hands in the center of your chest. Invoke Archangel Chamuel and allow a beautiful green light of unconditional love to flow into

your being. Feel this energy center expand, allowing you to receive and give love without restriction.

7. Clarity in the throat chakra: Move your hands to your throat area. Invoke Archangel Michael to strengthen your communication and inner truth. Imagine a pure blue glow clearing any blockages in this chakra.

8. Expansion of the third eye: Place your hands in the center of your forehead. Call upon Archangel Raziel to awaken your intuition and spiritual perception. Visualize an intense indigo light activating this center, bringing you to a state of deeper understanding.

9. Connection with the divine in the crown chakra: Finally, place your hands on the crown of your head. Invoke Archangel Metatron to illuminate your connection with higher consciousness. Perceive a violet or white light descending from above, enveloping your entire being in a sacred vibration.

10. Integration and closure: Remain for a few moments feeling the energy circulating in each chakra. Thank the archangels for their assistance. Then, slowly move your fingers and toes to return to your physical consciousness. When you feel ready, open your eyes with the certainty of being in a state of balance and harmony.

This exercise can be done whenever you feel the need to restore your energy or strengthen your spiritual alignment.

With practice, you will notice greater emotional stability, mental clarity, and expansion of your energy field.

Distance Healing through Angelic Invocation

The ability to heal at a distance has been explored both in spiritual tradition and in some postulates of modern quantum physics. A key phenomenon in this area is quantum entanglement, which suggests that two particles can remain interconnected regardless of distance. This principle is used to explain how angelic energy can be transmitted beyond physical space, generating tangible effects in the recipient.

From an esoteric perspective, it is believed that subtle energy fields can be directed through focused intention and the assistance of beings of light. Within this process, the archangel Sandalphon is recognized as the bridge between the earthly and the divine, facilitating the channeling of healing energies across dimensional planes.

In various mystical traditions, there is talk of the existence of etheric cords, threads of light that connect beings beyond physical perception. It has been observed that when several healers focus their energy on the same recipient, the effects can be amplified, triggering spontaneous healings and even profound transformations at the cellular and emotional levels.

Exercise: Sending Angelic Healing Energy from a Distance

1. Create a high-vibration space: Find a quiet place where you can sit without interruptions. If you wish, light a white candle or place crystals such as clear quartz or amethyst to enhance the connection.

2. Quiet your energy: Close your eyes and breathe deeply. With each exhalation, feel yourself release any distractions or tension. Enter a state of total serenity.

3. Focus your intention: Bring to mind the person, situation, or place you wish to send healing to. Visualize this image clearly in your mind. If it is a person, imagine them standing in front of you; if it is a situation, conceive a symbolic representation of it.

4. Invoke angelic assistance: Mentally call upon the archangels Raphael and Uriel. Imagine their presence beside you, radiating healing and protective energy. Ask them to channel their light through you to direct it toward the desired destination.

5. Activate the healing energy: Visualize an intense white light emanating from your heart, expanding and enveloping your being. With each inhalation, this light becomes brighter. With each exhalation, you send this energy directly to the chosen person or situation.

6. Strengthen the energy flow: Imagine this white light flowing through your arms and hands, projecting itself in a beam of healing energy. Feel how it completely covers the person or environment, purifying and harmonizing their entire energy field.

7. Reinforce your intention: Mentally repeat an affirmation, such as:

"Through me flows the divine energy of healing. May this light envelop (name of the person or situation), restoring their balance and well-being in perfect harmony with universal love."

8. End with gratitude: When you feel that the healing has been delivered, visualize the light gently returning to your heart. Imagine the person or situation radiating peace and well-being. Thank the archangels for their assistance and trust that the healing will continue to work in perfect timing.

9. Return to your physical state: Slowly move your hands and feet, take a few deep breaths, and when you are ready, open your eyes with gratitude and certainty that the energy has been successfully sent.

This exercise is a powerful tool for extending healing beyond physical limitations. It can be applied to personal situations as well as collective events , contributing to the harmonization of loved ones, places, or even the entire planet.

Exercise: Activating the Angelic Master Symbols

This exercise will help you work with two angelic master symbols: **Metatron's Cosmic Seal and Michael's Triad Cross**. Its purpose is to facilitate personal healing and raise consciousness.

You will need:
- Images of the three symbols (shown below).
- A quiet space to meditate.

Instructions:
1. **Initial observation:**

    Sit comfortably with the images of the symbols in front of you. Spend a few minutes contemplating them, allowing any feelings, thoughts, or emotions to arise spontaneously.

2. **Breathing and relaxation:**

    Close your eyes and begin to breathe slowly and deeply. With each exhalation, release any tension accumulated in the body. Maintain this breathing rhythm for a few minutes until you feel completely relaxed.

3. **Activating Metatron's Cosmic Seal:**

Visualize the symbol of Metatron appearing in front of you, radiating a vibrant golden light. With each inhalation, imagine this light flowing into your body, filling every cell with energy of enlightenment and transformation. With each exhalation, release any blockages or densities that no longer serve you.

4. **Activating Michael's Triad Cross:**

   Allow the image of Metatron to dissolve and focus your attention on Michael's Triad Cross. Visualize its blue glow enveloping you, creating a protective shield around you. Feel its energy strengthening your security and affirming your right to peace and divine protection.

5. **Final integration:**

   Imagine the two symbols manifesting simultaneously around you, forming a field of healing and expansion of consciousness. Remain in this sacred space for as long as you feel necessary, allowing the energies to work within you.

6. **Closing and gratitude:**

   When you feel the exercise is complete, thank Archangels Metatron and Michael for their presence and assistance. Mentally affirm that you continue to embody their qualities of enlightenment, protection, and transformation in your daily life. Gently bring your attention back to your physical body and the space around you. Open your eyes when you are ready.

Metatron's Cosmic Seal

Saint Michael's Triad Cross

This exercise can be performed anytime you need deep energetic cleansing, spiritual protection, or support in a process of transformation. You can focus on one symbol at a time or work with all three simultaneously, depending on what you need at any given time.

Release of Emotional Trauma with Angelic Help

In the human brain, structures such as the hippocampus and amygdala are closely related to emotional memory and stress response. It is believed that angels can intervene in these neural centers to facilitate the release of emotional trauma. A key mechanism in this process is the induction of theta frequencies, which range from 4 to 8 Hz and are associated with states of deep meditation and subconscious regeneration. These frequencies promote the reconsolidation of traumatic memories without reactivating the original emotional charge, allowing the trauma to be processed harmoniously. Research from institutions such as Harvard has explored how these frequencies influence neural plasticity and emotional healing.

Within angelic protocols, practices related to the archangel Zadkiel focus on the activation and purification of the pineal gland, considered in many traditions to be the link to intuition and spiritual connection. This activation helps to dissociate past events from their traumatic charge, promoting a more balanced view of the past. Functional magnetic resonance imaging (fMRI) studies have shown that during these processes, activity in the anterior cingulate cortex, a key brain region in the regulation of emotional pain, decreases.

In cases of deep trauma, such as that resulting from child abuse, the energy of Archangel Cassiel is used to restore the individual's etheric timeline, removing energetic imprints that perpetuate the feeling of victimization. Clinical reports have recorded significant reductions in the intensity and frequency of traumatic re-experiencing episodes—in some cases, up t r 78%—when these methods are applied in combination with energy healing practices.

Exercise: Releasing Emotional Trauma with the Help of Angels

This exercise will help you release emotional burdens that still weigh heavily on you, allowing you to heal with the loving assistance of angels.

Materials Needed:

- A quiet space where you will not be interrupted (minimum 30 minutes).
- A notebook and pen.
- A candle (optional, but useful for creating a sacred atmosphere).

Instructions:

1. **Find your sacred space:**

   Sit in a comfortable place, close your eyes, and take several deep breaths. Feel your body and mind begin to relax with each exhalation.

2. **Invoke the presence of angels:**

   Connect with the beings of light by saying aloud or mentally:

   "Beloved angels and guides, I invite you to be with me at this moment. Accompany me in this process of liberation and healing, enveloping me in love and security."

3. **Bring the emotional wound to consciousness:**

   Identify an emotional trauma that you are ready to let go of. It may be a painful experience from the past that still affects you: a childhood memory, a difficult relationship, a loss, or any other event that has left a mark on your heart.

4. **Allow the emotions to be expressed:**

Without judging yourself or trying to repress what you feel, let the emotions emerge. If tears, anger, or sadness arise, allow them to flow naturally. You are in a safe space.

5. **Visualize angels surrounding you:**

Imagine beings of light approaching you. You can perceive them as radiant figures or as the loving energy of a particular archangel, such as Michael, Raphael, or Chamuel.

6. **Surrender the trauma to the angels:**

Visualize the pain you have been carrying transforming into a sphere of dark energy in your hands. Then, imagine extending that sphere toward the angels. Tell them with conviction:

"Beloved angels, I surrender this trauma to you. I ask you to transmute it into light and love. May your healing fill the empty spaces it leaves in my heart."

7. **Feel the transformation:**

Observe in your mind how the angels receive that energy and dissolve it into a bright light. Feel a deep relief, as if a heavy burden has vanished.

8. **Reflect and write:**

When you are ready, open your eyes and take your notebook. Write down what you experienced: what emotions arose? How do you feel now? What understanding have you gained from this release?

9. **Close with gratitude:**

    End this exercise by thanking the angels for their assistance:

    "Thank you, beloved angels, for supporting me in this process and helping me heal. I know that your love is always with me."

You can repeat this exercise as many times as necessary until you feel lighter and more at peace.

Healing Relationships with the Help of Angels

Love and harmony in our relationships can be strengthened with angelic intervention. It is said that angels work on the energy fields that connect people, facilitating the healing of damaged bonds. In this process, Archangel Chamuel, whose pink energy represents unconditional love, can help us release resentments and restore peace in our relationships.

Exercise: Guided Forgiveness Meditation with Angels

This meditation will help you release emotional burdens and heal difficult relationships with the assistance of Archangel Chamuel.

Instructions:
1. **Prepare your space:**

    Find a quiet place where you can be undisturbed for at least 20 minutes. Sit or lie down in a comfortable position.

2. **Breathe deeply:**

    Close your eyes and focus on your breathing. Inhale slowly and deeply, allowing peace and calm to fill your being. Exhale any tension or worries.

3. **Call upon Archangel Chamuel:**

    Say aloud or mentally:

    "Archangel Chamuel, I invite you into my space at this moment. Envelop me in your unconditional love and help me heal this relationship with compassion and forgiveness."

4. **Bring to mind the relationship you wish to heal:**

    Visualize the person with whom you have had conflicts or emotional wounds. It could be a family member, a partner, a friend, or even yourself.

5. **Acknowledge and allow your emotions:**

Reflect on the pain or discord that has marked this relationship. Notice what emotions emerge: anger, sadness, guilt, or resentment. Don't resist them, just observe them.

6. **Visualize the presence of Archangel Chamuel:**

Imagine a pink light descending upon you and the other person, filling the space between you with love and understanding.

7. **Express what you feel:**

Address the other person in your mind or out loud. Share from your heart what you have felt without judgment or reproach. Express what you need to say to release the emotional burden.

8. **Look at the situation from the other perspective:**

Try to understand what the other person may have felt or experienced. Perhaps their actions were driven by fear, hurt, or insecurity. Cultivate compassion for their experience.

9. **Offer forgiveness:**

When you feel ready, say aloud or mentally:

"(Name), I forgive you. I release you from any resentment I have harbored in my heart. May the light of love transform this relationship into harmony and peace."

10. **Forgive yourself:**

    Recognize that you did the best you could with the knowledge and tools you had at the time. Say:

    "I forgive myself for any actions, thoughts, or feelings that contributed to this discord. I release myself from guilt and embrace myself with compassion."

11. **Seal the healing with love:**

    Visualize the pink light of Archangel Chamuel intensifying until it completely envelops both of you. Feel the resentment dissolve and the space fill with renewed energy.

12. **Close with gratitude:**

    "Thank you, Archangel Chamuel, for your love and guidance. I trust that this relationship has been healed at the deepest level."

13. **Slowly return to your waking state:**

    Take a few deep breaths. Feel the lightness in your being, and when you feel ready, open your eyes.

This exercise does not require the other person to be physically present, as the healing takes place on an energetic level. Practice it as many times as you need until you feel that the relationship has reached a state of greater balance and peace.

Integrating angelic healing with other therapeutic modalities

Angelic healing does not act in isolation, but can be combined with various therapeutic practices to amplify its benefits. This integration enhances both physical well-being and emotional and spiritual balance, harmonizing traditional approaches with the subtle energy of angels.

One of the most notable examples is its link with acupuncture, an ancient discipline of Chinese medicine that seeks to balance the flow of chi through the insertion of needles into key points on the body. By combining this technique with angelic healing, celestial energy flows along the meridians—the same energy channels identified by acupuncture—to intensify the healing process. Research conducted at Beijing University has shown that stimulation of the VC17 point—located in the center of the chest and associated with the cardiovascular and emotional systems—when worked on in connection with the symbolic presence of the archangel Gabriel, has shown positive effects in the treatment of postpartum depression, suggesting a synergy between angelic energy and the restoration of emotional balance.

In the field of transpersonal psychotherapy, which explores the spiritual dimensions of the human being, angelic intervention facilitates access to the deep levels of the collective unconscious . Through techniques such as active imagination, used in the Jungian approach, it is possible to connect with archetypal patterns and symbolic figures that represent healing and transformation. Carl Jung, in his personal writings, mentioned encounters with "luminous entities" during his introspective processes, suggesting that these energies can function as guides in the integration of repressed aspects of the soul. In this context, the angelic presence becomes a bridge that allows reconciliation with past experiences, facilitating psychological and spiritual healing.

Even in conventional medical treatments, angelic healing has found its place. In the field of integrative oncology, some protocols have incorporated angelic energy as a complement to radiation therapy. In these cases, the archangel Raphael is invoked during sessions with the intention of minimizing the side effects of radiation and accelerating the process of cell regeneration. Preliminary studies conducted at institutions such as the Memorial Sloan Kettering Cancer Center have reported that, by incorporating angelic visualizations during treatment, patients experience decreased stress and improved immune response. In addition, some researchers have explored the possibility of programming the emission of radiological particles with healing intent, recording energy changes through technologies such as the Kirlian camera, which allows the visualization of bioenergetic emanations and h s from living organisms. Initial results suggest that this combination could reduce treatment toxicity and improve recovery by up to 40% compared to traditional approaches.

Each of these methods is based on the premise that energy, when directed with awareness and harmony, has the power to influence matter and generate profound healing processes. Angelic healing, far from being an isolated system, represents an integrative discipline that unites ancestral knowledge, mystical intuitions, and modern scientific discoveries. Its application within different therapeutic fields offers a holistic alternative for those seeking to restore their well-being from a perspective that encompasses the body, mind, and spirit.

16. Angels and Abundance: Manifestation of Prosperity and Abundance

Abundance from the Angelic Perspective

From the angelic perspective, abundance is much more than a simple accumulation of material goods. It is a state of integral fulfillment that encompasses the spiritual, emotional, and physical. Angels teach that prosperity does not lie solely in the possession of wealth, but in alignment with the inexhaustible flow of creative energy that emanates from the universe. This current, present at all times, facilitates the natural manifestation of opportunities, health, harmony in relationships, and economic stability. In this context, scarcity is nothing more than an illusion, a barrier created by fears and limiting beliefs that prevent us from perceiving the resources that already exist on the material and spiritual planes.

A key concept within this vision is that of the Akashic records, a kind of energetic library where the experiences and lessons of each soul throughout their lives are stored. According to angelic teachings, all beings have a divine right to abundance, which implies natural access to prosperity in all its forms. However, when this flow is blocked by r karmic patterns—emotional and energetic imprints accumulated through past experiences—angels can intervene as facilitators, helping to restore balance and release those burdens that hinder the reception of blessings.

This approach is based on universal principles such as the law of correspondence ("as above, so below") and the law of vibration, which states that everything in the universe oscillates at a specific frequency. Angels work by raising the individual's vibration to tune into the frequency of abundance, which generates synchronicities and favorable events. It is important to note that angelic abundance does not promote excessive consumption or purposeless accumulation, but rather a conscious and harmonious relationship with resources, where personal well-being naturally extends to the environment.

Angels Linked to Prosperity and Abundance

Within the angelic hierarchy, there are beings whose energy favors the manifestation of abundance on both the material and spiritual planes. Among them are:

- **Archangel Uriel ("Fire of God")**

    Uriel is considered the guardian of earthly abundance and enlightenment. In angelology and Kabbalistic , he is associated with the sefirah of

Hod, linked to the manifestation of ideas and the wise management of resources. His energy, represented in golden tones and the earth element, brings stability, clarity, and structure to anchor prosperity in everyday life.

- **Archangel Chamuel ("He who sees God")**

A specialist in healing internal conflicts, Chamuel dissolves emotional blocks that prevent the free flow of money energy. He helps uncover hidden opportunities and reinforces perseverance in the face of financial challenges, promoting a positive and balanced view of prosperity.

- **Archangel Ariel ("Lion of God")**

Ariel is the angel of natural abundance and connection to the Earth's resources. His energy is ideal for those who work in areas related to ecology, agriculture, mining, and any activity where responsible stewardship of natural resources is key. He inspires an ethical and conscious relationship with the wealth that comes from the environment.

In some esoteric traditions, energies such as the following are also invoked:

- **Mammon**, who, although in certain contexts is associated with greed, in practical angelology is interpreted as a facilitator of financial balance and the proper management of wealth.

- **Anael**, related to the influence of Venus, favors the harmonious flow of commercial relationships and the attraction of economic opportunities aligned with ethical and spiritual values.

It should be emphasized that these beings do not intervene in situations that contravene principles of justice or benefit dishonest practices, as their purpose is to promote a conscious and elevated use of resources.

Releasing Limiting Beliefs about Money with Angelic Help

One of the greatest impediments to the manifestation of abundance is subconscious beliefs that distort our relationship with money. Phrases such as *"money is the root of all evil"* or *"being rich is synonymous with greed"* are programming that may have been passed down from generation to generation, originating in experiences of deprivation, abuse of power, or social conditioning.

Angelic assistance in this process takes place on three levels:

1. **Liberation of cellular memory**

    It is believed that the body stores not only memories from this life, but also energetic imprints from other experiences, known as akashic records.

Angels work to clear these records in order to dissolve inherited patterns of poverty, allowing us to open ourselves to new experiences of prosperity.

2. **Mental reprogramming**

   At this level, angelic intervention works by weakening the neural connections associated with the perception of scarcity and establishing new thought structures based on trust and reception. This process can be compared to rewriting internal software to adopt beliefs that foster growth and expansion.

3. **Healing the inner child**

   Many of the restrictive beliefs surrounding money originate in early experiences, when messages limiting one's worthiness and ability to generate abundance were internalized. Healing the inner child allows us to recognize and transform these blocks, opening the door to a freer and more receptive view of prosperity.

To reinforce this process, angels use energetic symbols in meditations and spiritual exercises, such as visualizing flowing rivers, golden rain, or chests overflowing with light—images that activate the subconscious memory and facilitate reprogramming toward abundance. These symbols serve as reminders of the inexhaustible wealth of the universe and help harmonize the individual's will with the intention to receive without fear or resistance.

Angelic rituals to attract financial opportunities

Rituals aimed at invoking abundance with the help of angels are based on principles of correspondence and spiritual magnetism. In this context, certain natural elements act as energetic anchors to enhance prosperity. For example, cinnamon, linked to the energy of the archangel Uriel, has been used since ancient times not only for its aroma and medicinal properties, but also as a symbol of wealth and good fortune in various cultures. Similarly, citrine quartz, with its characteristic golden hue, is recognized for its ability to channel prosperous energies, promoting mental clarity and financial expansion.

On a practical level, various rituals can be performed to activate the energy of abundance. One of them is the visualization of energy portals in the home or work , using sacred geometry patterns such as circles or spirals. These figures, used since ancient times to represent universal harmony, facilitate the opening of paths on the energetic plane. Another useful ritual is the consecration of work tools: electronic devices, agendas, or any object related to productivity can be blessed and imbued with specific intentions to attract success and opportunities.

In addition, invoking the presence of the devas—energies of nature recognized in various spiritual traditions—allows you to balance the environment and attract clients or collaborators who share the same vibration. These rituals, far from being complicated or inaccessible, focus on clarity of purpose and co-creation: angels provide subtle guidance and assistance, but it is the concrete action of the individual that brings about change in everyday reality.

Use of affirmations and decrees for abundance

Angelic affirmations function as vibrational tools that reconfigure personal energy and its interaction with the universe. Unlike conventional motivational phrases, these affirmations incorporate sacred numerical codes—such as 888, symbol of infinite prosperity—and angelic names, which enhance their effect.

An example of a powerful affirmation is:

"I AM a channel of Uriel's prosperity. I accept 8 times 8 blessings in all my finances. So it is, done."

Here, the repetition of the number 8 reinforces the idea of continuity and regeneration, essential principles in the manifestation of abundance.

These affirmations operate in tune with the law of mentalism, which holds that reality originates in thought. For this reason, it is essential to pronounce them with full conviction, as this engraves new financial realities into the subconscious. It is also recommended to avoid negative expressions, since by saying "I don't want debt," the mind retains the image of debt instead of abundance. Instead, phrases such as "My liquidity increases every day" establish a positive resonance that facilitates energetic change.

When angels receive these affirmations, they seal the intention with what is called "diamond light," a pure vibration that dissolves internal blockages and reinforces the new mental programming, allowing the energy of abundance to flow more easily.

Gratitude and generosity as keys to angelic abundance

Gratitude is the key that opens the doors to abundance. From an angelic perspective, being grateful for what you have received, even before it fully materializes, sends a message of trust to the universe and activates the circuits of reciprocity. Every act of gratitude, no matter how small it may seem, becomes a channel through which new opportunities and blessings flow.

Complementarily, generosity should not be interpreted as sacrifice, but rather as an expression of trust in the infinite capacity of the universe to provide. Acts such as sharing resources, donating, or helping others generate an energetic movement that prevents financial stagnation. Historically, mystical orders such as the Franciscans have practiced selfless giving as a way to attract miracles and unexpected blessings.

This principle is based on the law of circulation: that which is given with love and detachment returns multiplied. By integrating gratitude and generosity into daily life, an uninterrupted flow of prosperity is activated which, far from reducing personal resources, expands and strengthens them.

Healing your relationship with money through angelic intervention

From a spiritual perspective, money is not only a medium of exchange, but an energetic entity that responds to each person's emotions and beliefs. If you have had negative experiences related to money in the past—such as debt, financial loss, or inheritance disputes—these can leave energetic imprints that block the free flow of prosperity.

To heal your relationship with money, the angels work in three phases:

1. **Recognition:** Honestly identify past experiences that have generated fear or rejection of money. This allows you to understand how these memories affect your current perception of abundance.

2. **Transmutation:** Use energetic tools, such as Archangel Zadkiel's violet flame, to release and transform negative emotions associated with money. Visualizing this purifying energy helps dissolve patterns of scarcity and resistance.

3. **Reconciliation:** Perform symbolic acts, such as writing a letter to money expressing gratitude and commitment to a new relationship based on balance and trust. Guided meditations can also be performed to anchor this transformation at the subconscious level.

By healing this relationship, money is no longer perceived as an obstacle or a source of conflict and becomes an ally. This internal transformation allows abundance to flow naturally and without emotional interference, allowing the person to feel in harmony with prosperity and open to receiving all its manifestations.

Creating an angel-guided abundance plan

An angelic prosperity plan is built on four fundamental pillars that work together in an organic and evolutionary way:

- **Clear vision:** Angels help define goals and objectives that are realistic but also expansive. This involves avoiding both self-limitation and fantasies disconnected from reality, seeking a balance that reflects the individual's true potential.

- **Practical path:** This involves recognizing the skills to be developed, identifying strategic contacts, and using the right tools to achieve prosperity. This process is often enriched by revelations that can manifest through dreams, intuitions, or meditations, thus integrating the spiritual with the practical.

- **Energy protection:** Creating shields of light or energy barriers helps to avoid blockages and sabotage, both internal and external. These shields can be visualized as luminous armor that protects personal energy and keeps the focus in the right direction.

- **Continuous evaluation:** Maintaining an active connection with angels facilitates strategic adjustments as circumstances change. This evaluation is done intuitively and in tune with the natural rhythm of life, ensuring that each step is aligned with the individual's higher purpose.

Unlike the rigid models of traditional financial coaching, this plan adapts to the personal and spiritual evolution of each being, ensuring that the prosperity obtained contributes to integral growth and the fulfillment of one's life purpose.

Candle Ritual to Attract Financial Opportunities

This ritual invokes the energy of Archangel Raphael and prosperity, using fire as a channel to amplify the intention of abundance.

You will need:

- A green candle (or a conventional candle on which you will draw the money symbol $ with a pointed object or marker).
- A candle holder.
- The highest denomination bill you have on hand.
- Peppermint or cinnamon essential oil (optional).

Instructions:

1. **Purify the space.** Before you begin, energetically cleanse your surroundings. You can visualize a white light enveloping the room or use a bundle of sage or palo santo to harmonize the energy.

2. **Prepare the candle.** If you are using essential oil, apply a few drops to the candle from the base to the tip while focusing your intention on attracting abundance. If you don't have a green candle, use a conventional candle and draw the $ sign on it as a symbolic anchor of prosperity.

3. **Place the bill under the candle holder.** This acts as an energetic magnet for prosperity.

4. **Light the candle and recite the invocation:**

    "Archangel Raphael, I invoke you now. Please bring opportunities for prosperity and financial growth into my life. Guide my actions so that I may manifest abundance in ways that are for my highest good and the highest good of all involved. Thank you."

5. **Visualize your life in abundance.** As the candle burns, close your eyes and focus on how prosperity

feels. What changes does it bring to your life? How does money flow with ease and purpose? Allow this image to permeate your energy.

6. **Remain receptive to angelic messages.** As you watch the candle, pay attention to any intuitions, thoughts, or ideas that arise. If you keep a journal, write down any feelings or messages you receive.

7. **Allow the candle to burn completely.** When the candle has gone out, keep the bill in your wallet as a constant reminder of your intention to attract abundance.

Repeat this ritual when you feel you need financial reinforcement, are starting a new project, or want to strengthen your connection with the energy of prosperity.

Money Relationship Healing Ritual

This ritual guides you through a process to heal your relationship with money, releasing limiting beliefs and fostering an abundance mindset with the help of Archangel Uriel.

You will need:
- A quiet space where you can sit comfortably.
- A journal and pen.
- A citrine stone, white crystal, or coin on which to focus your intention (optional).

Instructions:
1. **Find a comfortable place to sit and relax.** Close your eyes and take deep breaths, allowing each exhalation to dissolve any tension in your body.

2. **Invoke the presence of Archangel Uriel:**

   "Archangel Uriel, I ask you to assist me in this process of healing my relationship with money. Help me to see and release any beliefs or patterns that are preventing me from living in abundance. Fill me with your light of wisdom and guide me toward a new perspective."

3. **Reflect on your current relationship with money.** How do you feel when you think about your finances? Do you feel fear, anxiety, guilt, or resentment? Allow yourself to acknowledge these emotions without judging them.

4. **Ask Uriel for clarity.** Ask him to show you the source of these emotions. Ask yourself:

    - Is there an experience from the past that has shaped my relationship with money?
    - Have I absorbed limiting beliefs from my family or society?
    - What recurring thoughts do I have about prosperity?
    - Remain attentive to any images, memories, or feelings that arise.

5. **Visualize these beliefs as ropes that bind you.** Now, imagine the archangel Uriel cutting them

with a sword of golden light, freeing you from these energetic ties that prevent you from flowing with abundance.

6. **Feel the transformation.** As these ropes dissolve, notice how a new energy of confidence, fluidity, and prosperity fills your entire being. Imagine this golden light enveloping your heart and expanding into all areas of your life.

7. **Create a new affirmation that reflects your renewed relationship with money.** It could be something like:

    - *"I am a magnet for abundance."*
    - *"Money flows to me with ease and grace."*
    - *"My finances grow steadily and harmoniously."*
    - Repeat this affirmation several times, feeling it with conviction in every word.

8. **Slowly open your eyes.** Take your journal and write about your experience. What did you discover? How do you feel now compared to when you started the ritual? Write down any messages or feelings you received.

9. **Seal your intention with a tangible object.**

    If you have a citrine stone, hold it while repeating your affirmation, as this stone is known for its connection to abundance.

If you don't have citrine, you can use a white crystal—a symbol of clarity and renewal—or even a coin. Charge this object with your new intention and keep it in your wallet or in a special place as a reminder of your financial transformation.

This adjustment maintains the essence of the ritual, offering more accessible options for those who do not have citrine, without losing the power of the healing process with the guidance of Archangel Uriel.

20 affirmations and decrees for abundance

1. With each breath, I inhale prosperity; with each exhalation, I release scarcity and anxiety.

2. I am a magnet for wealth and abundance, attracting opportunities in every circumstance.

3. Money flows to me in waves of abundance; I always have more than enough in every instance.

4. My relationship with money is healthy and prosperous; my abundance mindset will never be postponed.

5. Every day, in every way, my prosperity grows more and more.

6. My bank account grows and expands, my financial abundance never runs wild.

7. I release all blocks and limitations, embracing abundance in all its manifestations.

8. I am worthy of wealth and prosperity; my value is not tied to my solvency or property.

9. My income increases in unexpected ways, my earning potential is never underestimated.

10. My life is full of financial opportunities, my chances of success are infinite and real.

11. Every investment I make is wise and prosperous; my financial intuition is never postponed.

12. I am open to receiving abundance in all its forms; my finances grow like waves in storms.

13. The universe provides me with everything I need, my faith in abundance is never misplaced.

14. My work is valued and well-paid; my efforts are always appreciated and well-rewarded.

15. I am a wise and responsible steward of my wealth; my financial decisions are sound by law.

16. I use my prosperity to benefit others, sharing my abundance with my brothers and sisters.

17. Every financial challenge is an opportunity to grow; my economic resilience never ceases to flourish.

18. My relationship with money is balanced and healthy; my peace of mind is not disturbed by money.

19. I celebrate the abundance of others, knowing that there is more than enough for everyone.

20. I live in an abundant and prosperous universe, where all my needs are always met with care.

17. Angelic protection

The energetic universe is in constant interaction with our auric field, the subtle envelope that surrounds the physical body and connects us to different vibrations. However, this balance can be affected by various influences that alter our internal harmony. These threats are classified into three main categories: residual energies, conscious entities, and psychospiritual attacks.

Residual energies are accumulations of dense emotions that remain impregnated in physical spaces after intense or traumatic events. They manifest themselves in "cold spots" within certain environments, generating a feeling of discomfort or decay. On the other hand, conscious entities include autonomous thought forms and disembodied beings that, according to esoteric tradition, remain on the energetic plane and can attach themselves to the auric field, affecting people's vitality. Finally, psychospiritual attacks correspond to energetic aggressions intentionally directed by other people, motivated by envy or unconscious emotional conflicts.

The recognition of these influences is based on certain recurring patterns: persistent fatigue with no apparent medical cause, sudden mood swings associated with specific places, or disturbing dreams with unsettling presences. Quantum physics, through the study of morphogenetic fields—organizational energy patterns that influence matter and consciousness—has begun to explore these types of interactions from a scientific perspective.

The Protection of Archangel Michael and His Vibrational Power

Throughout history, invoking Archangel Michael has been an essential practice for energetic protection. Michael, whose name means "Who is like God?", is recognized in various spiritual traditions as the guardian against dark forces and discordant energies. His iconic image carrying a flaming sword symbolizes the ability to cut energetic ties and dissolve negative patterns that limit spiritual evolution.

In mystical theology, Michael's presence is related to the activation of the diamond body, an upper layer of the auric field that reinforces energetic boundaries and protects against unwanted influences. Comparative religion studies have identified parallels between Michael and other protective figures, such as India in the Vedic tradition, known for his mastery over the forces of chaos, and Horus in Egyptian mythology, whose eye symbolizes vigilance and divine protection.

From a metaphysical perspective, Michael's energy is associated with the solar plexus chakra, the center of will and personal h . In apocryphal texts such as the Book of Enoch, his role in the fight against fallen angels is detailed, while Kabbalah links him to the sefira of Hod, which represents organization and splendor. His influence, therefore, not only provides protection, but also helps to structure personal energy to strengthen inner security.

Creation and Maintenance of Angelic Energy Shields

Angelic energy shields function as protective filters that regulate the flow of energy in our environment. The effectiveness of these shields depends on three fundamental factors:

1. Clarity of intention: This is based on the observer theory in quantum physics, which points out how consciousness influences energetic outcomes.

2. Vibrational alignment: This involves tuning into higher frequencies that promote stability and protection.

3. Consistency in practice: Related to neuroplasticity, the brain's ability to adapt and sustain energy patterns through repetition.

Sacred geometry has been used to establish structural foundations in these protective fields. Shapes such as the tetrahedron and dodecahedron are used to construct light matrices that filter and reorganize surrounding vibrations. Research in quantum biology suggests that these shields interact with the human electromagnetic field, which has been recorded with devices such as GDV (Gas Discharge Visualization), capable of capturing the extent and behavior of the aura.

Energy shields can be classified into different categories according to their function:

- Reflective shields: They bounce back discordant energies and prevent their influence.

- Absorbent shields: They capture and dissolve negative vibrations.

- Transmuting shields: Transform dense frequencies into harmonious energy.

Cleansing and Consecration of Spaces with the Angelic Presence

The physical environment also stores energy, making it necessary to cleanse it periodically to prevent the accumulation of dense vibrations. Environmental physics has explored this phenomenon through the Hutchison effect, which suggests that electromagnetic fields can alter the material properties of a space. Angelic cleansing seeks to restore the vibrational purity of the environment and remove energetic residues.

One of the most effective methods is the use of sound frequencies, such as 528 Hz, which has been widely studied for its impact on DNA structure and cell regeneration. This frequency, combined with angelic invocations, enhances the cleansing and harmonization of spaces.

The consecration of a place involves establishing a unique vibrational signature aligned with higher energies. This practice has been applied in various cultures, from the Celtic Druids, who used natural elements in their rituals, to Gothic architects, who designed temples based on astronomical alignments to channel higher energies.

In contemporary angelology, the concept of dimensional anchoring is used, where the four cardinal archangels—Michael, Gabriel, Raphael, and Uriel—act as pillars of energetic stability in a space, consolidating its protection and harmony.

Angelic Symbols and Seals as Methods of Protection

Esoteric semiology has explored the power of angelic seals, symbols that operate as vibrational antennas to channel protective energies. There are two main types:

- Passive symbols: These act as receivers of protection, such as the Eye of Horus, associated with perception and spiritual security.

- Active symbols: Designed to project energy, such as angelic sigils, which can be activated through meditation or sacred chants.

One of the most widely used seals is the seal of Michael, represented by a circumscribed hexagram—two interlocking triangles symbolizing the union of opposites. This seal is believed to generate a torsion field, an energetic structure that organizes the vibration of space.

Energy Protection During Travel and Dangerous Situations

Physical displacement can generate instability in the auric field, which has led to the development of specific protection rituals for travelers. From Roman amulets to shamanic staffs, various traditions have used consecrated objects to protect those who venture outside their usual environment.

Modern angelology introduces the concept of the dynamic silver cord, a flexible energetic connection that links the traveler to their vibrational origin, using the toroidal form—a geometric structure that represents the continuous flow of energy.

In situations of extreme danger, the limbic system of the brain generates intense reactions that can weaken the energy field. At such times, many have reported the presence of angelic beings assisting in near-death experiences. This phenomenon has been analyzed by the Monroe Institute, where common patterns have been identified in testimonies of spiritual protection at critical moments.

Protection Exercise with Sacred Symbols

This exercise will guide you in using sacred symbols to create an energy shield that protects you from negative influences. Symbols have a deep archetypal power and can be powerful tools in your spiritual protection practice.

Protective Symbols:

The Pentagram: A pentagram surrounded by a circle, representing harmony and mastery over the elements. It is a widely recognized symbol for spiritual protection.

Pentagram

The Eye of Horus: Originating in Egypt, this symbol represents perception, protection, and health. It is effective in protecting against negative energies.

Eye of Horus

The Star of David: Formed by two overlapping equilateral triangles, this hexagram symbolizes the union of heaven and earth and is a powerful symbol of protection.

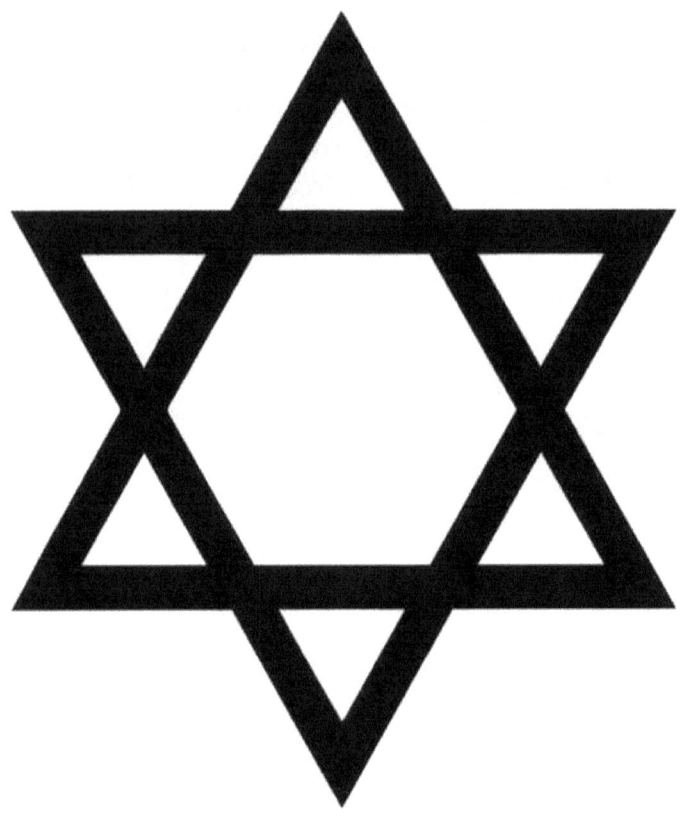

Star of David

The Tree of Life: A symbol representing connection, strength, and spiritual growth. It is universally recognized as a protective symbol.

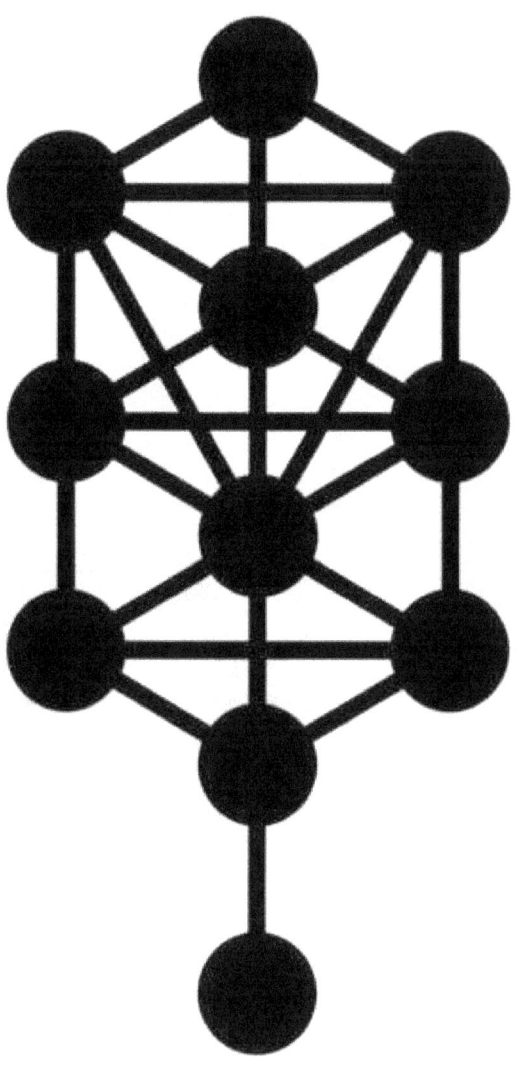

Simplified diagram of the Tree of Life

The Celtic Knot: Also known as the Witches' Knot, this intertwined Celtic design symbolizes protection against evil and negative energies.

Celtic Knot

Instructions:

You will need:

Paper and pencil or pen

A quiet place where you can concentrate without interruptions

Find a quiet space where you can be alone and free from distractions.

Sit comfortably and close your eyes. Take three deep breaths, focusing on releasing any tension with each exhalation.

Selecting and Drawing the Symbol:

Choose one of the protective symbols mentioned above, the one that resonates with you or appeals to you the most at this moment.

On a piece of paper, draw the symbol you have chosen. Don't worry about perfection; what matters is the intention you put into the process.

As you draw, visualize the symbol emanating a bright, protective light.

Activating the Energy Shield:

Once you have finished drawing the symbol, place your hands on it.

Close your eyes and visualize the symbol projecting a sphere of light that completely surrounds you, enveloping you in a protective energy field.

Repeat the following affirmation mentally or aloud (or create your own): *"Through this sacred symbol, I activate my shield of protection against all negative energy or discordant influences."*

Strengthening the Shield:

With your eyes closed, visualize the sphere of light becoming stronger and brighter with each breath you take.

Imagine that any negative energy that comes into contact with this shield is instantly transmuted or dissolved into light.

Maintain this visualization for at least five minutes, or until you feel a sense of safety and protection enveloping you.

Closing the Exercise:

Take a moment to thank the energy of the symbol and any guides or angels you feel have assisted you in this process.

Gently open your eyes, returning your attention to the physical space around you.

Keep your drawing in a special place, or carry it with you as a reminder of your protective shield.

18. Angels in Nature

Difference between angels, devas, and nature spirits

Angels are direct manifestations of divine consciousness that operate under universal cosmic principles. Their role transcends cultures and beliefs, being recognized as messengers of the divine and guardians of spiritual light. Their presence is documented from the Judeo-Christian tradition to contemporary mystical interpretations.

Devas, on the other hand, are considered the invisible architects of nature. They act as subtle forces that organize and sustain ecosystems, imbuing them with divine order. Their existence is manifested in the vitality of flora and fauna, as well as in the interconnection of natural cycles. Their origin is linked both to Eastern teachings, where the term *deva* refers to benevolent celestial beings, and to Western esoteric currents that identify them as guardians of planetary life.

On the other hand, elementals represent the primary energies of nature in their purest form. They are the entities that give life to terrestrial processes and have been described in popular imagination as gnomes (earth), sylphs (air), undines (water), and salamanders (fire). Each of them embodies the essence of their element and acts within the etheric plane, serving as intermediaries between the physical and the subtle.

These three categories of beings operate on different levels of existence. Angels reside in high-vibration celestial planes, radiating light and divine wisdom. Devas work from the archetypal world, where the primordial energies that shape life flow. Elementals, on the other hand, are found in the etheric web that connects matter with spirit, acting as active agents in the manifestation of nature. From the Rosicrucian perspective, devas are described as *angels of nature*, guardians of planetary cycles and the ancient wisdom that governs ecosystems. Meanwhile, elementals are seen as the invisible hands that sustain the harmony of the natural world, intervening in every leaf that sprouts, every stream of water, and every spark of fire.

Communication with the angels of the four elements

Each of the elements of nature is associated with an angelic hierarchy that embodies its principles and transmits specific teachings:

- **Earth Angels:** They represent stability, firmness, and abundance. Their energy is reflected in the solidity of mountains, the fertility of the soil, and the persistence of trees that take root deep in the earth.

- **Angels of Water:** They symbolize fluidity and emotional wisdom. Their teaching is manifested in the flow of rivers, the softness of rain, and the purity of springs, reminding us of the importance of adapting and allowing ourselves to feel.

- **Angels of Fire:** They embody transformation and willpower. They are the spark of inspiration, the force that purifies and renews, just like fire that consumes the old to make way for the new.

- **Angels of Air:** They represent mental clarity, communication, and spiritual elevation. Their energy is that of the wind that carries ideas, the breeze that refreshes, and the open skies that invite us to expand our consciousness.

These forces are associated with the four cardinal archangels of esoteric tradition: Uriel, linked to Earth and practical knowledge; Gabriel, connected to Water and the emotional world; Michael, representative of Fire and protective force; and Raphael, linked to Air and healing. Each of them is a manifestation of the balance between the divine and the elements of creation.

To connect with these elemental angels, it is recommended to observe the patterns of nature and learn from them. The patience of the mountains can teach us about endurance and stability, the flow of a stream speaks to us of the need to adapt, the dance of the flames reminds us of transformation, and the wind whispering through the trees invites us to clear our minds. Each of these elements holds a lesson for balancing our lives with the rhythm of the cosmos.

Working with devas for the healing of the planet

Devas are guardians of ecosystems, responsible for preserving harmony among all forms of life. Their work is essential in the regeneration of nature when it suffers damage, as they are dedicated to restoring the original energy patterns that sustain biodiversity.

Collaborating with them involves developing a deep ecological awareness, understanding that every human action has an impact on the web of life. By adopting attitudes of respect for the environment and tuning into natural energy, we can contribute to the restoration of damaged spaces and promote planetary regeneration.

Rituals for connecting with angels in natural environments

Sacred natural spaces—ancient forests, crystal-clear springs, or mountain peaks—act as portals where the barrier between planes of existence becomes thin. Celebrating rituals in these places enhances the connection with angels, as the energy of the environment intensifies at key moments, such as sunrise or under the soft light of the moon. A simple practice is to express gratitude to the guardians of the place while visualizing a bridge of light connecting the human heart with the crystalline core of the Earth, considered in many traditions to be the soul of the planet.

Symbolic offerings, such as songs, rhythmic movements, or the harmonious arrangement of stones in geometric patterns inspired by mandalas, serve as vibrational keys that open channels of communication with angels. Beyond physical objects, the key lies in pure intention and a reverent attitude, allowing the energy of the environment to guide and direct the exchange. Ancestral cultures have passed down ways of interpreting angelic messages through nature, such as observing the flight of birds or ephemeral patterns in the clouds, thus revealing the presence of these subtle beings.

Angelic gardening: co-creation with plant devas

Each plant possesses a subtle consciousness that safeguards the essence of its species, and by interacting with them consciously, it is possible to establish a connection with their invisible guardians. Angelic gardens are not mere spaces for cultivation, but living manifestations of ordered energy, where geometric arrangements—such as the golden spiral or sacred circles—favor the harmonious flow of vibrations. These forms are not random, but reflections of the balance that underlies all creation.

Connecting with plant devas requires a special sensitivity to grasp their silent language: paying attention to their cycles, recognizing their needs, and perceiving the healing wisdom they emanate. Those who cultivate in deep communion with nature often receive "intuitive flashes," subtle impressions that reveal combinations of plants capable of enhancing each other. These revelations are considered direct messages from the guardians of the plant kingdom, who act as allies in the work of sowing life and restoring the balance of the ecosystem.

Healing ecosystems through angelic invocations

When an ecosystem is damaged—whether by deforestation, pollution, or human disturbance—angelic invocations can activate regenerative forces on subtle planes. These practices combine visualization, verbal decrees, and intonations designed to harmonize the energy of the environment, based on the premise that the universe responds to concentrated intention. In indigenous communities, there are rituals in which the wounded forest is "sung" to, using ancestral melodies to invoke the presence of healing angels who restore the vital flow of the forest.

The ritual process begins with acknowledging the living consciousness of the place, followed by asking permission from its guardians and projecting networks of light that rebuild the broken bonds of life. Many Earth healers have reported perceiving "luminous entities" working in degraded areas, especially during group ceremonies where unified intention acts as a catalyst for regeneration. More than a symbolic act, this practice seeks to restore natural harmony, reminding us of the interdependence between all beings.

Communication with animals through angelic mediation

The angels who guard the animal kingdom—known in some traditions as zoo angels—facilitate understanding between species, establishing a bridge of consciousness that transcends verbal language. To connect with them, it is essential to cultivate mental stillness and adopt respectful observation, in which judgment dissolves and the heart opens to intuitive communication. Throughout history, there are accounts of mystics and saints who claimed to speak with animals, testifying to a connection beyond the ordinary.

In deep meditative states, some people describe receiving messages from animals, not in words, but in clear impressions about their needs, warnings, or expressions of affection. Park rangers and naturalists have reported experiences in which unusual behaviors of certain animals seemed to guide them at critical moments, interpreting them as angelic manifestations in defense of the natural balance. This silent communication responds to the cosmic law of interconnectedness, where every creature, regardless of size or species, contributes to the energetic fabric of the planet.

Eco-spirituality practices guided by angelic presences

Angelic eco-spirituality invites us to perceive the Earth not only as a physical environment, but as a conscious entity that communicates through its elements and landscapes. By interacting with nature from a sacred perspective, it is possible to tune into the network of vital energy that runs through it, awakening in us a sensitivity that transcends the material.

Simple practices, such as walking barefoot with full awareness on the grass, hugging trees while feeling their energy, or meditating next to a body of water, allow us to adjust our vibrational frequency to that of the planet. This alignment facilitates the perception of subtle presences that safeguard natural harmony.

Pilgrimages to places of power—sacred mountains, healing springs, ancient forests—activate cellular memory codes, energetic records that contain the ancestral wisdom of the Earth. Many people who have participated in these experiences report perceiving angelic manifestations in the form of ethereal lights, harmonic sounds that seem to emanate from hidden dimensions, or spontaneous inspirations that reveal ways to contribute to the care of the planet. These experiences not only deepen our connection to the Earth, but also remind us that every conscious act in its honor is an offering of love and gratitude to life in its purest and most sacred state.

Exercise: "Dialogue with the Elements"

This exercise invites you to establish communication with the angels through the natural elements, turning them into a board of divine messages.

Before you begin, reflect on three specific questions you would like to ask the angels. They can be related to any aspect of your life where you need guidance or clarity.

The exercise:

1. **Choose a natural space** where you can find a variety of elements: trees, flowers, stones, birds, insects, water if possible. It can be a park, garden, or forest.

2. **Establish your code of signals.** Before you begin, define how you will interpret the messages you receive. For example:

    - A bird flying to the right: affirmation, keep going.
    - Leaves moving in the wind: patience, it is not yet time.
    - The sound of running water: flow with confidence.
    - An insect crossing your path: pay attention to details.

- Finding a feather on the ground: angelic confirmation.
- Discovering a flower on the path: something new is blossoming in your life.
- Stones blocking the path: challenges you must overcome.

3. **Formulate your first question mentally** and begin walking mindfully. For exactly seven minutes (you can use a timer), observe what elements appear on your journey and in what order.

4. **Decipher the message.** The sequence in which the elements appear will be the angelic answer. For example, if you first see a butterfly, then a feather, and finally hear water, you could interpret it as follows: *"Trust the subtle signs, you are on the right path, keep moving forward with faith."*

5. **Repeat the process for the other two questions,** choosing a different path each time and new elements to interpret.

Variations of the exercise:

- Do it at **sunrise** if you are seeking guidance about beginnings and opportunities.
- Do it at **sunset** for answers about closing cycles or deep reflections.
- During the **full moon**, focus on messages about fulfillment and manifestation.
- During **the new moon**, explore questions related to projects or paths to embark on.

A lively conversation with nature and angels

Unlike traditional meditation, this exercise is dynamic and participatory. It allows you to interact with the natural world in an intuitive way, creating your own symbolic language to dialogue with the angels. Thus, each journey becomes a unique experience of connection and revelation.

19. Angelology in everyday life

Incorporating the angelic presence into your daily routine

The presence of angels is not a phenomenon reserved for extraordinary moments; it is found in the simple, everyday things, in the details that we often overlook. The divine is not only experienced in solemn rituals, but also when we wake up with gratitude, when we share a kind word, or when we contemplate the beauty of the ordinary. Angels, as manifestations of luminous energy, filter into reality in subtle ways, finding spaces in the rhythm of daily life to make themselves present.

Every action, no matter how insignificant it may seem, can become a sacred act when performed with full awareness. Lighting a candle in the morning, preparing food with intention, walking in silence and perceiving the environment—all of these can be channels for angelic presence. By allowing ourselves to be more attentive to the small signs around us, we become receptive to the subtle communication these beings offer: a feeling of certainty in the heart, an unexpected synchronicity, a sudden breeze at a meaningful moment.

This form of connection does not require superhuman effort, but rather a change in perspective. When we stop expecting grandiose signs and learn to perceive the divine in the everyday, we discover that the presence of angels has never been absent, but was simply waiting for our willingness to recognize it.

Creating an altar or sacred space in the home

The home is a reflection of the inner world, and within that space, it is possible to establish a meeting point with the angelic dimension. An altar is not a simple ornament, but an invitation to spiritual presence. Its size or complexity does not matter; what is essential is the intention with which it is constructed.

Placing a candle representing light, a container of water symbolizing fluidity, a stone anchoring the energy of the earth, and incense or a feather evoking the air is enough to create a center of harmonization. But beyond the elements, what transforms this space into a bridge to the celestial is dedication. The repetition of gestures, the renewal of offerings, and serene contemplation reinforce the altar's vibration, turning it into an energetic beacon.

There is no need to follow strict rules; each person intuitively knows which objects and symbols resonate with their own spiritual connection to the . An altar not only facilitates dialogue with angels, but also acts as a tangible reminder that the sacred is always accessible. A refuge of calm amid the hustle and bustle of everyday life, a meeting point between the visible and the invisible.

Morning and evening invocations for protection and guidance

The beginning and end of the day are auspicious times to establish contact with angels. The transition between wakefulness and rest allows for a clearer connection, as the mind is not as preoccupied with external demands. In the morning, a simple invocation may be enough to open the way to clarity and protection: a thought of gratitude, an affirmation of light, a sincere request for guidance.

During the night, accumulated worries can weigh on the mind, so surrendering those burdens before sleep helps one rest in peace. Invoking the angels at that moment allows one to let go of what is no longer needed and receive inspiration in sleep. It is not a matter of reciting rigid formulas, but of speaking honestly, as if conversing with a friend who always listens.

Words spoken with intention create an energetic bridge that strengthens the perception of angelic presence. Sometimes the answer comes in the form of a clear dream or , a feeling of tranquility, or the certainty of being accompanied. And even if it seems like nothing is happening, the simple act of calling on the angels is, in itself, an opening to their influence.

Using angelic intuition in decision-making

The language of angels is rarely expressed in direct words; instead, it manifests itself in hunches, in impulses that seem to come out of nowhere, in an inner sense of knowing without the need for reasons. Intuition is one of the clearest ways in which their guidance is experienced.

When doubt arises and the mind becomes entangled in confusing thoughts, the body often gives more honest answers. A feeling of expansion or tension, a slight tingling in the stomach, or sudden relief can be clues as to which path to follow. Angels do not impose decisions, but they provide signs to make discernment clearer.

Observing repetitive patterns, paying attention to recurring symbols, or simply listening to that inner impulse that suggests an unexpected direction are ways to receive their influence. Sometimes angelic intuition has no apparent logic, but over time, you discover that it guides you to exactly where you needed to be.

Angels at work: improving the work environment

The workplace is not always perceived as a place conducive to spiritual energy, but in reality, it is one of the settings where angelic intervention can be felt the most. Pressure, conflicts, and constant responsibilities generate tensions that can be alleviated by the presence of the divine.

Visualizing the work area enveloped in light, placing a symbolic object that reminds us of angelic protection, or simply starting the day with a clear intention can make a difference in the quality of the environment. The energy of angels is reflected in harmony among colleagues, in fluid creativity, and in the resolution of difficulties without unnecessary friction.

It is not uncommon for unexpected solutions to arise when invoking their presence, or for certain meetings or conversations to flow more easily. Sometimes, angelic intervention is not perceived as a grand event, but as a subtle adjustment in daily dynamics that facilitates well-being and collaboration.

Angels also act through others. A word of encouragement at the right moment, a kind gesture in the midst of stress, an opportunity that appears when it is most needed. As the connection with them strengthens, it becomes easier to notice how their influences seep into everyday life, even in spaces where one would not expect to find them.

No boundary between the sacred and the mundane

There is no specific time to connect with the angelic presence, nor is there an exclusive place where their energy can manifest. Angels are in every silent pause, in every choice made with the heart, in every moment when a space opens up to perceive them. It is not necessary to do something extraordinary to receive their guidance; it is enough to be present, to maintain the willingness to recognize their influence in everyday life.

In the end, life itself is a stage where the sacred and the mundane intertwine. It all depends on how we choose to look at it, on how open we are to feeling the company of those beings who, although invisible, are always near.

Conscious driving with angelic protection

The act of driving can become a practice of spiritual connection when done with full attention and a conscious intention of protection. When behind the wheel, alertness not only translates into quick reflexes and sound decisions, but also into an intuitive openness that allows us to perceive subtle warnings. Conscious driving is not just about applying safety rules, but about embracing the journey as an experience in which the body, mind, and energy align to create a harmonious flow on the road.

Guardian angels and guides manifest themselves in many ways while driving. Sometimes, a sudden feeling to stop for a few more seconds at a traffic light can prevent an accident, or a sudden inspiration can lead you to change your route for no apparent reason, only to discover later that you avoided a traffic jam or an accident. These interventions are not coincidences, but subtle responses from forces that watch over your safety and well-being.

To reinforce this protection, visualizations can be used before starting a trip. Imagining a field of light enveloping the vehicle or visualizing an energy shield that acts as a barrier against any negative influences helps to strengthen the feeling of protection. Some drivers are accustomed to invoking the archangels Michael or Raphael, asking for mental clarity, protection against any eventuality, and a safe journey. Turning driving into a conscious act, in which the environment is perceived with serenity and respect, creates a more harmonious experience, aligned with the angelic energy that watches over those who travel with high intentions.

Angelic cooking: preparing food with celestial energy

Cooking is much more than a domestic task; it is a process of transformation where ingredients come to life through intention. Since ancient times, many cultures have viewed food preparation as a sacred act, a bridge between the material and the divine. It is no coincidence that in monasteries, temples, and spiritual communities of various traditions, cooking is practiced as a ritual of gratitude and elevation.

The influence of energy on food can be perceived in the way it is prepared. A dish cooked with love and dedication nourishes not only the body but also the spirit. Prayers, mantras, or simple words of gratitude while washing vegetables, kneading bread, or serving food can imbue the food with a higher vibration, harmonizing its composition with beneficial energies. The angelic presence in the kitchen is felt when the preparation process is done with full awareness, when each ingredient is valued as a blessing, and when the act of sharing food becomes a manifestation of love and care.

In esoteric tradition, the archangel Metatron is seen as a mediator of divine energy in matter, helping to refine the vibrations of everything that nourishes the body. Invoking him before cooking or visualizing his light transforming food into carriers of well-being and balance can be a powerful practice. Beyond any belief, the truth is that the way food is prepared and consumed influences vitality and emotional state. Eating with gratitude, cooking with presence, and offering each dish with generosity opens a space where the everyday becomes sacred and where celestial energy intertwines with daily life.

Conscious parenting: involving children in angelic awareness

Children have a natural connection to the subtle world. Their free imagination and capacity for wonder allow them to perceive realities beyond the visible, something that adults have often forgotten over time. For them, contact with the angelic is a spontaneous experience that requires no explanation or proof, only openness to the marvelous.

Many children talk about "invisible friends," describe lights or presences in their rooms, or feel comfort in difficult moments without knowing why. In various traditions, this has been understood as a sign of their closeness to angels, who accompany them especially in the early years of life. It is not necessary to correct this perception or try to rationalize it; rather, it is an opportunity to strengthen their trust in the sacred and help them cultivate a natural relationship with these presences of light.

Encouraging this connection does not mean imposing beliefs, but rather accompanying their spiritual sensitivity with respect and openness. They can be invited to light a candle with intention before going to sleep, to express gratitude for the day that has passed, or to recognize the small signs of help and guidance that appear in their environment. Music, play, and stories are powerful tools for conveying the idea that they are not alone, but surrounded by beings who care for and guide them.

In angelic tradition, the archangel Sandalphon is seen as a special protector of children, helping to preserve their connection to the Earth and the divine. His subtle and harmonizing energy is associated with music, natural sounds, and creativity, aspects that can be incorporated into parenting as ways to strengthen children's connection to their own spiritual essence.

Ancient cultures have understood the importance of raising children with a sense of the sacred, not as a dogma, but as a way of reminding them that life is a mystery full of beauty and protection. Allowing them to grow up with this perception gives them a solid foundation for facing the world with confidence and harmony, always feeling the presence of those invisible guardians who accompany them on their journey.

The Angelic Map of the Home: Transforming Everyday Spaces

Every space in your home is an energetic microcosm, a reflection of the purpose it serves in your life. By connecting each room with the appropriate angelic presence, you not only harmonize the environment, but also turn your home into a refuge of light and protection. This exercise will guide you in creating a vibrant home, where every corner has its celestial guardian and every daily action is transformed into a conscious act.

Materials needed:
- A simple floor plan of your home (you can draw it by hand)
- Colored sticky notes or small pieces of paper
- A marker or pen

- A moment of calm to perform the exercise with intention

Step by step:

1. Draw an energy map of your home

Draw a simple diagram of your home, marking each room, hallway, and common area. Architectural precision is not necessary; the important thing is to capture each space where your life unfolds.

2. Assign a guardian angel to each space

Each room has an energetic purpose, and angels can enhance its function:

- **Kitchen:** Angel of abundance and nutrition—bless the food and fill the home with provisions.
- **Bedroom:** Angel of rest and renewal—watches over sleep and regenerates the body and soul.
- **Living room:** Angel of family harmony – strengthens communication and unity.
- **Bathroom:** Angel of purification—cleanses and renews energies.
- **Study or office:** Angel of wisdom – guides learning and work with clarity.
- **Entrance:** Guardian angel – protects the home and its inhabitants.

- **Hallways and corners:** Angels of fluidity – allow energy to circulate without stagnating.

Write the name of the corresponding angel on a sticky note and place it discreetly in each room (behind a door, under a piece of furniture, on a shelf). This not only reinforces the intention, but also acts as an energetic anchor.

3. Activate the angelic presence in each space

It is not enough to assign an angel to each room; you must welcome its role in the house. To do this, establish a **symbolic gesture** that will help you remember it every time you enter that space. Some ideas include:

- **Kitchen:** Before cooking, place your palm on the table and say quietly, "Thank you for the abundance."
- **Bedroom:** When you go to bed, visualize a soft light enveloping the bed and mentally repeat: "May this rest renew me."
- **Living room:** When you turn on a lamp or candle, feel the light activating the energy of harmony.
- **Bathroom:** When turning on the shower or faucet, imagine a blue glow purifying your entire being.
- **Study or office:** Before you start working or studying, gently touch the surface of your desk and repeat: "May wisdom guide my mind."

- **Entrance:** Each time you walk through the door, touch the frame and visualize a protective shield enveloping the home.

4. Interact with angels through daily actions

For one week, perform each activity with the awareness that you are not alone in space, but in collaboration with the angels who guard you. Each daily task becomes a sacred act:

- When preparing food, feel how the angel of nutrition infuses the food with vitality.
- When cleaning, perceive the presence of the angel of purification helping to clear dense energies.
- When conversing with your family, invoke the energy of the angel of harmony to strengthen understanding.
- When working, feel how the angel of wisdom inspires ideas and wise decisions.

5. Observe the changes in the environment

As the days go by, you will notice how the energy in your home becomes lighter, spaces feel more welcoming, and everyday tasks cease to be automatic and become rituals of connection. Angels do not need grand ceremonies to manifest themselves; it is enough to make space for them in your daily life and recognize their presence in every corner.

At the end of the week, you can review your home map and make adjustments if you feel it is necessary. You may find that certain spaces require more attention or that another angel feels more appropriate for a particular room. Allow the energy to flow and adapt the exercise to your own intuition.

Over time, this angelic map will become a living guide, reminding you that every action in the home can be imbued with light, presence, and protection.

20. Akashic Records and Angels: Accessing Universal Wisdom

The Akashic Records and Their Relationship to Angels

The Akashic Records can be imagined as an immense etheric library where every experience, thought, and learning of the soul throughout its multiple incarnations is preserved. More than just an archive of the past, this cosmic memory also encompasses future potentials, paths not taken, and lessons still pending. In this subtle plane of information, time is not linear, but rather a web of intertwined possibilities, accessible according to the degree of consciousness and evolution of the seeker.

Angels play a fundamental role in safeguarding this sacred knowledge, ensuring that only the appropriate information is accessed at the right time. This is not an arbitrary restriction, but a loving protection that prevents access to data that could be misinterpreted or used without adequate preparation. Among these guardians, the archangel Metatron stands out, known in various esoteric traditions as the celestial scribe. According to apocryphal texts such as the *Book of Enoch*, Metatron was the patriarch Enoch in life, who, due to his wisdom and connection with the divine, was transformed into a high-ranking angel. This account, although not part of the biblical canon in many traditions, offers clues about the transmission of divine knowledge and the angelic role in its safeguarding.

The interaction between angels and the Akashic records is not limited to the custody of knowledge. Their work goes further, as they act as mediators who filter and interpret information so that each soul receives exactly what it needs in its growth process. While the records store information objectively, angels transmit it with a loving wisdom that takes into account each person's level of evolution and capacity for understanding.

Guardian Angels of the Akashic Records

Although Metatron is the best-known guardian of these cosmic archives, he is not alone in this task. Various mystical traditions mention other custodians, such as the Kumaras or Lords of the Records, described as beings of light with high consciousness who operate on a plane of pure existence. These guardians are said to maintain the integrity of the records and prevent unauthorized access or selfish distortions. Their presence is perceived as spheres of crystalline light, symbols of the purity and transparency of the information they protect.

Another group of angels involved in this protection are the so-called *angels of memory*, linked to the choir of Thrones within the celestial hierarchy. Their function is to facilitate access to akashic memories relevant to the soul's learning process. Their intervention often manifests through synchronicities, those seemingly fortuitous events that actually act as signs: the repetition of certain numbers, unexpected encounters, or symbolic dreams that awaken deep intuitions. Every human decision and experience is recorded in what could be called a karmic map, and these angels use it as a reference to guide the individual in their evolution.

Techniques for Accessing the Records with Angelic Guidance

Tuning into the Akashic Records requires a vibrational adjustment that allows you to connect with their subtle frequency. To achieve this, it is essential to open the channel of spiritual perception, activating key energy centers such as the third eye chakra—considered the portal of intuition—and what mystical traditions call *the diamond soul*, a symbol of purity and spiritual strength.

There are several techniques to facilitate this connection, many of which have been used since ancient times. One of them is the recitation of angelic mantras, among which the *Yod-He-Vav-He* stands out, known in Kabbalah as the Tetragrammaton, a powerful sacred name that acts as a vibrational key to access higher states of consciousness.

Sacred geometry is also used, in particular the *Metatron cube*, a figure composed of geometric intersections that encapsulate universal patterns of creation and serve as a gateway to higher dimensions.

Another fundamental resource is the invocation of the archangel Gabriel, recognized in various traditions as the divine messenger. The Bible describes him as the angel who announced momentous events, such as the birth of Jesus, which associates him with the transmission of revealed knowledge. His energy facilitates the reception of information in symbolic forms, through colors, archetypal images, or internal sensations. From a contemporary perspective, some researchers have compared this process to the theory of *quantum information fields*, in which angels act as intermediaries who decode and transmit data stored in a universal energy matrix.

Reading and interpreting Akashic information

Accessing the Akashic records is only the first step; understanding the information that is revealed is an art that is developed on different levels. There are three fundamental planes in the interpretation of these records:

- **The historical level**, which focuses on past events and experiences, allowing us to understand how previous decisions have shaped our current reality.

- **The symbolic level**, where karmic patterns and cycles of learning emerge that repeat themselves throughout different incarnations.

- **The soul level**, the deepest of all, which reveals the soul's essential purpose and its evolution within the divine plan.

Angels play a crucial role in this process, serving as guides and interpreters of information. Through psychic abilities such as **clairsentience** (sensitivity to perceive subtle energies), **clairaudience** (the ability to receive messages in the form of sounds or words that do not come from the physical environment), and **clairvoyance** (vision of symbols and images of spiritual origin), they help the client translate the akashic data into knowledge applicable to their life.

A notable phenomenon in this field is **"mirror reading,"** in which, when interpreting another person's records, the reader simultaneously receives revelations about their own path and challenges. This suggests that the Akashic records are not isolated individual files, but rather part of a vast network of shared experiences where each soul can see itself reflected in the story of another, thus finding new perspectives and lessons.

It is important to note that time in the Akashic records does not follow a linear sequence. Instead of presenting a fixed past, present, and future, the angels show the information in the form of **constellations of possibilities**, allowing the client to visualize different potential futures. Research in the field of **transpersonal psychology** has documented cases in which individuals access memories that seem to correspond to parallel lives, experiences that, although they may seem metaphorical, the angels help to contextualize in order to facilitate personal growth and the resolution of blockages in the current life.

Healing past lives through records and angelic guidance

The Akashic records not only store the individual history of the soul, but also memories of transgenerational traumas and karmic pacts that can manifest in the present life as energy blockages or recurring patterns. These knots in the energy field can affect both emotional and physical well-being, preventing the natural evolution of the being.

Healing angels intervene in these healing processes, with Archangel **Raphael** as the main figure. His energy, recognized in various traditions for its healing capacity, acts in conjunction with forces such as the **violet fire** ( ), a transmuting principle capable of dissolving negative charges and reconfiguring the vibration of the soul. There are testimonies from people who have managed to overcome inexplicable phobias or emotional blocks by identifying and healing memories of traumatic experiences in other lives recorded in the Akashic Records.

This healing process takes place in three key phases:

1. **Revelation**: the client accesses the original cause of the trauma or blockage, which may manifest itself in images, sensations, or intense emotions.

2. **Understanding**: the angels offer a higher perspective on the situation, helping to integrate the experience from a learning and evolutionary approach.

3. **Liberation**: the energetic ties that maintain pain and limitation are cut, allowing for a profound transformation.

From a scientific perspective, neuroscience studies have shown that profound healing experiences can influence the **amygdala**, the region of the brain that regulates responses to fear and stress. This would explain why those who undergo liberation processes in the Akashic records may experience a decrease in anxiety and a greater sense of inner harmony.

Discovering your life purpose through the records

Before incarnating, each soul establishes what is known as a **"divine contract,"** a sacred agreement that defines the fundamental experiences, talents to be developed, and key relationships that will mark its evolutionary path. This record is guarded by **guardian angels**, who assist the individual in their search for meaning and mission on Earth.

One of the most relevant angels in this area is the **archangel Chamuel**, known for his loving energy and his ability to illuminate the essence of personal purpose. In moments when earthly circumstances have obscured the vision of the path, Chamuel helps restore the connection with the soul's original intention, guiding the client toward their true calling.

Numerical and symbolic clues can also be found in this process of discovery. Birth dates, names, and important events can contain patterns that reveal information about one's life purpose. **Angelic numerology** suggests that numerical sequences such as **11:11** or **333** appear at moments of alignment with the soul's destiny, functioning as signs of confirmation when a person is on the right path.

This approach has its roots in ancient cultures that used numerical systems to interpret divine designs and understand the cosmic order. As in ancient civilizations, angels use these codes to help the consultant recognize their mission and move forward with greater clarity.

Ethics and responsibility in accessing the Akashic records

The knowledge that emanates from the Akashic Records is not an absolute right, but a sacred tool that must be used with deep respect and responsibility. The **law of free will** is the supreme norm in this field, and angels, although willing to assist, will only reveal information with the conscious and voluntary consent of the client.

Among the **fundamental ethical standards** are:

- **Do not access another person's records without their permission**. Doing so without consent violates the right to spiritual privacy.

- **Avoid making immutable predictions**. Records should not be used to impose a fixed future, but to offer clarity and guidance.

- **Maintain absolute confidentiality** regarding the information obtained.

History has demonstrated the consequences of misinterpreting prophetic revelations. A clear example is the case of **Nostradamus**, whose visions have been the subject of multiple misunderstandings over the centuries, generating confusion and unnecessary fear. This underscores the need to handle any information received when accessing the records with caution.

Esoteric tradition teaches that the **Kumaras**, guardians of sacred wisdom, establish three essential filters for accessing Akashic information:

1. **Pure and selfless intention**, free from selfish motivations.

2. **Adequate vibrational preparation**, achieved through meditation, purification, and spiritual practices.

3. **High discernment**, avoiding interpretations based on assumptions or personal desires.

Interestingly, this principle finds a parallel in **quantum physics**, through the **observer principle**, which suggests that the state of consciousness of the observer can influence the outcome of what is observed. Similarly, angels block access to the records when they detect that the inquiry is motivated by ego or personal interests that do not contribute to soul growth.

Integrating Akashic wisdom into everyday life

Applying Akashic wisdom in daily life involves developing **soul memory**, an intuitive ability to access relevant information at the right moment. Through this connection, angels act as mediators, providing guidance through subtle signs and synchronicities that can go unnoticed if not given due attention.

These signs manifest in various ways: the unexpected appearance of a feather in moments of uncertainty, a melody that resonates at just the right moment, spontaneous memories that bring clarity in complex situations. Their function is to reinforce the presence of angels and their support in daily life, reminding us that Akashic wisdom is not distant knowledge, but a stream of information accessible at every moment.

To strengthen this connection and allow akashic information to flow naturally, it is recommended to adopt **daily practices that anchor consciousness in this subtle knowledge**. Some of these include:

- **Record coincidences and perceptions in a synchronistic journal**, which helps you recognize patterns and better understand the language of angels.

- **Create a personal altar** with symbolic elements such as feathers, white quartz crystals, or angelic figures that act as anchor points for spiritual connection.

- **Practice meditation with intention**, focusing on receiving guidance and clarity on specific issues.

Beyond formal practices, the true integration of this wisdom occurs when the client recognizes that every thought, emotion, and action is being recorded in the Akashic Records and that their evolution depends on the conscious decisions they make. In other words, the application of this knowledge is not passive, but rather a continuous process of transformation in which each choice shapes the future and contributes to the expansion of the soul.

Exercise: "Surrendering Emotional Traumas to the Angels"

This exercise facilitates the release of emotional burdens with the assistance of angels, allowing pain to be transformed into inner peace.

Materials needed:
- A quiet space without interruptions for at least 30 minutes.
- A journal and pen to record the experience.
- A candle (optional, to create a sacred atmosphere and raise the vibration of the space).

Instructions:

1. **Find a comfortable place and close your eyes.** Take several deep breaths, allowing your body and mind to relax.

2. **Invoke the presence of angels and spiritual guides**, either silently or aloud, with words such as:

3. *"Beloved angels, I invite you to be with me in this healing process. Help me feel protected and supported as I release this emotional burden."*

4. **Bring to your awareness an emotional trauma that you are ready to release.** It may be a childhood experience, an unresolved conflict, or any event that still causes discomfort within you.

5. **Allow the emotions to arise without repressing them.** If you feel sadness, anger, or fear, observe them without judgment, letting them flow without resistance.

6. **Visualize the presence of angels surrounding you with healing light**. You can imagine beings of light, or connect with specific archangels such as **Michael** for protection, **Raphael** for healing, or **Chamuel** for compassionate love.

7. **Surrender the trauma to the angels**. Imagine the pain turning into a sphere of dark energy in your hands and the angels lovingly taking it away. You can say mentally:

    "Beloved angels, I surrender this pain to you. Help me release it and transform it into light."

8. **Watch as the angels dissolve this energy into pure light**. Feel the lightness that this release leaves in you.

9. **Take a moment to record the experience in your journal**. Write down any feelings, messages, or insights you may have received.

10. **Close the exercise with a prayer of gratitude**, such as:

    "Thank you, beloved angels, for your love, guidance, and healing. I know you continue with me on my path."

21. Angels and Karma: Release of Patterns and Ancestral Healing

Karma from the angelic perspective

From the angelic perspective, karma is not an inescapable destiny or an imposed punishment, but a system of learning and evolution of the soul based on the cosmic law of cause and effect. Every thought, emotion, and action generates a vibration that returns in the form of experiences, with the purpose of providing opportunities for growth and healing. Angels teach us that the situations we face, whether harmonious or challenging, are part of a conscious process of spiritual evolution in which we can actively participate.

In this sense, karmic debts are not imposed burdens, but lessons yet to be integrated. Before incarnating, each soul establishes certain karmic agreements or pacts that will define the key challenges and lessons on its path. These agreements are recorded in the so-called Akashic records, a universal vibrational memory where the soul's past, present, and future experiences are archived. Archangels such as Metatron, the celestial scribe, and Raziel, guardian of divine mysteries, help interpret and access these records, providing clarity about the purpose behind each experience and how we can align ourselves with our highest evolution.

Unlike the linear perception of time we have on the physical plane, angels operate from a timeless vision in which the past, present, and future are intertwined. Archangels such as Sachiel, associated with the transformation of life energy and abundance, and Zadkiel, master of transmutation and forgiveness, facilitate the simultaneous healing of events that might seem disconnected from each other. In this way, blockages or patterns that repeat themselves at different times in life can be released through conscious intervention, since karma is not static, but flexible and malleable according to each being's awareness.

Identifying karmic patterns with the help of the angels

Karmic patterns often manifest as recurring situations in different areas of life, such as conflictive relationships that seem to follow the same pattern, persistent financial difficulties, or illnesses that return again and again without apparent cause. Angels help us recognize these signs so that we can transform them into opportunities for evolution and healing.

One of the methods they use is numerical synchronicities, where repeated sequences such as 1212 or 711 function as vibrational codes that indicate ongoing karmic learning. They can also communicate through bodily sensations, such as pressure in the solar plexus—an energy center related to willpower and self-esteem—or a feeling of warmth in the hands, indicating an energetic activation in the healing process. Another common channel is recurring dreams, where symbols, emotions, or scenarios are revealed that reflect karmic lessons yet to be integrated.

Each archangel has a specialty in identifying and releasing these patterns:

- Chamuel, archangel of unconditional love, helps to uncover blockages in emotional relationships, revealing dynamics of dependency, abandonment, or low self-esteem that may stem from past lives or early experiences.
- Raphael, the heavenly healer, guides us in understanding illnesses whose origin may be linked to karmic memories, allowing the restoration of physical and emotional balance.
- Jofiel, guardian of enlightenment, reveals limiting beliefs that prevent personal growth, facilitating the expansion of consciousness to higher levels.

Karmic patterns emit an energetic frequency that angels can detect with precision. Celestial entities specializing in the Akashic records, such as Akashiel, act as guardians of this information, revealing key details such as when the pattern originated, its initial purpose, and how it has evolved over time. By developing what is known in the

Hermetic tradition as causal vision—the ability to perceive the spiritual roots behind what happens on the physical plane—it is possible to make decisions more aligned with the soul's mission and accelerate the process of inner transformation.

Working with angelic guidance in identifying and healing karma allows us to break out of repetitive cycles and move toward a freer, more conscious, and harmonious life, in which we stop reacting to circumstances and begin to co-create our reality from wisdom and divine love.

Healing ancestral lines with family guardian angels

In angelology, it is recognized that the karmic burdens of a lineage can be divided into three broad categories: genetic karma, which is transmitted through DNA and influences physical predispositions and natural talents; psychic karma, which encompasses emotional patterns and inherited beliefs; and spiritual karma, which relates to soul commitments collectively assumed by a family throughout various incarnations.

Each family has a council of ancestral angels, guardians who safeguard the karmic memory of the lineage and facilitate its transformation. Often, this council is led by a specific archangel whose mission is to assist in healing recurring conflicts within the family history. For example, if a family has experienced generations of abandonment or emotional detachment, the presence of the archangel Ariel may be key, as his energy encourages the restoration of emotional balance and connection with nature as a source of stability and grounding.

The healing of these ancestral memories is guided by the Angel of Genealogy, identified in some traditions as Barachiel, who helps reveal hidden transgenerational patterns. These can manifest in descendants in various ways, from recurring challenges to inherited spiritual gifts waiting to be awakened. The key to this transformation lies in accessing the original light codes of the lineage, that is, the purity and purpose with which each family was conceived in the subtle planes, before the human experience distorted its energetic flow.

There are souls who, before incarnating, choose to be born into families with specific burdens in order to act as ancestral healers. These individuals often feel a natural h y connection to archangels associated with transformation, such as Zadkiel, whose energy helps release karma, or Metatron, who facilitates the restructuring of the lineage's energetic DNA. With angelic assistance, it is possible to perform symbolic ceremonies where the client acts as a representative of their family before the Celestial Court, a space of divine justice where forgiveness is asked for, balance is restored, and inherited patterns are released through compassion and unconditional love.

Resolution of karmic contracts through angelic decrees

Karmic contracts are agreements made between souls before incarnating for the purpose of promoting mutual learning and growth. However, in the course of physical life, these agreements can become restrictive, generating emotional dependencies, blockages, or repetitive cycles that hinder spiritual evolution. When this happens, it is possible to request the intervention of the archangels Juriel (linked to divine justice) and Eremiel (guardian of sacred covenants), who assist in the review and updating of these contracts through the use of angelic decrees.

Angelic decrees are verbal affirmations that, when spoken with conscious intention and celestial assistance, allow the vibrational codes imprinted in the Akashic records to be rewritten. Each word acts on the light structures that sustain karmic agreements, releasing unnecessary bonds and transforming burdens into learning opportunities. It is important to understand that these decrees do not eliminate the consequences of past decisions, but rather modify the way these experiences manifest, moving from cycles of repetitive suffering to processes of growth and conscious evolution.

The effectiveness of this method is supported by studies in cymatics, a discipline that demonstrates how certain sound frequencies generate geometric patterns in matter. Research has shown that certain combinations of vowels and consonants, especially those present in angelic names, generate harmonies that can reorganize energy fields. This suggests that angelic decrees, when intoned with precision and spiritual alignment, can modify the vibrational structure of karmic contracts, allowing their reconfiguration in tune with the evolution of the soul.

Since this work involves the manipulation of deep energies, it is essential to have the protection of Archangel Michael, whose vibration strengthens the practitioner's energy field and dispels discordant influences. With his assistance, it is possible to ensure that only those aspects necessary for spiritual advancement are transformed, always respecting free will and divine balance.

Transforming negative karma into lessons for growth

From the angelic perspective, negative karma is not a punishment, but rather the accumulation of experiences and choices disconnected from universal love and spiritual wisdom. Every karmic situation, no matter how difficult it may seem, holds a seed of learning that can be discovered and transformed through angelic alchemy, a process of transmutation that converts painful memories into conscious light.

A common example is the karma of betrayal. At first glance, this may seem like an unfair and painful experience, but at its core it may contain lessons about self-confidence and discernment. Angels help reinterpret these experiences from a higher perspective, considering the soul-to-soul connection of those involved, to reveal the hidden purpose behind each event. In this process, Archangel Gabriel, with his gift of communication and revelation, facilitates guided Akashic regressions to understand the spiritual origin of each situation, while Uriel, the bearer of divine light, brings clarity and understanding to integrate the teachings of each experience.

This approach finds a parallel in transpersonal psychology, whose studies have shown that reframing traumatic experiences can reduce stress nd increase spiritual resilience. Carl Jung called this process "individuation," referring to the conscious integration of fragmented aspects of the psyche into a harmonious whole. Through this perspective, the angels teach that the purpose of karma is not to perpetuate suffering, but to facilitate the evolution of the soul, allowing each individual to become a conscious co-creator of their reality.

Creating positive karma with angelically inspired actions

Positive karma is generated through conscious acts that expand the flow of love and harmony in the world. Angelic teachings emphasize that the intention behind each action is key: the same act can generate different effects depending on the energy with which it is performed. Therefore, the archangels Haniel (guardian of grace and beauty) and Raguel (mediator of harmony and justice in relationships) assist in aligning personal motivations with the greater good, ensuring that each action resonates with the divine essence.

Angelically inspired actions have three essential characteristics:

1. They occur in moments of synchronicity, when energy is aligned with divine purpose.
2. They flow naturally and spontaneously, without forcing circumstances.
3. They benefit on multiple levels, contributing to the well-being of the performer, the recipients, and the environment.

From a quantum perspective, it has been shown that the observer influences the observed reality, which resonates with the idea that consciousness, when guided by a higher intention, imprints an energetic footprint on the subtle field. This explains why simple acts, such as blessing food or expressing gratitude, can generate expansive effects on the collective vibration.

Even in the material realm, angels teach that sacred abundance does not depend solely on the quantity of accumulated goods, but on the quality of one's relationship with the energy of provision. The key to positive financial karma lies not only in generosity, but in the awareness with which economic energy is managed, honored, and shared, recognizing it as an expression of divine flow in matter.

Karmic release technique through angelic intervention: "Violet Flame of Liberation"

1. Close your eyes and breathe deeply. Invoke Archangel Zadkiel and ask him to envelop your entire being with his transmuting violet flame, capable of dissolving karmic burdens and releasing your energy.

2. Bring to mind a karmic situation that you wish to heal or release. Do not cling to the pain or conflict, simply observe it as a witness.

3. Repeat aloud, with conviction, three times:

4. *"By the power of the violet flame and angelic grace, I release this bond. What was, is no longer. What I learned strengthens me."*

5. Visualize how the situation begins to dissolve, transforming into violet light until it disappears completely. Feel your heart lighten and the energy of liberation envelop you.

6. Thank Archangel Zadkiel for his assistance and allow his light to remain in you, helping you to sustain this new freedom.

Ancestral Line Healing: "The Luminous Family Tree"

1. On a sheet of paper, draw a simple family tree, placing the names of your known ancestors. Don't worry about the perfection of the drawing; the important thing is the intention.

2. Call upon Archangel Michael, asking him to cover the entire process with his protection. Visualize his blue light enveloping the tree and your entire family.

3. For each ancestor you name, say aloud:

   "[Name], I honor you, I bless you, I release you."

4. Feel the energy of recognition and love flowing through the lineage.

5. Imagine a golden light descending from above, enveloping each branch of the tree, healing wounds, releasing burdens, and restoring balance.

6. End by saying:

   "With love and gratitude, I heal my lineage."

   Feel the connection with your ancestors in harmony and allow the healing to continue beyond this moment.

Resolution of karmic contracts: "Decree of Freedom"

1. Close your eyes, breathe calmly, and invoke Archangel Metatron to witness the process. Visualize his luminous energy at your side, holding a golden scroll containing the records of your soul contracts.

2. With firmness and from the heart, pronounce the following decree:

   "I, [your name], in full consciousness and love, decree the dissolution of all karmic contracts that no longer serve my evolution. With gratitude for the lessons learned, I free myself and all those involved. So be it."

3. Visualize how the scroll lights up and its contents transform into particles of light that dissolve into the universe.

4. Feel the peace of this new freedom in your heart and thank Archangel Metatron for his guidance.

Transformation of negative karma: "Angelic Alchemy"

1. Identify a difficult situation you are currently going through. Instead of focusing on the suffering, open your heart to the learning that this experience brings.

2. Call upon Archangel Uriel, master of wisdom and enlightenment. Imagine his golden light descending upon you, clearing your mind and expanding your understanding.

3. Ask aloud or within yourself:

4. *"What lesson can I learn from this?"*

5. Remain silent for a few moments, breathing mindfully. Do not rush to find answers. Trust that the revelation will come through an intuition, an image, a thought, or a feeling.

6. When you feel you have received the teaching, thank Archangel Uriel and let his light accompany you in the process of integration.

Creating positive karma: "Angelic Seeding"

1. When you wake up each morning, connect with your guardian angel and ask them to reveal three opportunities for you to generate positive karma throughout the day.

2. Maintain an attentive and receptive attitude. It may be a kind gesture, a word of encouragement, or an unexpected act of service.

3. Act without expecting recognition. Perform every action out of genuine love, trusting that its impact will be profound, even if you don't see it immediately.

4. Before going to sleep, reflect on the opportunities you received and give thanks for them. Recognize the transformation that occurs within you each time you choose to sow light in the world.

Meditation to dissolve attachments: "Cutting Ties"

1. Find a quiet place and close your eyes. Breathe deeply and call upon Archangel Michael, asking him to help you cut the energetic ties that no longer serve you.

2. Visualize karmic ties as strings of energy that connect you to certain people or situations. Notice which ones feel heavy, worn out, or limiting.

3. In a clear and decisive voice, say:

   "Archangel Michael, cut all ties that do not serve me."

4. Imagine his sword of light gently descending and cutting each unnecessary bond. Feel how the release occurs without pain, only with love and peace.

5. Breathe deeply and allow Michael's energy to envelop you with a new sense of lightness and freedom. Thank him for his assistance and remain in this state of harmony for a few more moments.

23. Near-death experiences and angelic encounters: Evidence and testimonies

Overview of research on near-death experiences (NDEs)

Eben Alexander, whose academic training and scientific approach did not contemplate the possibility of realities beyond the material. However, in his book *Proof of Heaven* (2012), he recounted how, during a coma induced by severe meningitis, he experienced a journey to heavenly realms where he interacted with luminous beings. This episode completely transformed his perspective, challenging his previous skepticism and leading him to question the limits of human consciousness. His testimony sparked intense debate within the medical community, as it called into question conventional explanations of brain function and the nature of the mind, suggesting that consciousness could persist beyond neurological activity.

In 2019, the *AWARE II Project*, led by researcher Sam Parnia—one of the pioneers in the study of post-mortem consciousness—analyzed 567 patients who had suffered cardiac arrest. In the study, one patient described seeing a golden light and feeling the presence of a loving being while her brain showed no detectable electrical activity for five minutes. Most surprising about her testimony is that she was able to accurately recall details of medical conversations that occurred during her resuscitation, challenging the traditional view that memory and perception require an active brain. Such accounts have led some researchers to consider that NDEs could open a window into states of consciousness that science does not yet fully understand.

While some studies have attempted to explain NDEs in terms of cerebral hypoxia—the lack of oxygen in the brain that can induce hallucinations—or the release of dimethyltryptamine (DMT), an endogenous compound linked to altered states of consciousness, there are cases that seem to go beyond these explanatory frameworks. A notable example is that of Anita Moorjani, who in 2006 claimed to have been healed of terminal cancer after an NDE in which she received detailed information about her illness and her healing. Her case, considered extraordinary by the doctors who treated her, has inspired many to question the limits of conventional medicine and explore the possibility that consciousness and healing go beyond the physical body.

Common patterns in angelic encounters during NDEs

One of the recurring patterns in NDEs is the presence of luminous entities that convey messages of peace, protection, and guidance. In 1996, researcher Richard Bonenfant documented the case of a woman who, after nearly drowning at age 16, saw what she described as a "lady of light." This entity led her through a luminous tunnel, a recurring phenomenon in NDE accounts that is often associated with the transition to another state of existence. Fifteen years later, during a dog attack on her daughter, the same luminous figure appeared again to reassure her and assure her that the girl would recover. This phenomenon, known as "recurring angels," suggests that certain beings of light can manifest themselves at critical moments throughout a person's life.

Another notable case is that of orthopedic surgeon Mary C. Neal, who, after drowning in a river in 1999, reported being greeted by a choir of angels who not only offered her comfort but also imparted profound teachings about the purpose of existence and the interconnectedness of all souls. Based on the analysis of multiple testimonies, three main manifestations of angelic beings during NDEs have been identified:

- **Protective guides**: In 1975, Dannion Brinkley was struck by lightning and pronounced dead for more than 20 minutes. During his NDE, he described how angels appeared to him to show him fragments of his future life, helping him understand the impact of his decisions and guiding him toward a path of greater awareness and service to others.

- **Messengers**: In 1985, Betty Eadie recounted in her book *Embraced by the Light* that, after surgery, she experienced an NDE in which an angelic being taught her the spiritual purpose of pain. According to her account, this angel explained that difficulties are not punishments, but opportunities for growth that strengthen the soul on its evolutionary path.

- **Transformed family members**: Some testimonies suggest that deceased loved ones may appear in NDEs with a luminous and transformed presence. A moving example is that of Gaylen Cardwell's father, who appeared as a being of light during the euthanasia of the family pet. His appearance not only brought her comfort, but also changed her perception of death, showing her that existence does not end, but transforms into other planes.

Post-NDE life transformations and their relationship to angelology

One of the most fascinating aspects of NDEs is the profound transformation that many people experience after having one of these experiences. A paradigmatic case is that of Mellen-Thomas Benedict, who in 1982 was declared brain dead and, after his return, claimed to have acquired the ability to perceive what he called "earth angels": subtle entities that, according to his perception, protect ecosystems and maintain the balance of nature. His testimony coincides with the findings of the Seattle NDE

Research Institute, which reported that 68% of people who have experienced NDEs experience a significant increase in their connection to nature and their perception of an interconnected reality.

Another revealing case is that of Dr. George Rodonaia, a Soviet pathologist who, in 1976, was declared dead for three days. After waking up, his worldview changed completely: he abandoned his scientific skepticism and atheistic stance to organize his life from a spiritual perspective. He became a priest and founded an organization dedicated to researching the relationship between angels and collective consciousness. His studies revealed that 92% of NDE survivors claimed to have maintained contact with celestial beings long after the initial event, suggesting that the connection with these beings can become a constant in the lives of those who have crossed the threshold of death and returned with a new understanding of existence.

The relationship between NDEs and angelology remains a field of study that raises profound questions about the nature of consciousness, the continuity of life beyond the physical body, and the role of angels as mediators between planes of existence. As science and spirituality continue their dialogue, these accounts remain a source of wonder and exploration for those seeking to understand the mysteries of life and death.

Appendix 1 – Angelic Listing from Multiple Traditions

I. Canonical and Major Archangels

This section groups together the most recognized angels in the Judeo-Christian tradition and in sacred texts. They are considered divine leaders and messengers, responsible for leading heavenly armies and transmitting important revelations. Their iconography is widely disseminated in theology and sacred art.

Michael (מִיכָאֵל)

Function: Head of the heavenly armies.

He is the protector and leader of the divine forces, widely venerated in various traditions.

Gabriel (גַּבְרִיאֵל)

Role: Divine messenger.

He is known for announcing important revelations and acting as an intermediary between the divine and humanity.

Raphael (רְפָאֵל)

Role: Healer and guide for travelers.

His work is associated with physical and spiritual healing, and protection during journeys.

Uriel (אוּרִיאֵל)

Function: Bearer of divine light.

Linked to enlightenment, knowledge, and inner transformation.

Metatron

Function: Celestial scribe.

His name, of Hebrew origin (although subject to variations), relates his work to the transcription and organization of divine wisdom.

Raziel (רזיאל)

Function: Guardian of cosmic secrets.

He guards the mysteries of the universe and reveals esoteric knowledge.

Samael (סמאל)

Function: Angel of divine justice.

A complex figure in some traditions, associated with both justice and retribution.

Zadkiel (צדקיאל)

Function: Angel of benevolence.

Associated with mercy, forgiveness, and compassion.

Jophiel (יופיאל)

Function: Guardian of wisdom.

He is associated with inspiration, beauty, and sacred knowledge.

Camael (כמאל)

Function: Angel of strength.

He represents courage, discipline, and the ability to face adversity.

II. Angels of Kabbalah

This category includes those angels who, according to Jewish mysticism and Kabbalistic tradition, have specific roles in contemplation, mercy, and the transformation of energy. Their names and attributes come from esoteric interpretations of the Tree of Life and the sefirot.

Tzaphkiel (צפקִיאל)

Function: Inspirer of divine contemplation.

Stimulates meditation and deep connection with the divine.

Tzadkiel (צדקיאל)

Function: Mercy and freedom.

Associated with compassion and liberation of the soul in times of difficulty.

Khamael

Function: Martial energy.

Represents strength and dynamism in the spiritual realm, driving righteous action.

Haniel (חַנִיאֵל)

Function: Grace and harmony.

Linked to beauty, sweetness, and balance in human and divine relationships.

Ratziel

Function: Guardian of secret mysteries.

He guards hidden knowledge and reveals connections between the earthly and the transcendental.

Sandalphon (סַנְדַלְפוֹן)

Function: Earthly transformation.

Facilitates the conversion of energies in the material world, supporting processes of change.

Cassiel (קַסִיאֵל)

Function: Time and destiny.

Associated with the regulation of cosmic rhythms and the acceptance of destiny.

III. Apocryphal angels

This section brings together angels that do not appear in the official canons of the major religions, but which appear in apocryphal texts and esoteric traditions. Their presence is based on extra-canonical accounts and alternative theological studies.

Baradiel

Function: Deity of electricity.

He is associated with dynamic energies and the force that drives change.

Galgaliel

Function: Ruler of the spheres.

His domain encompasses the movements and cycles of the cosmos, reflecting the influence of the celestial spheres.

Hadraniel

Function: Divine spokesperson.

He acts as an intermediary, communicating sacred messages between the divine and the human.

Kemuel

Function: Guardian of portals.

Guards the thresholds and access points to spiritual dimensions.

Lailah (לַיְלָה)

Function: Angel of conception.

Associated with the beginning of life and the mysterious power of the night.

Nuriel

Function: Storms and hail.

Related to natural forces manifested in intense atmospheric phenomena.

Pravuil

Function: Celestial chronicler.

Records divine events and the fate of souls in the great book of heaven.

Radueriel

Function: Archivist of heaven.

Guards the sacred records and ancestral knowledge of the firmament.

Sahaquiel

Function: Stellar guardian.

He watches over and protects the stars and the cosmic energies that pass through them.

Zagzagel

Function: Guardian of the burning bush.

He is associated with the image of sacred fire, a symbol of purification and enlightenment.

IV. Angels of the celestial spheres

This category includes angels linked to celestial bodies or "spheres" according to ancient cosmologies. Each one is related to a planet or sphere, reflecting the influence of astrology and the Hermetic tradition in angelology.

Zafkiel

Function: Sphere of Saturn.

Linked to discipline, structure, and learning through time, characteristics associated with Saturn.

Zedekiel

Function: Sphere of Jupiter.

Related to abundance, justice, and expansion, in tune with Jupiter's energies.

Madimiel

Function: Sphere of Mars.

Represents the strength, energy, and action characteristic of Mars.

Shemeshiel

Function: Sphere of the Sun.

Associated with the vitality, illumination, and creative power that emanates from the Sun.

Nogahiel

Function: Sphere of Venus.

Embodiment of beauty, love, and harmony, reflecting the qualities of Venus.

Kokabiel

Function: Sphere of Mercury.

Related to communication, wit, and mental agility, characteristics of Mercury.

Levaniel

Function: Sphere of the Moon.

Associated with intuition, emotions, and mystery, in correspondence with the influence of the moon.

V. Angels of the Christian tradition

This section brings together angels who, although they may appear in various traditions, have a strong presence in Christian theology and iconography. They encompass roles ranging from comforter to intercessor and protector in various areas of life.

Verchiel

Function: Ruler of July.

His name is associated with the organization of time and cycles, and according to some texts, he is the patron saint of this month.

Hamaliel

Function: Protector against witchcraft.

Invoked to offer defense against negative energies and witchcraft practices.

Mumiah

Function: Terminal healing.

Known for his healing powers, especially in critical or terminal situations.

Ambriel

Function: Defense against negative energies.

Acts as a protective shield against harmful influences.

Azrael (עֲזְרָאֵל)

Function: Psychopomp (guide of souls).

Traditionally associated with the passage of souls and compassion in times of loss.

Cerviel

Function: Dominion over beasts.

His presence is related to protection from wild animals and order in nature.

Dumah (דֻמָה)

Function: Angel of silence.

He represents the mystery of silence and deep spiritual reflection.

Eremiel

Function: Guardian of Sheol.

Responsible for supervising and guiding in the underworld or realm of the dead.

Ithuriel

Function: Discerner of deception.

Gifted with the ability to reveal falsehoods and uncover hidden truths.

Jegudiel

Function: Patron of work.

Inspires effort, dedication, and fulfillment of daily responsibilities.

Jerahmeel

Function: Apocalyptic visions.

Associated with revelations about the end times and final transformation.

Phanuel

Function: Revealer of truths.

Recognized for unveiling hidden realities and promoting spiritual enlightenment.

Puriel

Function: Examiner of souls.

His task is to clarify people's spiritual state through a thorough examination.

Raguel

Function: Celestial mediator.

Promotes harmony and justice in both divine and human relationships.

Ramiel

Role: Comforter of the afflicted.

Provides support and comfort to those going through times of suffering.

Remiel

Function: Guide of visions.

Helps interpret visions and guides souls on their spiritual path.

Sachiel

Function: Provider of wealth.

Associated with prosperity and abundance in the material and spiritual realms.

Sariel

Function: Lunar instructor.

Related to wisdom and the rhythms of the moon, he promotes intuition and discernment.

Sealtiel

Function: Intercessor of prayers.

Acts as a mediator in communication between humanity and the divine through prayer.

Seraphiel

Function: Chief of seraphim.

Leader of the most devoted angels, associated with sacred fire and purification.

Simiel

Function: Spiritual uplifter.

Promotes the ascension of the soul and helps overcome earthly limitations.

Suriel

Function: Shield against plagues.

Protector against epidemics and harmful energies that may affect the integrity of the being.

Uzziel

Function: Strength of God.

Incarnation of divine power, confers strength and stability to those who invoke it.

Vehuel

Function: Divine exaltation.

Leads to the recognition of the greatness and glory of the divine in people's lives.

Zerachiel

Function: Patron saint of children.

Protector of innocence and growth, promotes well-being and generational continuity.

VI. Angels of regional traditions

This last category groups together those angels who are part of regional cultural or religious traditions, contributing their own nuances to the angelic image. It includes influences from currents such as Zoroastrianism and local mythologies, enriching the diversity of angelology.

Aeshma

Function: Pursuer of lies.

Associated with the punishment of falsehood and deception, according to Zoroastrian traditions.

Arariel

Function: Master of the waters.

Represents the power and importance of aquatic elements in nature and regional mythology.

Baraqiel

Function: Control of lightning.

Linked to electrical energy and intense atmospheric phenomena, he symbolizes the transformative force of nature.

Appendix 2 – Angel Numerology

Angelic numerology is a fascinating practice that connects us to the divine realm through the inherent power of numbers. Since ancient times, humanity has shown great interest in the profound meanings and messages hidden in numbers, using them as a source of guidance and clarity in life. This discipline gives you a unique insight into your spiritual journey, helping you to decipher your purpose and the path you must follow.

Within the celestial language of angels, each number has sacred vibrations and a profound meaning. The digits 1 through 9, along with the so-called master numbers 11, 22, and sometimes 33, emanate specific energies that have a significant influence on your life. By interpreting the combinations and sequences that form these numbers, it is possible to discover details about your past, present, and future, allowing you to align your path with the divine plan.

The origins of angelic numerology are lost in history, dating back to various ancient civilizations, each contributing its particular vision and interpretation of numbering. In Babylon, for example, priests integrated numbers into their sacred rituals, recognizing their potential to connect with the divine. The renowned Greek philosopher and mathematician Pythagoras believed that numbers were the basis of all existence, and his disciples explored the complex relationships between numbers and the observable universe.

In ancient China, the concept of Yin and Yang merged with their number system, emphasizing the delicate balance and harmony that numbers symbolize. The Egyptians, renowned for their imposing pyramids and enigmatic hieroglyphics, not only used numbers to perform advanced calculations, but also imbued them with spiritual meaning in their works and ceremonies.

The Jewish mystical tradition, through Kabbalah, attributes great significance to numbers, using gematria to reveal hidden meanings in the Hebrew Scriptures. In India, Vedic numerology is deeply rooted in astrological traditions, offering a unique perspective on the role numbers play in shaping destiny.

During medieval Europe, despite the Church's reservations about divinatory practices, Christian mystics incorporated numerology as a means of communicating directly with the divine. They recognized that numbers were the key to deciphering the language of the soul and receiving messages from God.

Today, angelic numerology has experienced a resurgence, especially within the New Age movement, which integrates Eastern and Western spiritual and philosophies. Modern numerologists not only draw on ancient wisdom and the vibrations inherent in numbers, but also incorporate intuitive interpretations, creating a personalized approach to understanding the divine messages communicated through numerical sequences.

This discipline proves to be a powerful tool for self-knowledge, personal growth, and spiritual enlightenment. Tuning into the energy of numbers and receiving guidance from angels allows you to navigate your life with greater clarity, purpose, and connection to your higher self. Whether you are seeking answers to everyday challenges, direction for momentous decisions, or a deeper understanding of your soul's journey, angelic numerology opens a sacred door to the wisdom and love of the divine realm.

The connection between numerology and angel numbers

The basis of numerology lies in the belief that each number radiates particular energies and vibrations that influence your existence. Each number has a unique meaning, and by understanding its vibrations, you can gain a deeper insight into yourself and your environment. Angels, as divine emissaries and protectors, use these numbers as a universal language to communicate with you and offer guidance on your spiritual path.

Angel numbers manifest themselves in the form of sequences that repeat themselves at unexpected times and places. Far from being mere coincidences, these appearances are orchestrated by your angels to capture your attention and convey meaningful messages. By applying numerology to decipher these numbers, you can uncover messages and teachings that the angels wish to share.

Decoding angel numbers

To interpret angel numbers through numerology, you can use the principles of Pythagorean numerology, which assigns a specific numerical value to each letter of the alphabet. By reducing an angel number to a single digit or identifying it as a master number (11, 22, or 33), you can reveal its core vibration and underlying message.

For example, if you repeatedly encounter the sequence 1234, the reduction is done as follows:

$1 + 2 + 3 + 4 = 10$

$1 + 0 = 1$

The result is the number 1, which symbolizes new beginnings, leadership, and the manifestation of ideas. This can be interpreted as a sign from your angels that you are about to start a new phase in your life or that it is the right time to take the initiative in a specific area.

Interpreting angel numbers with intuition

Although numerology provides a framework for understanding angel numbers, it is essential to trust your intuition when interpreting the messages these numbers convey. Angels communicate with you personally, and the meaning of a number sequence may have a particular connotation depending on your life situation.

Pay attention to the thoughts, emotions, and circumstances surrounding the appearance of an angel number. Reflect on what you were thinking or experiencing at that moment, and how it made you feel. These details can provide essential context that will help you decipher the message your angels are trying to communicate to you.

Angel Numbers in Spiritual Practice

Incorporating angel numbers into your daily life can be a powerful tool for enhancing your personal development and spiritual growth. By integrating them into your daily practices, you strengthen your connection to the divine and receive constant guidance and support from your angels. Some ways to work with these numbers are:

Keep a journal: Record the numbers you encounter, along with any associated thoughts, emotions, or perceptions. Over time, you will be able to identify patterns or recurring themes that will give you greater understanding and direction.

Meditate on the numbers: If you notice a number that catches your attention, pause and reflect on its meaning.

Close your eyes, breathe deeply, and let the energy of the number resonate within you. Ask your angels for clarity and trust the impressions you receive.

Express your gratitude: When you perceive a message through a number sequence, take a moment to thank your angels for their guidance and support. Acknowledging their presence strengthens your connection and opens the door to receiving even more divine guidance.

The Pythagorean System and the Numbers in Your Life

In addition to angel numbers, numerology offers a wealth of information about your purpose, talents, and challenges throughout your life. By calculating your core numbers, such as your Life Path number, Expression number, Soul Urge number, and Personality number, you can gain deeper insight into the energies and themes that shape your existence.

To determine your Life Path number, which represents your life purpose and the path you should follow, use your date of birth. For example, if you were born on September 15, 1985, the calculation is as follows:

9 (since September is the ninth month) + 1 + 5 (day) + 1 + 9 + 8 + 5 (year) = 38

3 + 8 = 11

In this case, the resulting number is 11, a master number associated with spiritual enlightenment, intuition, and inspiration.

To calculate your Expression number, which reflects your talents, abilities, and challenges, use your full birth name and the Pythagorean system. In this system, each letter of the alphabet is linked to a number from 1 to 9 in a cyclical pattern, based on the idea that letters and words have specific vibrations that can be interpreted numerically to reveal profound aspects of personality, destiny, and life path. The assignment is as follows:

1 = A, J, S

2 = B, K, T

3 = C, L, U

4 = D, M, V

5 = E, N, W

6 = F, O, X

7 = G, P, Y

8 = H, Q, Z

9 = I, R

To transform a full name into a single digit, add the numerical values of each letter and, if the result is a number with two or more digits, reduce it by adding its digits until you obtain a single digit. This process is known as reduction.

As an example, we will apply this method to the name "Natalia Martinez Arango":

Natalia: 5 + 1 + 2 + 1 + 3 + 9 + 1 = 22

Martínez: 4 + 1 + 9 + 2 + 9 + 5 + 5 + 8 = 43 : 4 + 3 = 7

Arango: 1 + 9 + 1 + 5 + 7 + 6 = 29 : 2 + 9 = 11 : 1 + 1 = 2

Adding the totals: 22 + 7 + 2 = 31 : 3 + 1 = 4

Thus, the resulting number for "Natalia Martínez Arango" in the Pythagorean system is 4, which is interpreted based on numerological characteristics that reveal aspects of the person's personality and destiny.

Exploring your fundamental numbers and their meanings allows you to deepen your understanding of your life purpose, strengths, and challenges, helping you make more aligned decisions and walk your path with greater clarity and confidence.

Discovering angel numbers in everyday life

As you begin to notice the presence of angel numbers, you will realize that life is full of moments of magic and synchronicity, in which the divine manifests itself in your everyday experiences. These heavenly "signs" appear in subtle ways, waiting to be recognized by those who are open and attentive to their surroundings. If you are wondering how and where you can identify these numerical synchronicities, here are some common places where they may become apparent:

Digital screens:

In today's technology-dominated world, screens are ubiquitous and offer multiple opportunities for numbers to manifest themselves to you. From your cell phone and computer to your wristwatch or even billboards, these devices can act as conduits for angelic communication. If, for example, you repeatedly glance at the clock at 11:11 or notice that your battery always stops at 44%, these "coincidences" could be messages from the divine realm.

License plates and addresses:

As you drive down the street, pay attention to vehicle license plates. Each plate has a unique alphanumeric code, and certain combinations may catch your interest in unexpected ways. If you are drawn to a particular license plate or repeatedly see the same sequence, it could be a message from your angels. Likewise, when driving through neighborhoods or looking for an address, the numbers on doors or streets may have special meaning, even if you end up in the "wrong" place, as a playful way for your angels to communicate with you.

Receipts, bills, and books:

Angel numbers can appear in the most everyday contexts, such as on shopping receipts or bills. Although these documents may seem trivial, they represent an opportunity for angels to send you a message. You may notice that your purchase totals often add up to specific numbers or that the order number repeats itself in different situations. Likewise, books can become a medium for guidance ; pay attention to page numbers that resonate with you or passages that align with the number sequences you have been noticing. The direction the plot takes, the chronology of events, or even the length of a chapter may have hidden meaning.

Special dates and dreams:

Pay attention to dates that are relevant in your life, such as anniversaries or memorable events. If you make an important decision or experience a profound moment on a date that coincides with an angel number, it may be a sign of divine intervention. In addition, your dreams can serve as a powerful channel of communication. Angels can use the dream world to convey messages and confirm their presence through specific numbers. If you notice numbers in your dreams or if they are mentioned by characters, analyze their meaning.

Nature and social media:

The natural environment is the canvas on which angels can paint their messages. From the number of leaves you find on your path to the formation of birds on a branch, nature offers countless opportunities for angel numbers to manifest. Even the number of petals on a flower or the recurring presence of a certain animal can have special meaning. In the digital realm, social media and online interactions can also be channels for angelic guidance. The number of likes on a post, the length of a video, or the date and time of a meaningful comment can all be ways for your angels to make themselves known.

Music, movies, and games:

Angels can integrate their messages into various forms of entertainment and media. When listening to music, pay attention to the length of the song or lyrics that have a special impact on you. In movies or series, a character's dialogue, the length of an episode, or even the number of seasons can have a particular meaning. If you are a fan of video games, pay attention to your character's levels, scores, or statistics, as the repetition of certain numbers may mean more than just a coincidence.

Tickets, barcodes, and everyday events:

From the flight number on your boarding pass to your hotel room number, the details of your travels can be loaded with angelic messages. If you are assigned a seat or room with a special number, it may be a subtle sign that you are being accompanied on your journey.

Guide to interpreting angel numbers

From 0 to 9, 11, and 22

Angelic numerology is an extremely powerful tool for interpreting the messages that our spiritual guides want to convey to us. Each number, with its unique vibration, carries a special message. Below is a guide to understanding these angelic numbers, from 0 to 9, including the master numbers 11 and 22.

0 - Totality and Infinite Cycle

0 symbolizes infinity, wholeness, the point of origin, and the return to the primordial essence. It is a reminder that we are intrinsically connected to the universe and that you are on the right spiritual path, supported by the cosmos.

1 - New Beginnings and Leadership

The number 1 invites action, representing new beginnings, independence, and the ability to create reality through our thoughts and actions. It is a sign that we are the architects of our destiny and that it is time to start new projects with determination.

2 - Faith and Harmony

The number 2 embodies faith, trust, balance, and harmony. This digit encourages you to keep faith in your spiritual path and to collaborate harmoniously with those around you, reminding you that everything will unfold as it needs to.

3 - Communication and Expression

With a creative vibration, the number 3 is associated with self-expression and communication. It invites you to express yourself clearly and use your creative abilities to realize your dreams, being a sign of divine support in your creative endeavors.

4 - Stability and Foundations

This number symbolizes building solid foundations, stability, and constant effort. The 4 reminds you that your angels are present to help you work steadily and patiently toward your goals.

5 - Change and Freedom

The number 5 heralds important changes in life, adventure, and the pursuit of freedom. It is a message that you should be receptive and adapt to change, which will bring personal growth and new opportunities.

6 - Balance and Responsibility

Representing harmony, responsibility, and service to others, the number 6 reminds you of the importance of maintaining a balance between the material and the spiritual, taking care of both yourself and those around you.

7 - Spiritual Development and Inner Reflection

The 7 vibrates with energies of spiritual awakening, reflection, and self-knowledge. It invites you to listen to your intuition and look deep within yourself to find answers and advance in your spiritual development.

8 - Abundance and Personal Power

Symbolizing abundance, success, and personal power, the 8 tells you that prosperity is on its way, reminding you of the abundance of the universe and your potential for success.

9 - Conclusion and Humanitarianism

This digit represents the closing of cycles, completion, and service to humanity. The 9 encourages you to close chapters and move forward to a new chapter focused on fulfilling your life's mission.

In numerology, the numbers 11 and 22 are considered master numbers and are not reduced to a single digit when appearing in a calculation.

11 - Inspiration and Spiritual Awareness

The master number 11 symbolizes inspiration, enlightenment, and heightened spiritual awareness. It is a call to connect with your higher self, to live authentically, and to inspire others on their spiritual path.

22 - Building Dreams and Global Reach

This master number, 22, combines the vision of 11 with a strong sense of realism and discipline. It holds immense potential for transforming dreams and visions into tangible realities, highlighting leadership, ambition, and the ability to manifest high ideals.

Each angel number carries a particular message designed to guide, inspire, and support you on your spiritual journey. By paying attention to these digits and their meanings, you can tune in more deeply to divine guidance, moving toward your true essence and purpose in life.

Interpreting angelic messages

When you repeatedly encounter angelic number sequences, it is a clear sign that your spiritual guides wish to communicate with you. These messages can manifest as warnings, confirmations, comfort, or inspiration to continue on your path. The key to deciphering them lies in conscious observation and reflection on how these numbers relate to your current situation.

How to Respond to These Messages

Observe and Record: Write down when and where these numbers appear. The context in which they manifest can be as relevant as the number itself.

Reflect: Take a moment to meditate or think about what you were doing when the number appeared; this can offer you essential clues about the message.

Research: While this guide offers a general meaning for each number, the interpretation may vary from person to person. Research and meditate to discover how these meanings apply to your particular situation.

Act: Angel numbers often indicate the need to take action or make a change. Consider how you can apply that message in your life; perhaps it's time to start a new project, let go of what no longer serves you, or simply trust in the process of life.

Trust: Above all, trust that these messages are signs of love and guidance from your angels. Even if the message is not immediately clear, keep your mind and heart open to receiving its meaning.

Angel numbers are gifts from the universe designed to remind us of our divine connection and to guide us throughout our earthly journey. By paying attention to these signs and trusting the guidance they offer, you can navigate life with greater clarity, purpose, and joy.

While the fascinating universe of angel numbers is so vast and profound that it could fill entire volumes, it is important to recognize that a comprehensive guide to every detailed meaning is beyond the scope of this book. The information presented here serves as a solid introduction to the power of numbers as messengers from the universe, intended to spark your interest and provide you with the basic tools to begin interpreting these divine signs.

Master Numbers: Elevating Vibrations

Master numbers in numerology are notably distinguished from simple digits by their intensified vibration. These numbers, such as 11, 22, 33, etc., enhance the essence of the individual digits they represent, and each has a unique meaning.

11 – The Intuitive Illuminator:

Recognized as the number of deep intuition, 11 symbolizes spiritual vision and enlightenment. It has the ability to inspire and reveal profound mysteries of existence, and people influenced by this number often possess wisdom and perception that transcends the ordinary.

22 – The Master Builder:

The number 22 merges the visionary aspects of 11 with a strong dose of realism and discipline. This number holds enormous potential for turning dreams into tangible realities, denoting leadership, ambition, and the ability to materialize lofty visions.

33 – The Master:

Hailed as the number of the Master, 33 vibrates with energies of compassion, healing, and the desire to bless others. Although it shares certain energies with 6 (since 3+3=6), its influence is magnified, aiming to elevate humanity through guidance and care, drawing lessons from shared experiences.

The relevance of these master numbers lies in their ability to intensify the energies of the single digits. For example, 11 not only reinforces the qualities of the number 1 in terms of leadership and innovation, but does so with a greater spiritual charge. Thus, someone whose life path is governed by the number 11 experiences life differently from someone who identifies with the number 2, even though both share the essence of partnership and harmony. In the case of 11, spiritual calling becomes even more prominent.

The sequence in which these numbers appear is significant. For example, a sequence of 1122 suggests an evolution from the spiritual awakening represented by 11 to the constructive action indicated by 22, implying a phase of enlightenment followed by the need to materialize that vision in practice.

Understanding master numbers involves seeing beyond mere numerical repetition, recognizing their role as carriers of spiritual frequencies that connect the earthly with the divine and act as channels for higher wisdom and purpose.

Master numbers in various contexts

In birth dates, those born under the influence of 22 often exhibit traits of a Master Builder, demonstrating natural leadership and the ability to conceive and carry out grand visions.

Those with 11 in their natal chart are more inclined toward intuition, experience intense dreams, and maintain a deep spiritual connection.

In names, the presence of a master number, such as 33, suggests great potential to inspire and heal, revealing a deep connection between numbers and personal destiny.

Addresses with master numbers can have a significant impact on the purpose and achievements of residents. For example, living at an address marked with 22 can give you focus and ambition, while 11 can encourage spiritual growth and enlightenment.

When master numbers are combined, as in the sequence 1122, it symbolizes a journey from spiritual awakening to practical fulfillment, offering a nuanced view of life stages, challenges, and spiritual evolution.

The influence of master numbers not only bestows strengths but also imposes challenges. The intense enlightenment that accompanies 11 can be overwhelming and anxiety-inducing, while 22 demands not only vision but also the ability to materialize that vision. Those who resonate with 33 must find a balance between their personal aspirations and the call to serve others.

This numerical dance reflects the spiritual energy of the universe, offering both talents and a call to grow and align with your own numerological path.

Repetition of Angel Numbers and Their Meaning

Zeros symbolize eternity, potential, and connection to universal energy, marking the beginning of a spiritual journey and the importance of starting anew, focused on growth and unity.

Ones represent initiative, leadership, and the essence of action. Their repetition is a cosmic sign to seize opportunities and focus your aspirations in a positive way.

Twos highlight duality, balance, and collaboration, inviting you to be patient and keep the faith in times of uncertainty, ensuring that harmony will prevail.

The threes indicate creativity, the affirmation of prayers, and imminent blessings, which translate into divine support and guidance.

The fours symbolize stability and the building of solid foundations, assuring you that your efforts will soon bear fruit.

Fives signal change and adventure, inviting you to embrace new experiences and leave behind what no longer serves you.

The sixes urge you to reevaluate your thoughts and balance the material and spiritual aspects of your life, asking you for harmony in all facets.

The sevens, with their mystical energy, indicate that you are on the right spiritual path, suggesting that, thanks to your practice, you are close to achieving enlightenment.

Eights represent power, abundance, and the endless cycle of energy and its consequences, preparing you for prosperity and a future of leadership.

Nines signal completion and humanitarianism, suggesting the end of one stage and the beginning of a new chapter focused on fulfilling your life's mission.

These sequences act as divine communications that guide, warn, and comfort you, offering you insight into both your earthly and spiritual paths.

Timing and frequency

The recurring appearance of angel numbers is not random; their repeated manifestation underscores the importance of their message. Encountering the same number, or different numbers, often signifies the presence of a guiding force that acts as a constant reminder of the spiritual communication being offered to you. The transition from one number to another may signal a change in the type of guidance being provided.

The frequency with which an angel number appears may indicate the urgency of its message. For example, if the number 111 appears in various contexts, it may be a sign from the universe for you to pay attention to certain aspects of your life. Similarly, if you see 555 in the midst of an important decision, the angels may be encouraging you to be open to change.

These random encounters act as subtle wake-up calls, prompting you to reflect or adjust your course. They are especially poignant during times of decision or transition, offering guidance if you are tuned in. They can also comfort you in times of emotional turmoil, serving as a heavenly hug when you need it most.

The timing and frequency of these appearances often align with key stages or decisions in your life, whether it's a job change, the start of a new relationship, or daily uncertainties. For some, the timely appearance of an angel number may even predict future events or transitions.

These numbers can also synchronize with specific phases of your existence, suggesting particular lessons or themes that require your attention. This idea relates to Carl Jung's theory of synchronicity, in which the manifestation of these numbers correlates with your thoughts, emotions, or significant events. Such synchronicities intensify during periods of deep reflection, meditation, or spiritual practices ( ), indicating that you are establishing a more intimate connection at those times.

To improve your ability to recognize angel numbers, consider the following strategies:

Increase your daily awareness: Pay special attention to repeating numbers, such as those on clocks, license plates, or receipts.

Recognize and record: Make a mental note of numbers you see frequently. Their constant appearance is often indicative of an urgent message.

Document: Keep a journal or use your phone to record angel numbers. This will help you identify patterns and meditate on their meanings.

Reflect on your emotional state: Think about what you were feeling or thinking when you noticed a particular number; context is essential.

Trust your intuition: If certain numbers are particularly meaningful to you, trust that feeling.

Meditate or contemplate in silence: This can increase your receptivity to picking up on these messages.

Observe your dreams: Angel numbers can also appear in the dream world, so keeping a dream journal can be very helpful.

Pay attention to digital media: In our technological age, keep an eye out for numbers in notifications, timestamps, and the like.

Do your research: Knowing the generally accepted meanings of the sequences you encounter can serve as a starting point.

Share your experiences: Talking to other people interested in angel numbers can offer you new perspectives and broaden your understanding.

Remember that the interpretation of angel numbers is not fixed or universal. A sequence that may imply financial aspects for you could have a purely spiritual connotation for someone else. The relevance of these numbers depends largely on your personal journey.

To decipher the message of angel numbers, trust your own intuition. While general guidelines can provide direction, the personal meaning of these numbers is paramount. Stay receptive to the ways in which the universe communicates with you, and as you delve deeper into the world of numbers, you will discover more about the various sequences and combinations through which the angels speak to you, thus enriching your understanding of this celestial dialogue.

Angel numbers, when they appear in sequences or patterns, convey messages and guidance from a higher realm, reflecting the precise and purposeful method of communication of the universe. These sequences, similar to the natural rhythms of the moon, the seasons, and life cycles, follow a progression. Ascending sequences symbolize growth and expansion, similar to the energizing sunrise that heralds a new day full of opportunities. In contrast, descending sequences reflect the culmination, introspection, and reflective energy of a sunset, indicating the closing of a cycle.

Ascending angel number sequences:

012: Indicates the beginning of a spiritual journey in which 0 signifies potential, 1 signifies leadership and new beginnings, and 2 signifies balance and collaboration.

123: Suggests an orderly progression in your personal or spiritual growth, emphasizing new beginnings, cooperation, and creative expression.

234: Proposes building a stable foundation based on growth and balance, with 2 representing harmony, 3 representing creativity and social commitment, and 4 representing structure and practicality.

345: Encourages you to move from stability toward change and exploration, integrating creativity (3), structure (4), and the desire for adventure and freedom (5).

456: Represents the transition from structured energy (4), through acceptance of change (5), to service to others with new insights (6).

567: Invites personal evolution through change (5), responsibility (6), and the search for inner wisdom and spiritual awakening (7).

678: Highlights your spiritual growth that leads to empowerment and abundance, demonstrating the realization of your personal power after a process of learning and introspection.

789: Denotes the culmination of a stage, suggesting that, after achieving power and abundance (8), a cycle closes to make way for a new beginning focused on service (9).

Descending sequences of angel numbers:

987: Symbolizes the end of a phase, emphasizing the transition from material or external achievements to a deeper spiritual exploration, marking the end of a cycle and the beginning of an inner journey.

876: Indicates a transformation from personal achievements and power to a more altruistic focus, highlighting the importance of community, responsibility, and service, inviting you to reorder your priorities.

765: Represents a period of transformation initiated by spiritual vision (7), followed by responsibility and community care (6), and culminating in significant change and freedom (5), implying a process of enlightenment that involves vital adjustments.

654: Points the way to regaining stability after significant changes, beginning with an emphasis on community (6), accepting change (5), and establishing solid foundations (4). It is indicative of a period of grounding and consolidation.

543: Describes the transition from transformation (5) and stability (4) to creativity and self-expression (3), highlighting the movement toward creative growth after a period of change.

432: Shows the transition from stability and order (4) to collaboration and teamwork (2), through creativity and expression (3). This sequence emphasizes the evolution from individual growth to collective efforts and harmony in relationships.

321: Indicates a cycle of renewal in which, after creativity and growth (3) and collaboration (2), the possibility of new beginnings and leadership (1) opens up, urging you to take the initiative again.

210: Suggests preparation for a new stage, emphasizing the importance of balance and harmony (2) as a foundation before embarking on a new journey.

The meaning of mirror or reflected numbers

Numbers that appear reflected within angelic combinations have a special place in numerology due to their unique structure, vibrational frequencies, and the profound concepts they represent. These reflected numbers evoke the idea of balance, harmony, and the interconnectedness of all things in the universe.

The arrangement of digits in a mirror pattern intensifies the energy of the central number, while the digits that frame it enhance its power. This configuration can be interpreted as a protective shield, suggesting that the central energy is especially powerful and requires deep reflection to fully understand it.

Reflected numbers symbolize cycles, integrity, and unity, resonating with the natural rhythms of life. They also act as reminders of the dualities and challenges that may arise, emphasizing the need to maintain harmony amid opposing forces.

These numbers serve as a gateway to deeper understanding and self-discovery, inviting you to explore your inner world and align your life with your purpose. The sequences evoke the continuity and eternal flow of universal energy, representing the constant dance of looking inward and recognizing connections with the outside world.

Since mirror numbers vibrate at particular frequencies, they often have a calming and balancing effect on those who are sensitive to energy. In addition, they can be gentle nudges from the universe to reflect on your thoughts, emotions, and circumstances.

The balanced structure of these numbers implies growth, evolution, and expansion, symbolizing the path of learning, transforming, and returning with new knowledge. They are emblems of cosmic perfection, reminding you of the intrinsic perfection of the universe and the potential for perfection that resides within you. The emphasis on the central digit underscores the importance of the here and now, encouraging you to remain present and recognize the crucial role of the moment in your life journey.

Specific meanings of the numbers reflected

101: As you begin a new chapter, this number reminds you that the universe supports you and confirms that you are on the right path.

121: Just as the calm surface of a pond reflects the trees surrounding it, the symmetry of this number invites you to trust the path you have chosen.

131: The sequence symbolizes both your individuality and your connection to a higher power, indicating a deep relationship with the mysteries of the cosmos.

141: It signals that positive changes are brewing; you have laid a solid foundation in your life, so you are encouraged to persevere.

151: This number invites you to embrace your authenticity and move forward at your own pace, celebrating your uniqueness and ability to chart your own course.

161: This number highlights the importance of partnerships; if you are collaborating with someone, it may be a very favorable union for achieving remarkable results.

171: This number underscores the importance of spiritual growth. The universe is guiding you on your path to enlightenment, encouraging you to continue exploring your spirituality.

181: Indicates that with experience comes renewal. Learning from the past opens the door to new beginnings, and the universe encourages this process of renewal.

191: Marks the end of one stage and the beginning of another, reflecting the natural cycle of life in which, when one chapter ends, the possibility of a new one opens up.

202: Highlights the importance of achieving balance and harmony in relationships and partnerships throughout your life.

212: Focuses on the union between individuals and the sense of unity, inviting you to understand different perspectives without losing your identity.

232: Encourages you to face new experiences with wonder and humility, prompting you to discover opportunities that will help you grow.

242: Is related to stability and satisfaction; when life feels balanced, everything flows naturally, giving you security.

252: Urges you to prioritize self-expression and adventure, inviting you to embrace new experiences and innovative ideas.

262: It suggests that successful collaborations are possible when there is mutual respect and shared visions, especially in the realm of business or joint projects.

272: Draws your attention to deep spiritual insights that are ready to emerge within you.

282: Indicates that transformative energies are brewing around you, making this an ideal time to renew yourself and start anew.

292: As one cycle ends, the universe assures you that new adventures and experiences await you just around the corner.

303: Encourages you to unleash your creative potential, urging you to express your deepest desires and dreams, as creative energy abounds around you.

313: This number invites you to consider the deep connections you can forge during your adventures and life experiences.

323: Although it may seem that you and your partner have different points of view, there is a common thread that connects both perspectives; you are encouraged to find it.

343: This suggests that a solid foundation is essential for growth; the universe emphasizes the importance of stability.

353: It highlights independence; the universe urges you to embrace your freedom to express yourself and experience the wonders of life.

363: Emphasizes teamwork and mutual respect, inviting you to approach your current relationships with optimism.

373: It is linked to spiritual seeking and the search for deeper meaning in life.

383: This number heralds changes and transformations in your spiritual life, which may also manifest in the material realm.

393: Marks the end of a chapter, paving the way for the next stage on your journey.

404: It suggests that before embarking on a new adventure, it is crucial to have a solid foundation.

414: It indicates that your efforts to maintain stability in a new project will be rewarded if you persevere.

424: Represents the balance between structure and harmony, especially in your interpersonal relationships.

434: Encourages you to maintain resilience as you explore new ways of approaching life.

454: Encourages you to maintain your independence and remain grounded, even if you feel lonely.

464: Suggests that cooperating with others and building trust will bring you great benefits.

474: Indicates that the spiritual path is made easier by building on previous experiences and lessons learned.

484: Points out that significant changes in your life are more likely to be lasting if they are based on your past experiences.

494: Reminds you that the structures that once supported you no longer serve their purpose, prompting you to create something new.

505: This is a nudge from the universe to broaden your horizons and delve into new knowledge.

515: It suggests that infusing your projects with your unique personality will make them much more special.

525: Maintaining balance during your travels ensures a peaceful and sustained exploration.

535: Expressing your independence requires courage; continue to forge your own path.

545: Even when embarking on a solo journey, you can find harmony in adventure.

565: Collaborations that arise along the way can evolve into enriching partnerships for your experiences.

575: Your unique path will bring you spiritual insights that will deepen your understanding of the universe that guides you.

585: Adventures undertaken or planned can trigger significant transformations, based on what you have learned over time.

595: As this adventurous phase concludes, the universe prepares you for new beginnings and unexplored horizons.

606: Emphasizes the importance of balancing romantic relationships, reminding you that trust and respect are essential to maintaining your authenticity even in collaboration.

616: Highlights the coexistence of independence and interdependence in healthy relationships, where the end of one stage creates space for a new beginning.

626: Indicates that romantic relationships should foster mutual growth; a solid foundation based on trust is essential.

636: Invites you to balance the physical and spiritual, embracing independence in your journey and taking a sincere look within.

646: Represents a deep bond between two souls, based on trust and genuine connection.

656: Serves as a reminder that every being possesses power, even when two hearts beat as one; it is important not to lose yourself in the union.

676: Announces that the truth you seek will be revealed, emphasizing the need for patience and trust.

686: Just as rivers change course, relationships also transform to enrich and deepen love and trust; trust in change.

696: Indicates that although stories come to an end, each ending opens the door to new beginnings; it is time to let go so that the new can emerge.

707: It suggests that you are about to discover mystical secrets that will transform your life in a positive way.

717: Reminds you that you are on a journey, so you must follow your heart's guidance to make your dreams come true.

727: Points out that learning to trust your spirit to manifest things is a beneficial change that will bring greater balance to your life.

737: Indicates that unlocking your creativity can be achieved by looking deep within yourself; devote time to spiritual work to facilitate other aspects of your life.

747: Urges you to connect with your roots, as doing so will allow you to receive heavenly insights and decipher the mysteries of existence.

757: Warns that only by deepening your spirituality and strengthening your roots will you achieve a higher understanding of the universe.

767: Collaborating with others on spiritual matters facilitates growth and the acquisition of new knowledge through shared experiences.

787: Significant changes in your spiritual perspective indicate that you are beginning to connect more deeply with the universe.

797: It signals that a period of intense spiritual insight is coming to an end, preparing you for new cosmic adventures.

808: Announces that renewal and change are essential, indicating that the universe is urging you to embrace transformation.

818: Invites you to accept the changes you are experiencing, assuring you that they are leading you to a beautiful destination.

828: Indicates that balanced change involves harmonious adjustments in all aspects of your life, allowing you to maintain stability during the transition.

838: Suggests that initiating change on your own terms is a sign of leadership in your renewal process.

848: It highlights that transformations based on what you have learned in the past underscore the importance of applying those lessons in the present.

858: Combines an adventurous spirit with change, marking the beginning of adventures that can profoundly transform your reality and manifest your highest aspirations.

868: Indicates that working alongside others during periods of change is essential for growing together and sharing experiences in life transitions.

878: Urges you to seek spiritual insights amid change to facilitate a smooth transition from your old self to the one you wish to be.

898: Announces that a period of transformation is coming to an end, signaling that new beginnings will open up once the changes are complete.

909: Represents the end of one cycle and the beginning of another, marking life transitions in which one stage closes to make way for another.

919: Suggests that the completion of certain personal goals can open the door to new stages, illustrating how different objectives alternate throughout life.

929: Emphasizes the importance of maintaining calm and balance during periods of change, facilitating smooth transitions.

939: Highlights independence when concluding one chapter and beginning a new one, inviting you to take control of your transformations.

949: Underlines that well-grounded endings and new beginnings are based on what has been learned, inviting you to recognize the lessons of the past as you move forward.

959: Indicates that exploration can mark the end of one phase and the beginning of another, suggesting that adventures can be both endings and beginnings simultaneously.

969: Warns that team efforts may come to an end, opening up the possibility for new collaborations and shared experiences in the future; remain open to working with others.

979: Places you on the cusp of spiritual greatness, indicating that continuing on your current path will lead to greater achievements and a positive impact in all areas of your life.

989: It advises you to allow everything that needs to end to do so, so that you can experience abundance and growth in all areas of your existence.

Unconventional Patterns

Angel numbers also appear in sequences that are out of the ordinary, offering meaningful messages through seemingly random combinations. These unusual patterns can provide you with personalized guidance, inviting you to look deeper within yourself to discover their full meaning.

Sequences such as 1234 or 4321 highlight progression and regression throughout the stages of life, representing the universe's encouragement to persevere and trust in the fluidity of the life path. Similarly, extended repetitions such as 4444 or 8888 intensify the essence of their individual digits, serving as a cosmic loudspeaker that draws your attention to crucial aspects of your life.

The interpretation of these atypical numbers depends largely on your intuition and the particular circumstances surrounding their appearance. While generally accepted meanings can serve as a starting point, personal context and emotions tied to these numbers are fundamental to a complete understanding. These patterns invite you to look inward and discover less conventional channels of communication through which the spiritual realm expresses itself.

When you encounter these strange angel numbers, consider them an invitation to explore forms of communication that transcend the traditional. Recognizing and interpreting these messages can enlighten you on your path, revealing the complex and multifaceted ways in which the universe guides and supports you.

Appendix 3 – Creating Angelic Sigils

Sigils are symbols of sacred power that act as vibrational keys to connect with angelic energies. Throughout history, from ancient Sumerian tablets to medieval grimoires, these symbols have been used as bridges between the earthly and the heavenly, condensing the vibrational essence of angels into geometric forms. Each stroke, each line, and each connection in a sigil represents a facet of the angelic energy we invoke, creating a visual language that transcends the barriers of time and space. When we create an angelic sigil, we are not only drawing a symbol, but we are weaving a web of intention and purpose that serves as an antenna to tune into the specific frequencies of each angel.

The creation of angelic sigils is significantly enhanced when done at times of natural power, such as during the full moon, which amplifies the energies of manifestation, or at the new moon, perfect for new beginnings and spiritual sowing. Equinoxes and solstices are also auspicious times, as they represent points of balance and transformation in the annual cycle. Personally significant dates, such as our birthday or the turn of the year, charge the sigil with a unique and personal resonance, as at these times our energy is naturally more receptive and attuned to the higher planes. By combining the r geometric precision of the sigil with the conscious choice of the moment of its creation, we establish a powerful and lasting bond with the angel we wish to invoke, creating a deeply personal and effective tool for spiritual connection.

1. Basic preparation:

What you need:

White paper without lines

Pencil and eraser

Compass or something circular to draw a circle

Ruler

Gold ink (optional)

2. The classic method for creating a sigil:

Start by reducing the name to its root letters. For example, for the angel *Raziel*:

Remove the vowels, leaving only R, Z, L

Each letter is used only once

Draw a circle:

It should be large enough to work comfortably (6-8 inches)

This circle represents the sacred space where the sigil will manifest

Divide the circle:

Draw a cross in the center, creating four quadrants

If you wish, you can subdivide each quadrant

Position the letters:

Place each letter at a point on the circle

Maintain a balanced distribution

Think about symmetry and visual balance

Connect the letters:

Connect the letters with straight lines

The lines can cross

Create patterns that you find harmonious

There are no strict rules for this; let your intuition guide you

3. Practical examples:

For the angel Michael (MKAEL):

Remove vowels: M, K, L

Place the letters at equal distances around the circle

Connect them to form a triangle

Add decorative details if desired

For the angel Gabriel (GBRAL):

Remove vowels: G, B, R, L

Distribute the letters around the circle

Connect them to form a square or diamond

Add additional lines to balance the design

4. Important considerations:

Intention: Keep your mind focused on the angel while creating the sigil

Cleanliness: Work in a tidy and quiet space

Time: There is no rush; take the time you need

Intuition: Trust your inner guidance as you connect the letters

Energy: The sigil should "feel" right when you finish it

5. Activating the sigil:

Once completed, you can activate your sigil in several ways:

Contemplating it while repeating the angel's name

Tracing it with your finger while invoking its presence

Meditating briefly with it

Charging it under the light of the full moon

6. Use and storage:

Keep your sigil in a special place

You can carry it with you

You can also place it on your altar

Treat it with respect as a sacred tool

Important note: There is no "wrong" way to create a sigil as long as you maintain a pure and respectful intention. Each person can develop their own style and method, always maintaining the basic principles of sacred geometry and balance.

Don't be discouraged if your first attempts don't look as you expected. What matters is the intention and energy you put into its creation.

You can also make sigils from an affirmation or decree. In this case, simply write the decree in a positive way and follow the same procedure, removing vowels, selecting unique consonants, and drawing them into a symbol that artistically integrates those letters. For example: "I am at peace."

I AM AT PEACE
~~I AM AT PEACE~~
M, T, P, C

Appendix 4 – Seals of the 7 Archangels

The following seals can be used to invoke angels and archangels. You can redraw them or simply focus on their image meditatively for any of the invocation, manifestation, and protection procedures described above.

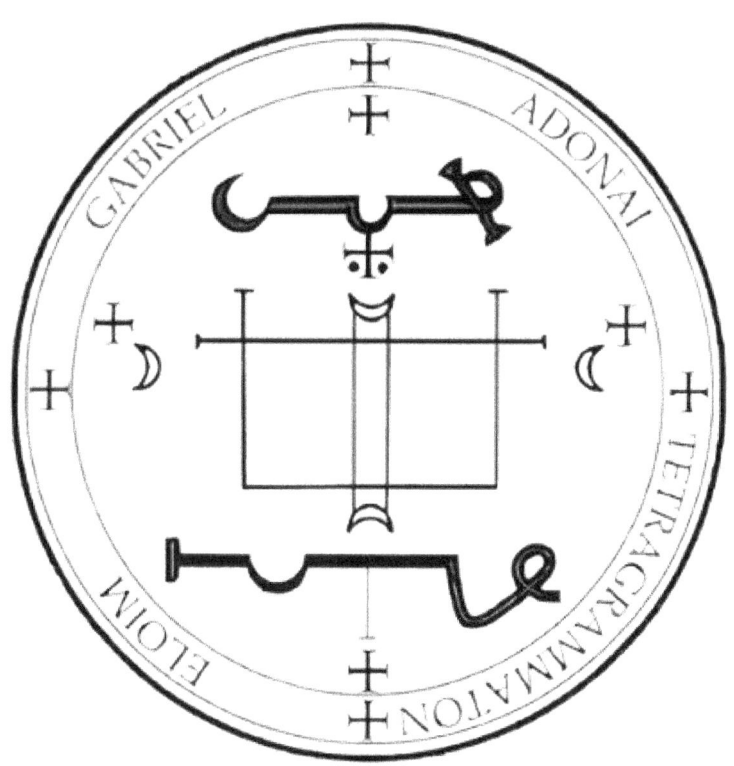

Seal of Archangel Gabriel

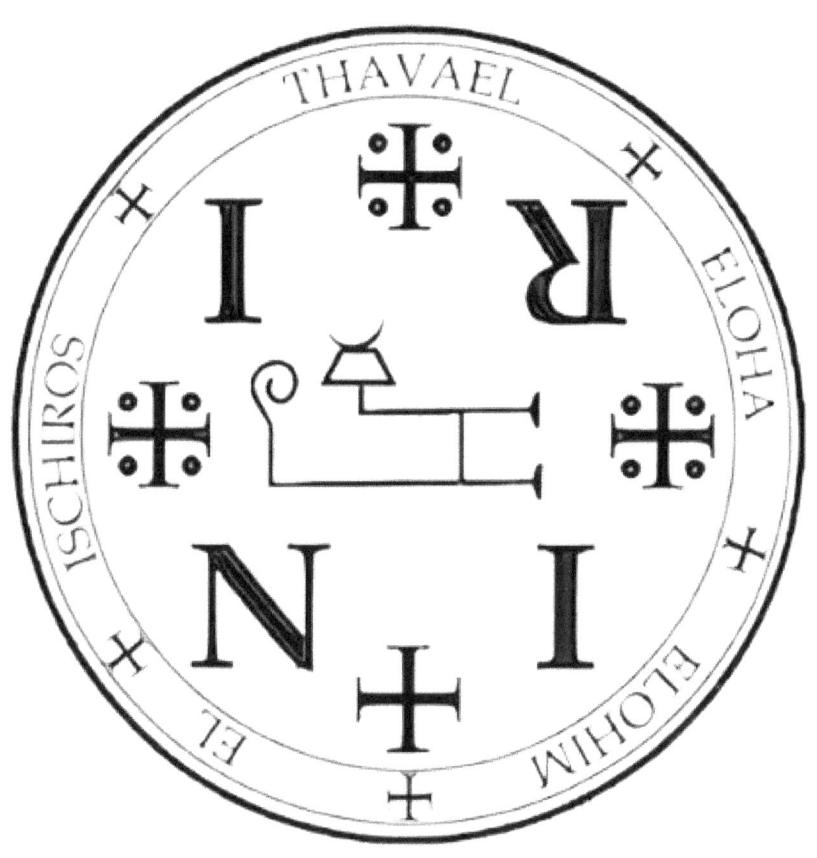

Seal of Archangel Jofiel

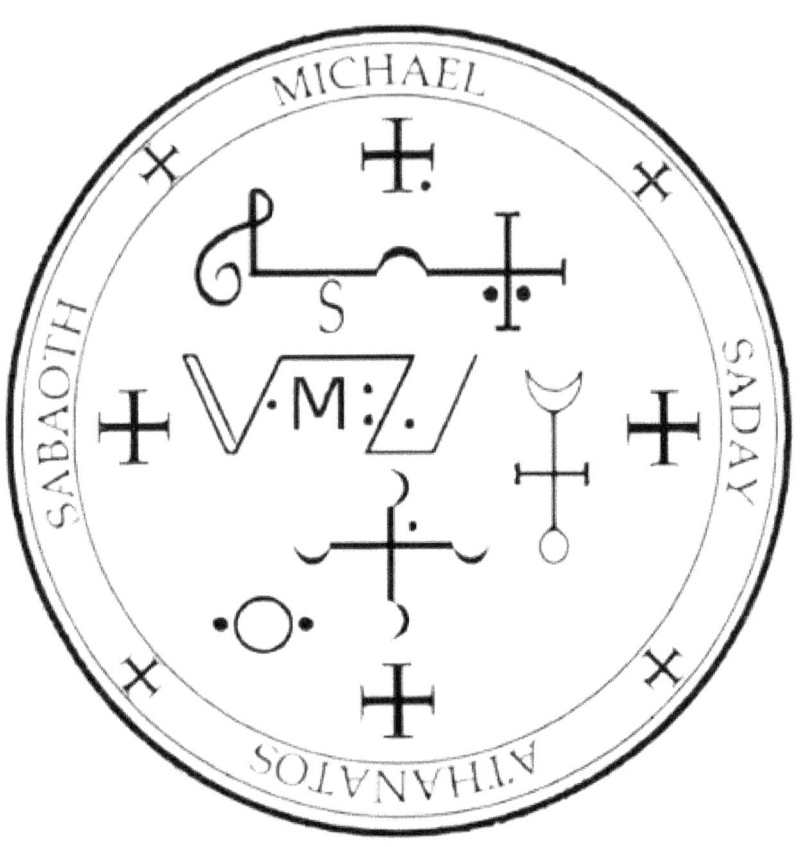

Seal of Archangel Michael

Seal of Archangel Chamuel

Seal of Archangel Uriel

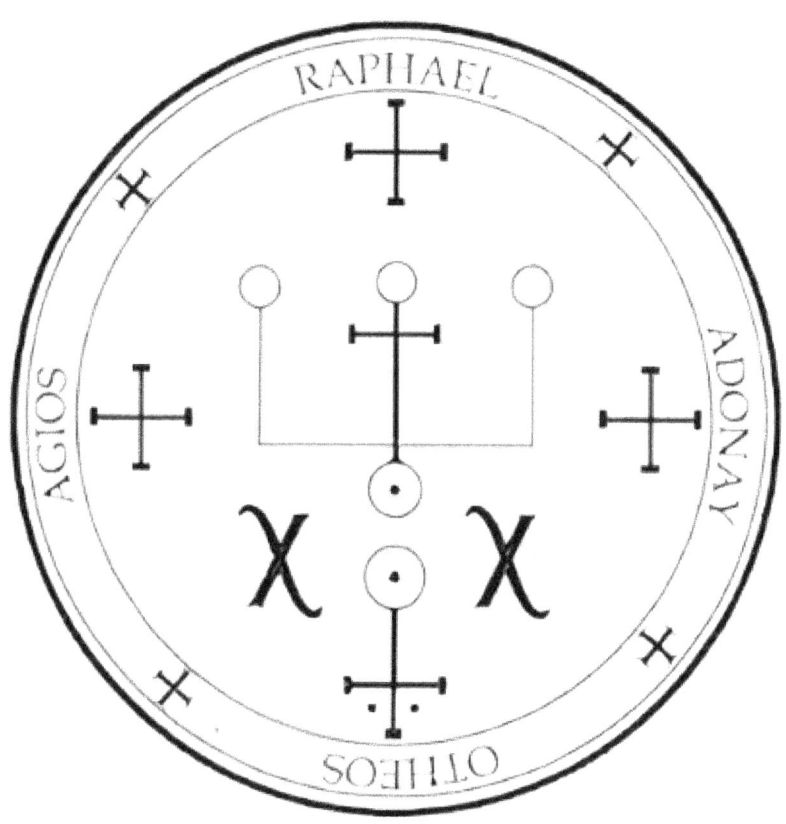

Seal of Archangel Raphael

Seal of Archangel Zadkiel

www.ingramcontent.com/pod-product-compliance
Lightning Source LLC
Chambersburg PA
CBHW050418170426
43201CB00008B/447